running
deep

AN AUSTRALIAN
SUBMARINE LIFE

First published 2023 by
FREMANTLE PRESS

Fremantle Press Inc. trading as Fremantle Press
PO Box 158, North Fremantle, Western Australia, 6159
fremantlepress.com.au

Cover images: Author image © Department of Defence; submarine:
EA Given / Shutterstock; background: Tina Dawson / Unsplash
Cover design by: Carolyn Brown, tendeersigh.com.au
Printed and bound in Australia by Griffin Press.

 A catalogue record for this
book is available from the
National Library of Australia

ISBN 9781760992002 (paperback)
ISBN 9781760992019 (ebook)

Fremantle Press is supported by the State Government through the
Department of Local Government, Sport and Cultural Industries.

Fremantle Press respectfully acknowledges the Wadjak people of the
Noongar nation as the Traditional Owners and Custodians of the land
where we work in Walyalap.

running deep

AN AUSTRALIAN SUBMARINE LIFE

COMMODORE **PETER SCOTT**

 FREMANTLE PRESS

This book is dedicated to Australian Submariners,

wherever they may be,

and to those who love and support them.

CONTENTS

FOREWORD

It is always an honour to be asked to write the foreword for a book, especially when the author is known to you and the story is one of importance to our nation. Peter and I first worked together when I was the Vice Chief of the Defence Force and Peter served as my Military Assistant. Our professional lives then parted, but reunited on occasion over time as is the way of service life. What I learned about Peter in that twelve-month period was that he was a moral and ethical man, intelligent and driven to do his best whatever the circumstances. He was extremely proud of the submarine service and therefore shared the ambition, and felt all the frustrations, as the Australian Defence Force worked hard to rebuild the Collins-class submarine capability. As his story tells, Peter played an important role in the revitalisation of the Collins-class.

The importance of *Running Deep* is that it will help Australians better understand why a submarine capability is an essential part of ensuring Australia's national security, the complexity of submarine operations and the quality of the people who serve in our submarine service. The narrative around the submarine service in Australia is often focused on the failure to logistically support the Collins-class submarines in their early years of service. But that is not the whole story. Australia now has a capable submarine service and Peter's story is very much about how that outcome was achieved. A central element of Peter's story is how our Australian submariners achieved that turnaround.

It is often stated as a truism that people are the heart of defence capability. Peter's description of his journey, the submariners with whom he interacted, and the impact of his service on his personal life expose us to both the strength and fragility of that beating heart. I found that Peter's description of his experiences on the submarine command course, ominously known as 'Perisher', demonstrated these competing characteristics very clearly as he described the wide range of emotions that many leaders in the military and naval services experience.

The 'loneliness of command', the vacillation between self-belief and doubt, the disappointment of failure and the euphoria of success are all discussed in Peter's forthright manner.

There are many lessons to be found on leadership under stress in the Perisher story. But Perisher is a training course. The dangers of submarine service and the demands on its leaders become crystal clear as Peter recalls a crisis at sea on board HMAS *Dechaineux* on 12 February 2003. The repeated alarm of 'Flood! Flood! Flood!' marked the beginning of an extraordinary story of terror, bravery, leadership and team response during a major life-threatening incident at sea. It is a story that draws together all the elements of life as a submariner that Peter has openly and honestly provided for us in this book. The implications for Peter and his family in later life remind us of the duty of care that we have to all our servicemen and women.

Running Deep is an important addition to the writings on Australia's defence capability and the people who are at its core. Peter covers many themes in his book – the training, education and development of our submariners; the importance of the submarine capability to our national security; the difficulties with the development and sustainment of the Collins-class capability over time; the reaffirmation of the importance of leadership; and the cost that some bear for their service. In doing so, Peter is clear in the statement of his opinions, and is not afraid to offer praise or criticism. He is true to himself and has given us a very candid history of his life and service.

Australians have a strong emotional attachment to their country's military and naval history which is evident, for example, in the attendance at Anzac Day ceremonies. There is a general understanding of the feats and sacrifices made by Australians in the three services. I would suggest though, that not many are familiar with the achievements of our submarine service and therefore, perhaps, have less of a relationship with it. I trust that *Running Deep* will help strengthen that relationship through greater awareness and understanding.

His Excellency General the Honourable
David Hurley AC DSC (Retd)
Governor-General of the Commonwealth of Australia

A NOTE FROM THE AUTHOR

In the four decades that have passed since I joined the Royal Australian Navy as a gangly youth, the world has shifted irreversibly across environmental, technological, societal and geopolitical dimensions. In these ever-changing surroundings, I have dedicated much of my life and most of my energy to furthering the security and prosperity of Australia as a nation. I chose to do that from within our Navy's strategic deterrent force, the Submarine Arm.

Life in uniform did not begin with grandiose notions or high ambitions. I joined as a hopeful, but uncertain, young man. The challenges and adversity I faced over the years at sea and ashore, in peacetime and at war have shaped and transformed me, generally for the better. In living a submarine life, I continually found purpose, meaning and connection. Over time, I developed into a proud and able naval officer, and eventually emerged as an elder with some hard-won wisdom.

Accepting that every sailor's story is a sea story and should be taken with a grain of salt, this memoir is an honest account of one man's naval and submarine career. While it is truthful, it is not the entire truth. If you have opened this book expecting to discover details of the classified operations of Australian submarines conducted at any time over the past fifty years, you will be disappointed. This is not an exposé on the where and when of our top-secret missions; to reveal the operational secrets entrusted to me would contravene the *Crimes Act 1914*, breaching the vital security net which safeguards and enables effective operations. It would place brave Australian men and women at even greater risk than they already face through the hazardous nature of their service.

What you will find are tales of service, daring and leadership drawn from a life beneath the waves – a life demanding courage, commitment and compassion in equal measure. They capture something of the mystery, thrill, occasional terror and enduring satisfaction of living and working with submarines and with those who take them to sea as warriors.

It is my fervent hope that I can, in some measure, inspire the next generation of Australian Submariners. At the very least, I wish to offer insight into what is a genuinely rare way of life, and a greater appreciation of the capabilities and tremendous value of our submarines as a strategic deterrent.

While the experiences are my own, they illustrate the struggles, failures and triumphs of a Submarine Arm that is vital to the nation in an era of rising uncertainty and challenge. This is the story of my life as an Australian Submariner – a quest for honour, living and leading among the warrior elite of the Silent Service.

PROLOGUE

'Flood, flood, flood! Flood in the lower motor room.'

We are dived, hundreds of metres beneath the sea surface and there are thousands of metres beneath us. It is light up there, but dark down here, and blacker still in the dense abyss.

Standing beneath a main hatch near the bows of the submarine, I meet Mango's eyes, just inches from mine. I meet Johnny's eyes; he is as close. They vanish, racing to their emergency stations, and so do I.

Within seconds, I am in the control room. My Executive Officer has the weight as Duty Commanding Officer, so today it's his boat. We are at Deep Diving Depth, the submarine is under immense pressure and flooding uncontrollably.

'Emergency Stations, Emergency Stations. Flood, flood, flood. Flood in the lower motor room.'

Strident but steady, the Ship Control Officer of the Watch picks up the alert from the sailors back aft, sounds the alarm and sends the report over the main broadcast again. No mistaking it this time, there was no mistaking it last time.

'Full ahead. 20 up. Midships. Blow main ballast. Blow emergency main ballast. Shut all hull valves.'

The emergency orders ring out and are immediately acknowledged by the operators. The panel watchkeeper cracks the valves to hear the rattle, blast and hiss of high-pressure air pushing into the ballast tanks. Our laconic Chief of the Boat is on the planes. He lifts and artfully holds the nose of the submarine. The revolutions come on and we start to surge forward. They know the drill and are already onto it. But this is no drill.

In an instant, we have gone from knowing the state of our submarine in intimate detail to endless unknowns. What failed and caused the flood? How fast are we flooding and how much weight have we already taken on? What is the state of our systems? What damage has been suffered and what is the ongoing risk? Where is the water? Are my people

12

drowning? Are they dead? Has it been stopped? Can it be stopped? Am I going to die?

Breathe.

My heart is beating through my neck. I imagine the unbearable shock, noise and damage happening aft, beyond the watertight bulkhead doors. I know – we all know – that if we go down in this depth of water, we will be crushed by the pressure before we hit the bottom. Once the pressure hull splits, the ocean's onslaught will be absolute in its violence. There's much more out there than we have room for in here. There is no coming back.

Breathe.

We've been here before. We've trained for this. Some of us have trained for this our whole adult lives.

'I have the submarine,' I say, resuming full command.

It's much quieter now. HQ1 reports they are closed up; sonar is calling sweeps for clearance; '20 up,' from the Chief on the planes.

But the reaction is over. All of the Emergency Operating Procedures are done and we're now pumping on anything that can draw a suction. Standing between the periscopes in the centre of the packed control room, I feel the eyes of one of my sailors fixed on me. I meet his gaze. He is searching for the answer to a singular question: 'Can we survive?' He sees that I don't know, but I am still in the fight. My eyes return to the depth gauge.

We're sinking. We're beneath Deep Diving Depth, and we're sinking.

PART I

SEAMAN AND SUBMARINER

CHAPTER 1
EARLY YEARS

Close alongside Mum, we passed through the open gate in the low brick fence framing my grandparents' three-bedroom cottage in Kingsford, Sydney. As we approach the narrow front door, planes overhead descend into the nearby airport and sparrows chirp on the ground under the hydrangeas. It's home, I love it.

For the first years of my life, I lived with Mum and Dad and my elder brother Mark at Grandma and Grandad's place. I knew every inch of the house – endlessly explored wardrobes, climbed pantry shelves, poked fingers down holes and into mouse traps. I also learned to keep my hands to myself in the small gas-fired kitchen, where there was a near permanent aroma of beef drippings, lamb chops and rice custard.

The tiny, secluded fern-shaded garden around one side of the house was my mini oasis. The buffalo lawn in the backyard tolerated all sorts of abuse and the brick driveway on the other side was a different playground again. The disused timber stables by the back fence were off limits until I was much older, on account of the jars of nails, assorted hammers, rusting saws and lengths of rope and chain adorning the walls. And we were never, ever to swing on the Hills hoist.

As we entered the house, I found Grandad relaxing in his armchair, listening to the call at Royal Randwick, feet warming by the bar heater, comfortable and content. His bright eyes smiled, and big hands ruffled my blonde top. Grandma gathered me up.

My grandparents, Jack and Gladys, married in 1923 and raised a family of three boys. My uncles, John and David, were born in the mid-1920s, and my dad, Michael, followed a decade later. The two elder boys emerged from their schoolboy days in the midst of the Second World War.

Uncle John, a talented athlete as a youngster and a wicked humourist throughout his life, joined the Royal Australian Air Force in 1942 and trained as a telegraphist. He deployed into Finschafen, east of Lae, during the campaigns to repel the invading Japanese forces from Papua New Guinea and the archipelagos further north. Surviving the war, he and his new bride, Elvery, raised their family in Epping, a suburb of Sydney. Uncle David took a different path, entering the seminary and becoming an ordained Catholic priest in 1950. As the parish priest of Winston Hills, he built the parish from the ground up over the course of forty years. And I remembered that he carried himself with great dignity and humility. I grew up wholly admiring his seemingly boundless compassion for others.

My father, Michael, grew up in a different world. An A-grade sprinter and rugby player, he initially followed Uncle David's footsteps into the seminary. Eventually deciding the priesthood was not his vocation, he nonetheless remained a devout servant of the church throughout his life. When he met my mum, Margaret, in 1958, his future path became clear. They married five years later, albeit without her family's blessing. Mum spent the next four decades almost completely estranged from her family. Undoubtedly painful for both Mum and Dad, they devoted themselves entirely to the security, wellbeing and happiness of their own little family.

Three younger sisters arrived in quick succession, and our tight-knit family of seven soon outgrew my grandparents' home, so we nestled into a new house in the recently created suburb of Riverview on the Lower North Shore. That family home was an anchorage for me for decades to come. Our block, and the vacant surrounds, made for a magical playground as foundations were laid and timber frames erected. In the earliest years, with no fences and few neighbours, we were at complete liberty to wander and explore. Ludowici's, a disused leather tannery nearby, was a dangerous but favourite playhouse. My brother and I spent countless hours with local lads re-enacting scenes from the late 1960s American TV action series, *Combat!*

The most difficult thing I had to deal with over many of my earlier years is that I was a bed-wetter. Hardly uncommon in children of preschool age, for me the torment persisted into my early teens. One thing after another was tried under the advice of the family doctor: being woken in the middle of the night, audible alarms, even electric shocks. Mum in particular showed the patience of a saint. As I became increasingly aware that this was not a problem my brother or younger sisters shared, the sense of difference and inadequacy grew in intensity, surmounting the physical discomfort and trauma of waking each morning soaked and stinking. As far as I knew, this was a closely held family secret, with my siblings loyal beyond their years. And I was desperate that it remained so, terrified by the prospect of my shame being discovered and reaching the ears of school friends.

I learned to think of my bed-wetting as a central and deficient piece of me that needed to be boxed up, hidden away and protected. This was the only way I could cope with it. The depth of caring, connection and trust I felt with my family, as well as the ability and willingness to keep parts of my life separate from others, has endured across the ensuing decades.

At the local convent school, the Sisters of Mercy nuns imposed a gentle order on our day. Generally letting us run free in the dust and the puddles during 'little lunch' and other breaks, they guided us through our early days in the classroom with a kind hand and an occasional swat from a feather duster. In later years, I was adequately caned and strapped by the Marist Brothers and Jesuits in succession. Corporal punishment aside, I was well cared for and well taught.

One fateful day in Year 6, I was in the Headmaster's office doing chores with two of my closest mates, Anthony and Mark. The misdemeanour that landed us there has long since faded, but what I remember most was our high-spirited conversation, inspired by the *Battle of Britain* block-buster, about joining the Air Force together to become fighter pilots – a far-sighted commitment for lads who generally saw nothing beyond next weekend's game of footy.

'Together, to the skies!' we pledged in unison.

We were absolutely resolved to do whatever it took to gain selection, earn our wings and fly. On subsequent holidays to Port Stephens, I insisted that Dad stop at the airfield in Williamtown to watch the Mirage fighter jets taking off and landing over our heads. My brother and sisters soon tired of this, but I was mesmerised by the sight and sound of the roaring jets.

Occupying an entire headland of the Lane Cove River since 1880, the grounds of Saint Ignatius' College were close to home and boasted rugby fields, cricket pitches, tennis and basketball courts and bushland fronting the water. The appeal for Mum and Dad was the high-quality Jesuit education emphasising humanistic studies, justice and compassion. The challenge was the money this type of high school education required. Dad had made career decisions, declining roles in Canberra and advancement in favour of family stability, and as a career statistician and public servant, he was on a modest salary. Mum took on multiple jobs over the ensuing years, working nights and weekends, to make ends meet.

Short and slight for most of my schoolboy days, I ran some track and was thrilled to play low-grade rugby through the winters, but I found a home away from home at the rowing sheds. Over four seasons, I enjoyed tremendous fun and excitement on and off the water, meeting with both triumph and failure. Selected as the coxswain of the Second Eight in Year 11, we achieved mixed early results.

Our performance peaked at the penultimate race of the season in our home event, the Gold Cup Regatta. The course was built for climactic finishes with a short dogleg turning around a pile adjacent to our sheds and a dash to the finish line at the ferry wharf. With our nemesis, Shore School, close aboard on my right and moving ahead, a clash of oars threatened. Deft handling of the boat came at a critical moment, bringing us nimbly round the pile. They lost rhythm as we powered up, the crew straining beyond exhaustion with the thrill of the race. With the river bubbling beneath the sleek timbers of the shell, we drove through to a win by a canvas. Passion, teamwork, skill, dedication. Returning alongside the pontoon and receiving our miniature silver oars, the collective and individual pride was immense.

Our ultimate race that season, the Head of the River regatta at Penrith, was starkly different. A flooded Nepean River, awash with flotsam, threatened cancellation of the event. Assigned an outside lane, our oars were fouled by floating beds of weed as we lined up for the race. Despite this, I allowed the officials to fire the starting gun. Having trained all season with a strategy built on winning the race with our explosive start, we were doomed and finished at the back of the pack. The disappointment, exacerbated by our high expectations, was crushing.

Arriving at the week-long summer rowing camp the following January, I had minimised my part in our failure at the Head of the River. *We could never have won with that lane on that day.* Rating myself a better-than-even chance for selection in the First Eight, I joined the throng to find my name as the crew lists were posted on the noticeboard in the Quadrangle. Not the First Eight. My heart sank. Not the Second Eight. *What?!* Dropped to the First Four I cried myself to sleep that night, sick with disappointment and humiliation. By morning, I had a new resolve; I would never again be the weak link in a team.

Grandad passed away a couple of days before my thirteenth birthday. As a young boy, I knew nothing of the trauma and loss of his war. He rarely spoke of his experience as a soldier, and only a little more often of the chums he had sailed to war with and fought alongside. But never to me of those mates he lost on the front or on their return. Never to me of the grim realities of war.

What do I know of his war now? Jack Scott, my father's father, enlisted in the Australian Imperial Force two days before his sixteenth birthday in March 1917. Departing on the troopship HMAT *Marathon* in May, he spent four months training on the Salisbury Plains before 'proceeding overseas' to the Western Front in France. Reinforcing the 34th Battalion in November after the heavy losses suffered at the Third Battle of Ypres, he endured months of trench warfare along the river Lys in Flanders. Late in March of 1918, Jack entrained for the Somme (having celebrated his seventeenth birthday a fortnight earlier), moving inexorably into the path of the German army advancing towards Amiens and the railway network so vital to the defence of Paris and the rest of France.

Arriving at Villers-Bretonneux, the 33rd and 34th Battalions were deployed to Hangard Wood on the evening of 30 March as counter-attack troops to stem the German onslaught. The retreating British infantry reported the enemy were approaching from the east in overwhelming strength.[1] Lacking artillery support, but in company with the cavalry of the 12th Royal Lancers, three companies of the 33rd Battalion

---

1   Bean, C.E.W. *Official History of Australia in the War of 1914-1918, vol. V*, 8th ed., Angus & Robertson Ltd, 1941, Sydney, p.304.

emerged from cover to advance across a field and attack the German line. They came under intense machine gun fire from the German troops entrenched along the crest of a bare spur.

Jack's company, A Company, were brought in to reinforce the left flank, which suffered heavy casualties, and attacked the ridge in one line as night fell. Driving the Germans from their picquet-line and capturing two machine guns, they continued the advance, forcing the enemy from their main continuous trench at the point of the bayonet. Pressing on to follow the fleeing enemy, a German machine gun opened heavy fire on them from the north, killing one officer and inflicting most of the Australian casualties suffered in the attack.

With the German trench occupied, but the 33rd Battalion unable to push forward to join them, A Company conducted a tactical withdrawal and filled a gap in the line where the 33rd had dug in. Having captured a number of prisoners and with an estimated sixty enemy killed and wounded, Jack's A Company was relieved before dawn.

Across the entire action, the Australians lost nine officers, with 191 others killed or wounded. In the turmoil of overrunning the German trench, Jack was felled by a machine gun bullet to the head. Brought back into the line later that night, he was evacuated to the Australian Hospital in Rouen the following day. Several weeks later, he was further evacuated from France to the Bath War Hospital in England.

A month on, when writing a letter to home, Jack said of his steel hat and the bullet that nearly ended his life, there were 'two nice little peepholes in it where it went in and came out'. After four months of rehabilitation in England, he was repatriated home to Sydney and reunited with his beloved childhood sweetheart, Gladys.

⊕

My grandparents' experiences of that war were stale by half a century before I had any exposure to them. Nonetheless, they ran quiet and deep as an influence on the family. As youngsters, my brother Mark and I were occasionally gripped by puerile fascination with Grandad's barely visible pie-slice scars. They delineated the section of skull removed by the surgeons and replaced with a metal plate. On a rare occasion, worn down by a week-long school holiday visit and with Grandma out of sight, he acquiesced to our badgering. We poked the dimples of his entry and exit wounds with our prying little fingers.

Although seemingly unmarked beyond his head wound, Grandad's wartime experience shaped who he was to the family, and who he was to me. I adored him as one of many courageous young Australians who stepped forward and put their young lives on the line. I was less consciously aware of his apparent ability to deal with the consequences, including blinding headaches for many years hence, with both pride and equanimity. As a paragon of survival, resilience and leadership, and the centre of our close and loving family, Grandad was my childhood hero – a status that lived on long into my adult life.

Over time, my determination to join the Air Force evolved. One of my school mates organised a career guidance trip to the Royal Australian Naval College at Jervis Bay on the New South Wales coast. We toured the heritage-listed buildings, walked the immaculate grounds and spoke with the officers and sailors. The magnetic sea was tantalisingly close. This one day enthused me no end as I had glimpsed something of the person I might become and a life I might lead. It sharpened the sense of destination that carried me through the final years at school.

During that time, I heeded Dad's advice to aim for acceptance as an officer. Conscious of the competition and difficulty of achieving selection, I applied to join both the Army and the Navy. Thinking that I was giving myself some real options here, in fact I was simply committing to a life of service in uniform. But one final question, asked by the Colonel chairing the Army Selection Board, disclosed a surprising revelation – they already knew I had applied for the Navy as well! If I was successful in both applications, which service would I join? Hesitation betrayed me and my soldiering career was curtailed before it began.

With just enough courage to quell my inner doubts and fears, I joined the Navy as a Midshipman on 17 January 1983. Setting forth in search of my place in the world, I was convinced that my life would matter and determined to make my family proud.

CHAPTER 2
SETTING SAIL

Stepping up onto the bus at the Defence Recruiting Centre at Central Station in Sydney, my ambitions were not lofty – simply making it to the end of the year would suffice. We made an early stop at Randwick Barracks to be issued our kit. I was no more than six hundred yards from my grandparents' old home, yet it seemed a world away. We rumbled south down the Princes Highway and along the coast to the Royal Australian Naval College.

Over the final miles, the wide and glorious bay, framed by Point Perpendicular and Bowen Island, came into occasional view through the low scrub. I craned my neck for a fresh glimpse of the distinctive heritage clock tower I remembered so vividly from my last visit, now more than a year hence. It appeared briefly, standing proud and tall among the Norfolk Island pines and presiding over the felt green turf of the quarterdeck, the main parade ground. Excitement, anticipation, trepidation and an overriding sense of adventure filled that first day of my new life.

The charter of the college was to 'train young men and women for service to their country as officers in the Royal Australian Navy … in an environment that demands professional excellence and stimulates personal endeavour', while the college motto was 'Honour, Virtue, Integrity.' The whole prospect was brimming with challenge and gave shape to my otherwise formless aspirations. As one of eighty-three young men to join the college with that intake, I was assigned to Phillip Division, named for the first Governor of New South Wales, Admiral Arthur Phillip, RN. By close of day, I had a stiff blue shirt on my back, a meal in my belly, a 'cabin' with my name on it and a new clan. I laid my head down that night with a deep sense of personal accomplishment in having arrived at this place. What I could not yet imagine was the degree to which every step and misstep over the next month would be directed and scrutinised by others. But I had chosen my path, taken the first steps and made the grade, thus far.

Commissioned as an officer of the Royal Australian Navy from the day of entry, such airy status was heavily obscured during these early weeks as the Navy set about transforming our self-image. We were formally referred to as 'new entry Midshipman' however 'new grub' was the less affectionate and more frequently barked form of address. We appeared to have no meaningful credibility whatsoever.

Our initial efforts were guided by the harmless looking, but soon to be dreaded, Task Book. Individually issued on Day One, it might as well be written in a foreign language for all the sense it offered. Progressing through this ledger of knowledge and experience, to be studiously acquired and duly demonstrated, ruled our daily lives. Our days commenced with physical training, gently described as 'early morning activity', and were filled to the brim with swim tests, medical and dental checks, firefighting training, boat work, sword drills and endless squad drills. In spare moments, we pursued the completion of our tasks and final sign-off by the Divisional staff or second-year Midshipmen.

It's clear that these first few weeks were confronting by design, as we were deliberately thrown off kilter and slapped back into shape to hopefully present ourselves as something resembling naval officers. Minor failings were brought to our attention with high volume and punished with laps of the Quarterdeck at double pace, rifle carried in front and overhead. The rewards for a completed Task Book were permission to wear the rank insignia of a Midshipman, access to bar privileges and the prospect of weekend 'shore leave' beyond the gates. Inspired by all three, I collapsed into my bunk at the end of each day and muttered a quiet prayer for the gumption to climb this first peak.

Heading home on leave one densely packed month later, among the first in Phillip Division to achieve this milestone, I was full of quiet pride when Mum picked me up from the station. It was surpassed three weeks later when my parents and sisters travelled down to witness our first formal parade, grandly billed as 'Ceremonial Divisions'.

'Chin up, Mr Scott. Be proud of yourself,' was the Commanding Officer's encouragement as he passed in review.

The pace shifted as the academic year began and work commenced towards a university degree. History, political science, mathematics and oceanography were on my plate as a first-year Arts student. During the university breaks we were saturated with purely military training: naval history, relative velocity, communications, gunnery, seamanship, nuclear, biological and chemical defence, navigation and other essential subjects. I found it all fascinating, but my efforts were definitely impacted by the distraction of social and sporting pursuits.

Weekends were spent either racing up and down the highway to Sydney in a car packed with other Midshipmen or travelling to play sport for the college. We found our way to every village with a set of rugby posts on the Far South Coast of NSW. Lacking any tremendous talent but always willing to have a go, I made the cut and enjoyed my first overseas trip in June 1983, flying to Auckland for a short rugby tour.

Hosted by the New Zealand Naval and Military College at HMNZS *Tamaki*, our First and Second Fifteen teams were respectively outgunned by a full Royal New Zealand Navy Colts (under-21s) side and a combined *Tamaki*/Fleet Midshipman side. The pummelling we received did nothing to diminish the fun and excitement of traveling to foreign (enough) shores to represent Navy with a bunch of lively mates.

Back at our college, the 'Gunroom' was my haven during the week. Traditionally the Midshipmen's mess in a warship, this simple bar was our onboard escape from the scrutiny of the staff. I revelled in the camaraderie and jocularity as we wound down and let loose. Heavy mid-week drinking became my norm as I regularly downed nine beers in ninety minutes, taking pride in my ability to skull a beer much quicker than most.

With a skinful one night, I uncharacteristically lost my temper and punched a hole in a wall. Not the worst offence in the world, but the ensuing discipline was swift. Hauled in front of my Divisional Officer, the Training Officer and the Executive Officer (XO) in quick succession early the next day, I was 'awarded' a bill to cover the damages, as well as a month's loss of leave and bar privileges. The frustration of being confined to the base stung less than being exiled from the Gunroom and the self-inflicted wound to my self-esteem. The irony was not lost on me that this punishment was brought down a week before my eighteenth birthday, when I had intended to celebrate with my first age-legal beer!

By the middle of the year, I have enough savings to secure a loan for a car. Dad gets a deal on a Valiant from a mate and, just $1,200 poorer, I am on the road. Five months later, an afternoon at the Huskisson Hotel is followed by a rowdy gathering at a local's house in Vincentia. Sure that I had been drinking sensibly throughout the day, I drive a friend home. Heading back to pick up my remaining mates, the narrow streets of the small coastal village are dark and quiet. I slide Fischer-Z into the tape deck, crank it up and hit the accelerator, immediately rewarded with the deep rumble of the big V-8 opening up.

Tracking the old speed dial towards 60 mph, I look up too late to line up for a fast-approaching S-bend. Tyres screeching, the car spins and careens off the road, flipping over as it ploughs through half a dozen timber posts and off a small bridge. Colliding head on with the stone embankment on the far side, the car drops into Vincentia Creek, wheels up. With the windows smashed, the shallow creek is running through the roof of the car. Hanging upside down, I have an unexpected view through the crumpled bonnet to the engine – where orange flames lick ominously at the carburettor. Releasing the seatbelt, I scramble under the bench seat, out through the rear window, over the upturned wreck and onto the road above. And run.

Arriving back at the party house, my tale is met with scepticism. It seems a ridiculous story, particularly as I am virtually unscathed. Confident that I have merely tipped the car on its side around some gentle sandy bend, my mates set off to put the Valiant back on its feet. Not possible – it would take a crane the following day to retrieve the car and a tow truck to drag it away. At the crash site, my well-intentioned buddies assure the concerned gathering of neighbours – who kindly put out the fire – that I was the sole occupant and am safe in a nearby house. Coincidentally, this ensures the success of the police who set out to hunt me down.

Within the hour, I'm breathalysed, arrested and taken to the station. Exhausted and forlorn, at 3 am I am released on bail, undertaking to appear in the Court of Petty Sessions in Nowra. Nine days later, standing weakly before the magistrate, I am humbled, ashamed and defenceless. I cop a hefty fine and six-month disqualification of my licence. More crucially, I earn a criminal record and am wholly certain that my naval career is at an end.

Standing at his disciplinary table after the Vincentia crash, the CO shows me mercy. I am censured – a serious black mark against my name – but not discharged from the Navy. I get no insight into his deliberations and can't fathom the outcome but am exceedingly relieved. Having come so close to losing control over my destiny, I realise just how attached I've become to my identity as a young naval officer and the depth of connection with my Navy mates.

I carry a photo of my wrecked Valiant in my wallet for the next thirty years as a reminder to never drink and drive. Regrettably, the even simpler lesson that was on offer – a lesson on my relationship with alcohol – went begging.

As the year drew to a close, our exposure to 'the real Navy' had been low, with only one or two days at sea in warships and the occasional visit to ships at anchor. A glimmer of my future appeared in the form of HMAS *Oxley* sailing into Jervis Bay late one afternoon. Two mates and I were tasked with a boat trip out to the submarine. Having surfaced off Point Perpendicular, she appeared on the far horizon, periscope fully raised. Solid black and initially pencil thin, the sleek form of her fin and the outer casing of her hull slowly emerged, as a low fog of diesel exhaust trailed away to the south.

Coaxed onboard by the crew once we got alongside the submarine, we clambered over the smooth ballast tanks and up onto the slippery casing, climbed warily down through a forward hatch and made our way through dark and impossibly cramped passageways and confined spaces. It felt like we were moving through the floor of an industrial rainforest, dense with hefty machinery, teeming with dials and valves and alive with snaking pipework and cabling. Living within the confines of this undergrowth, people appeared again and again. A freckled arm breached a bunk curtain, hanging motionless; a bearded head peered up through a hatch in the deck, growling something as we step over; a glaring cook guarded his tiny galley, dangling cigarette adding to the fug. I couldn't comprehend what I was seeing, hearing or smelling. The contrast between the external simplicity of form and the internal complexity of systems left a deep impression.

Lewd and crude jokes were made at our expense. My sense was that the sailors just wanted to mess with a couple of Midshipmen for their own amusement. A happy lot, they gave an impression of total indifference as to how we regarded them or their boat. In later years, I understood that they were most assuredly assessing us, as they took the mark of any officer or sailor who came into their submarine. I was not immediately hooked, but I was absolutely intrigued.

Journal note, November 1983. *I love subs – so black and Christ their [sic] our teeth*

After surviving the year at Jervis Bay, the shift up to Sydney was a welcome change. Living on base at HMAS *Watson* on South Head and attending the Kensington campus of the University of New South Wales, I had another two years of academic and professional studies ahead of me. I was delighted to be closer to family, and to an ever-widening set of social circles, while still surrounded by most of the mates the Navy had issued me the year before.

Having fallen hard for a beautiful and lively girl over the summer, I was thrilled to be at the front end of my first serious relationship. The fact that she lived in Melbourne didn't seem to matter much at first; bus tickets were cheap, and time was free. Life was looking decidedly rosy heading into a second year in the Navy. I was determined to keep it in order and excel; I was determined to do many things. I leaned into some a lot harder than others.

Through those next two years, my life became a series of wild oscillations as I leapt into the freedom seemingly on offer while striving to meet the expectations of myself and others. The beginning of every academic semester, and the first days of each Navy course, were invariably linked with a new determination to lift my game and get back on track. The enthusiasm was easy to bring because I genuinely enjoyed both the university work and the Navy training immensely. However, the foundations of my good intent invariably crumbled under the pressure of other attractions.

Whenever possible, I lived a nocturnal existence – spending my time in a string of pubs, seeing bands and going out to parties, night after night, week after week. I was desperate to remain within Navy's protective and respectable bounds, but led a solo, out-of-hours rebellion against authority and convention. Simultaneously craving both total independence and boundless connection with others, life was an absolute riot. I had an indecent amount of fun, meaning collateral damage was inevitable. A pattern of failed commitments emerged: lectures, assignments, rugby training and family gatherings fell by the wayside in the haze of drunken indulgence. Noses were broken and eyes were blackened in brawls. I needlessly trashed more than one romantic relationship along the way. My favourite sports – drinking, smoking and revelling – became my continual torment.

Journal note, October 1984. *Must quit smoking/drinking or I'll go down in a pile of shit.*

By the back end of 1984, I was running full pelt and having the time of my life, but also 'on Qs' – a formal warning for lack of 'officer-like qualities' earned through a string of misdemeanours. Reports from my seniors spoke to my 'engaging personality and natural ability' but delivered blunt appraisals of my 'lack of maturity and responsibility'. After being without a car for a year, I regained my licence and arranged three-year terms for a $3,000 loan. We were the highest paid students on campus but drank the cheapest beer and spirits in town at our Officers' Mess. And yet, four months later, I still had no car and remained firmly in debt. The cash, pissed up against the proverbial wall, was gone.

Over time, I ended up investing the absolute minimum of effort into my studies. I deliberately selected subjects so that my weekends began on Thursdays during one semester, then on Wednesdays and eventually on Tuesdays. Any academic work was crammed into the desperate days and nights ahead of deadlines and exams. Living on the razor's edge, I passed only one examination during my final two years, scraping through on marks from assignments to achieve my Bachelor of Arts by the barest of margins.

Somewhat surprisingly, I was still in one piece to graduate at our Passing Out parade in December 1985, presided over by the Governor-General and our Commander-in-Chief, Sir Ninian Stephen. Replete with armed guards, drum bands, fly-pasts, march-pasts and royal salutes, it was another splendid day and another inspirational beginning. Now degree-qualified, with three years of professional training and seniority as a Midshipman under my belt, I was supposedly ready to enter the Fleet as a leader. Yet my efforts to simply lead myself as a responsible adult – continually ambushed by a high-spirited and unquenchable thirst for excitement and social acceptance – were failing spectacularly.

Captain Morton's view was: 'Midshipman Scott lacks any sense of responsibility, application or interest in his training and development as a naval officer.'

The Navy had my measure, and I had been found decidedly wanting.

CHAPTER 3
LEARNING THE ROPES

In late 1985, I met and fell instantly in love with my future wife, Shaunaugh. As a wild romance erupted around us, Shaunaugh was thrown roughly into the deep end of Navy life. Within weeks of our first meeting, I deployed for a month and a half to join HMAS *Bendigo* and later HMAS *Launceston*; Fremantle-class patrol boats running out of Darwin and Cairns, respectively. Personally, it was the beginning of two years of difficult and extended separations at the outset of our relationship that would both test and prove our commitment to each other. Professionally, although I was still under training, it was a first forward step towards finding a place in the Navy as a member of a Ship's Company, with both the competence and the confidence to do it justice.

To date, my sea experience had been highly orchestrated and structured around individual training objectives, tasks and progress. Joining *Bendigo*, the boat had distinct operational roles to fulfil and we – myself and my two Midshipman buddies – immediately took hold of our part in that. Our fairly simple mission was to take *Bendigo* to her new home port in Cairns, conduct a crew swap with *Launceston*, and retrieve her to Darwin. Sailing across the Gulf of Carpentaria and through the Torres Strait on Australia Day, I carried a quiet pride in being out at sea, 'defending the nation' as it were. Having safely navigated the reef and arrived in Cairns, the whole endeavour received a shot in the arm when we were recalled to the ship and crash sailed. Tropical Cyclone Winifred, building in intensity as it tracked south-east through the Coral Sea over the past several days, suddenly turned towards the coast to bear down on us.

The most imminent danger we faced was that our small flotilla of patrol boats might break up against the wharf and be sunk where they lay. Safer at sea than alongside, our entire crew hastily gathered onboard, then slipped lines. Only half the crew had their personal belongings onboard, and the formalities and ceremony of the handover were foregone. Steaming out through the leads and into the cyclone, all five patrol boats turned to port in formation astern. Although we reached the relative safety of the open ocean, the entire scene was bracing as the twin V-16 diesel engines pushed our little 220-tonne warship into the maelstrom.

With sustained winds of over 70 knots and gusts of over 85 knots whipping the ocean into a blinding frenzy of foam and spray, these were without a doubt the worst seas I had encountered thus far. Though exhilarating, I was uncertain as to how confident I should be of our survival. As Winifred crossed the coast, it killed three people and wreaked havoc as the most disastrous cyclone to hit Queensland in a decade and a half. Amid the turmoil, the other patrol boats were dispatched to search for two missing trawlers while we were sent north to board and inspect Thai fishing boats for illegal catches.

In April of that year, I crossed the gangway of HMAS *Vampire*, the last of the Daring-class destroyers. A proud ship and a veteran of both the Indonesia-Malaysia Confrontation and the Vietnam War, she was nearing the end of her distinguished service days. Joining for her decommissioning cruise, I was one of the last two Midshipmen to serve within her Ship's Company. The ship's program laid out several months of single ship steaming before us, with port visits up and down the east coast of Australia, and across to Fiji, Western Samoa and New Zealand. It was a dream posting on the ideal ship for a couple of lads looking for more challenge and adventure.

Notwithstanding *Vampire*'s age and the relatively soft, non-operational nature of her final tasking, the ramp up in complexity and intensity aboard a destroyer was a steep one. As the only officer trainees embarked, we lacked for nothing when it came to the attention and energies of the officers and crew. Encouraged by the passion and pride coursing through the Ship's Company, I worked with a determination and zeal that I could not have previously mustered.

While keeping watch on the bridge was our main fare, we threw ourselves into every aspect of shipboard life. Under the watchful eye of the XO, we practised no end of seamanship evolutions, including man overboard drills, rigging for tow, laying danbuoys and boat handling.

We grappled with the intricacies of astronavigation, and shot sun, moon and stars to plot the position of the ship. We prepared meals with the chefs, dispatched signals with the communicators and relayed ammunition through the gun-bay up to one of the three twin 4.5-inch gun turrets. Standing watch in the fiercely hot boiler rooms at sea was rewarded with the rare chance to enter and clean out the oil-fired boilers while alongside. Emerging through the furnace manhole after hours of backbreaking toil, our white officers' overalls were indelibly blackened, and our skin drenched from head to toe in the oily soot from the brick interior walls. The Chief Stoker assures us that someone had to do it.

It was during this time in *Vampire* that I celebrated my twenty-first birthday. Alongside in Fiji on the day, the officers organised a party at the home of one of the resident ex-pats. Lairy green 'Beam me up, Scotty' T-shirts featuring a vampire bat logo were worn by all for the occasion. By coincidence, my younger sister Cath was in Fiji on a high school excursion and able to join in. The officers did everything they could to recognise the significance of the day and substitute for the absence of wider family and friends, engendering a real sense of Navy as family.

I held most of the *Vampire* officers in particularly high regard and was eager to impress them as we sailed through these idyllic waters. I was also captivated by the warmth of the people who welcomed us to their island homes and by the astonishing beauty of the reefs, beaches and tropical mountains of the islands in the Southwest Pacific. Yet not all was calm in paradise, with rates of crime and social unrest high. The charming streets fronting the picturesque port of Apia, Western Samoa became dark, dangerous and lawless by night. Standing watch on the gangway one night, I helped seven of our sailors clamber back onboard after a savage assault by local youths. One of our number, a young Fijian Midshipman embarked with us for sea experience, was scarred for life after copping a full beer bottle smashed over his head.

After a brief weekend in Sydney to reconnect with loved ones, I carried my duffle bag off *Vampire*, across the wharf and up a long, steep gangway to embark in HMAS *Stalwart* and circumnavigate Australia. For the next three and a half months, *Stalwart*, a destroyer tender and the Flagship of the Fleet, led a group of warships visiting coastal capital cities on the mainland to celebrate the Navy's 75th anniversary, often with much fanfare in each port. To my professional benefit, this whole venture provided more seatime and more time in company with other warships. Sailing with the destroyer HMAS *Hobart*, fleet oiler HMAS *Success* and destroyer escorts HMAS *Stuart*, *Parramatta* and *Derwent*, we were the linchpin of a highly capable task group heading through the Bass Strait and into the Southern Ocean. New experiences came thick and fast as the ships manoeuvred throughout the days and nights.

I was on the bridge one night when we came dangerously close to a collision with *Success*. As we altered course to port, *Success* appeared close on our port bow. Her navigation lights suddenly clear and bright, she was on a steady bearing, and we were on a collision course. We needed to use full rudder and stop the port shaft to tighten our lumbering turn and avoid impact. Holding my breath on the starboard bridgewing as *Success* sailed by, beam to beam and far too close, we turned to starboard again, close astern of her. There would have been no victor in a collision between the two largest ships of the Fleet in the middle of the night.

From the bridge, eight decks above the waterline, *Stalwart*'s substantial bulk towered over the other warships as they closed to within 50 yards to conduct replenishments at sea, taking on stores and munitions. During daylight hours, I occasionally waved to a grinning classmate on the bridgewing of another ship close aboard. To reduce the total time that she was constrained in her ability to manoeuvre, *Stalwart* routinely replenished two ships at once, one on either side. While these were tightly controlled evolutions requiring the attention of almost everyone onboard, they were thrilling for the proximity of the ships and the forces involved, particularly among the hard blows and big swells of the Bight. Those forces became all the more real when I experienced a transfer as the cargo.

Stepping through the guardrails and off the starboard side of the ship, I clutched a strop and dangled from the jackstay between the two ships some 70 feet above the waterline. The sailors lining the decks of *Parramatta* and *Stalwart*, sporting life jackets and hard hats, heaved in and checked away on their lines, steadily hauling me across a seemingly canyon-like space between the ships. The seas surged and broke between the two hulls, peaks rising to lick my boots and troughs falling away to reveal the black underbellies of the ships. As I reached the other side, my feet scrabbled for the deck. On a calmer day, I would likely have been a candidate for a deliberate dunking.

Thrills and excitement notwithstanding, *Stalwart* was a somewhat sombre ship. The spectre of a fatal incident at sea the previous year, where three sailors succumbed to hydrogen-sulphide gas, still menaced those embarked at the time. There was a gravity and formality aboard the Flagship that I was not cut out for yet. That said, the posting finished on an absolute high with the ultimate celebration of the 75th anniversary – a Fleet Review by His Royal Highness Prince Philip of more than forty warships from six nations and the most spectacular fireworks display yet seen on Sydney harbour. Our Navy had the attention of the nation and we had the party of our lives. It was the kind of day that cemented the career choice of a young officer.

The following week I was thrilled to be included in the Navy Colts rugby side to tour the United Kingdom and France early in the new year. My selection had been something of a gamble, as I was still recovering from an operation conducted at the Naval Hospital in Balmoral, a month prior. Several years of ad hoc games with minimal preparation had left me with a right shoulder that suffered recurrent dislocations.

What the Navy rugby selectors did not yet know was that the operation had been botched. The surgeon had nicked an artery that continued to bleed into my shoulder after I had been sewn up. Within an hour, my right upper arm and chest was so grotesquely swollen that my skin was stretched taut and peeling off me in layers. Unable to recall the surgeon or get me back to theatre in time, the duty medical officer gathered a handful of trainee medics close around my bed to observe the procedure, then took a scalpel to the stitches binding the wound. As the pressure in my shoulder suddenly released, a fountain of clotted blood erupted from the wound, spraying the ceilings nearly five metres above. All but one of the medics fainted and hit the deck. Shaunaugh, a registered nurse herself, had come in to see me post-op and witnessed the whole ghastly scene. Floating on some heavy-duty pain killers, my careless fascination became hysterical laughter in the ensuing chaos.

While we met with only moderate success on the field, the Colts tour proved an adventure of a different sort, particularly as it was my first foray to Europe and my first travels to countries with vastly different culture and language. Despite the surgical mishap, the gamble paid off.

Over these years, my professional ability and aspirations were steadily on the rise. Despite my tendency to test the loyalty of my friends and an occasional abrogation of responsibility, an overriding, if somewhat ill-defined, motivation towards service pushed me forward, and I craved the respect of others. Quips such as 'Scotty, are you going for dux of Stage 3?', delivered with blokeish good humour, cut deeply into my ego. I knew that I was capable of more and used the taunts to bolster my determination to do well and prove myself professionally. This was all the more challenging as I was increasingly caught in the paradox of rising professional satisfaction grinding against the miserable loneliness of being separated from loved ones, particularly Shaunaugh.

At a time when communication with home was limited to written letters and the occasional expensive phone call, I became more practised at packing up my feelings. Placing them in a metaphorical corner of my cabin made it easier to get through the long days and nights of isolation. The other paradox of living in close proximity to hundreds of souls yet feeling isolated and adrift from the ones you love was an ever-present challenge. I drew some inspiration from an address on Navy life delivered by Rear Admiral David Martin, RAN, then the Naval Support Commander and later Governor of New South Wales. His theme of 'the deeper the downs, the richer the highs' struck a chord, and helped me accept the dichotomy and build some capacity to fully experience both.

In January 1987, I was genuinely delighted and relieved to 'stripe up' as a Sub-Lieutenant. By April, I had hauled myself through the Fleet examinations and ranked sixth in the class, substantially surpassing the low expectations of my classmates and more closely matching what I knew I could achieve. But it felt as if the improvement came too late.

While the front runners were dispatched to destroyers or exchange postings with other Commonwealth navies to achieve Bridge Watchkeeping Certificates – the licence to drive a warship and the core qualification for a seaman officer – I was sent to HMAS *Jervis Bay*, a former merchant ferry converted to operate as the training ship for officers. As a member of the Ship's Company, I convinced myself of the ship's valuable role, but it was hardly a plum posting. A saving grace, her home port being Sydney meant I was near Shaunaugh and family, and I resolved to make the most of what she offered.

My previous experience in *Jervis Bay* had been on my initial training cruise a couple of years earlier. Embarked for four weeks, the program looked typical of a luxury cruise liner. Our days were spent sailing around New Zealand, including through the Bay of Islands, exploring the far reaches of the Marlborough and Queen Charlotte Sounds, or marvelling at the majestic fjords of the South Island. Weekend port visits included the wholly engaging towns of Whangerai, Tauranga, Nelson and Lyttleton. On arrival at each new port, I took myself for a run around the waterfront or into town, scoping out the local scene. It was a chance to escape the confines of the ship, stretch my legs and capture some daylight memories ahead of the certain descent into drunken revelry with the locals. It was a routine that endured through countless port visits over the years.

All that charm and fun was somewhat eroded by the pressure of putting into practice at sea the skills we had learned ashore, albeit in a totally benign tactical environment. Time on passage was consumed by a never-ending series of training tasks, while conning and navigating the ship in pilotage waters was daily fare once in New Zealand waters. Coming to grips with the ship's handling characteristics or the effects of wind and tidal streams, bringing the ship to anchor, conducting man overboard drills and learning to safely lower and hoist seaboats were challenges that kept us leaning forward every day.

This time around, although it did nothing for my warfare skills, watchkeeping as a billeted officer in *Jervis Bay* provided a phenomenal opportunity to consolidate and extend my mariner skills. We conducted multiple training cruises, combing every navigable inch of the Whitsundays in Queensland, the D'Entrecasteaux Channel in Tasmania, and the old hunting grounds in New Zealand. As the trainee Midshipmen conned the ship from the specially constructed training bridge above (under the watchful gaze and direction of the Navigating Officer), the team on the actual bridge were continually checking for any risk of collision or grounding to maintain ship's safety for the CO.

Over the course of multiple cruises, I conducted hundreds of runs and anchorages in a vast array of conditions, building depth of experience and a complete confidence in my ability to plan and execute pilotage. Beyond this, the Navigator insisted that I practise the science and art of astronavigation morning, noon and night during every ocean passage. While this felt excessive, it resulted in some tremendous skill and culminated in the award of an Ocean Navigation Certificate, of which I was exceptionally proud. I also witnessed an abject lesson in how not to do some things – like how not to introduce women to a seagoing naval fleet.

The Women's Royal Australian Naval Service (WRANS) was established during the Second World War as a non-combatant branch of the Royal Australian Navy. When the WRANS was disbanded by an Act of Parliament during the early 1980s, WRANS personnel were integrated into the Royal Australian Navy. While they were permitted to serve aboard naval ships from that time, government policy of the day stipulated servicewomen not be employed in combat duties, severely restraining the options to ships such as the unarmed *Jervis Bay*. It wasn't until a decade later, in 1992, that any women were posted in billet into a combatant frigate, HMAS *Sydney*.

For many years, *Jervis Bay* had carried female Midshipmen on training cruises to gain sea experience. And the standards of behaviour and professional relationships expected between the Ship's Company and trainees were well enough established and generally abided. However, the introduction of women into the permanent strength of the Ship's Company created a different dynamic onboard altogether. All of us were ill-prepared. It was a clumsy, half-hearted and experimental gesture towards true integration into the Fleet, and I experienced it as a miserable failure.

Professionally and personally, I was offended by the ship's popular moniker of 'The Love Boat', yet it was impossible to credibly decry it. One senior officer was dismissed from the ship following an intimate and persistent affair with a female junior sailor, and I knew that similar liaisons onboard were commonplace. While I had an early opportunity to serve with some truly excellent female officers and sailors, I was also quick to unleash my Catholic morality in the silent judgement of others. Importantly, still struggling to achieve a degree of professional credibility, the last thing I needed was to be serving in a ship that was jeered at by my destroyer sailing pals.

Although she was a training ship and non-combatant, real-world operations were never far away for *Jervis Bay*. In early June, we departed Sydney to relieve HMAS *Success* on station off Fiji as part of Operation Morris Dance, the Australian Defence Force (ADF) operation responding to the first Fijian coup d'état of 1987. Regrettably, from my perspective, the operation was suspended as we completed flight trials for the helicopter landing deck that had been hurriedly fitted to the ship in the weeks prior. My hopes of seeing operational service were raised again in late September as the second coup erupted and we were recalled to the ship in readiness for an evacuation of Australian nationals. Although it was fortunate that we were not needed, it was a definite anti-climax being diverted to Queensland for a sealift exercise with the Army.

Our collective skills were tested in a meaningful way during February 1988, my last month onboard. Alongside in Wellington, New Zealand we were recalled to the ship late on a Saturday night and crash sailed into a fierce storm to respond to a distress call from a Korean fishing vessel, the *Dong Chang No.3*. Working with a mother ship, they had been at sea for more than a year. The vessel had sent out her mayday call moments before foundering and sinking in the renowned Cook Straits, which separate the North and South Islands.

Closing the search area at our best possible speed in heavy seas and degrading conditions, we joined the aircraft and passing merchant vessel already engaged in the search. Shortly after daybreak, the bridge was electrified as we sighted the boat's inflatable life raft appearing momentarily on the crest of a distant wave. Shaping course and closing the distance, we manoeuvred the *Jervis Bay* to provide a lee from the weather. Suffering from the horror of their boat capsizing and sinking underneath them, the survivors had endured a fearful night battered by the sea.

Completely exposed to the elements, they clung desperately to each other and to any handhold on the upturned and shredded inflatable life raft.

Launching the zodiac, we retrieved twelve wretched fishermen, including the skipper. He doggedly made his way up three more decks to the bridge to shake the hand of our Captain and thank the crew. He beamed with gratitude and the ecstasy of a life restored. But he was also grief stricken. While we remained at sea throughout the day continuing the search, we never found the three remaining crew who were trapped and taken down with the boat. While proud to be part of this outstanding Ship's Company that was willing to respond and had the competence and skill to save lives in such foreboding circumstances, I was also marked by the wholly indifferent and indiscriminate nature of the ocean.

As my time in *Jervis Bay* drew to a close, my awareness and understanding of the world around me deepened, and I wondered how I could and would make my mark. The competence of the Ship's Company was recognised in late 1987 with the award of the Duke of Gloucester's Cup, a highly prized trophy presented annually by the Governor-General of Australia to the most proficient ship in the Fleet. Increasingly competent and confident as a mariner, I took the distinction to heart and began looking to prove myself as a warrior.

Despite some professional credit to my name, I remained unsure of and in conflict with myself. A complete inability to limit my drinking had plagued me throughout the past two years. The damage I had inflicted on myself had been both contained by the extensive seatime and amplified by overindulgence in the seemingly endless runs ashore in distant ports. My steadily expanding beer coaster collection covered an entire wall in my apartment. It was both a tribute to a frenetic social life and testament to the tightening tentacles of drink. Before Shaunaugh – my moderating influence – departed for the United Kingdom for a few months of travel, I promised her I would turn over a new leaf.

Journal note, December 1987. *I can't fail at reform again.*

CHAPTER 4
YOU DID *WHAT*?

After serving in patrol boats, a destroyer, the Flagship and the training ship, I came to realise that life in the Navy wasn't all beer and skittles. The Navy demanded a great deal more than just hard work; it imposed real personal sacrifice, both on myself and those closest to me. For their sake and mine, I decided that as long as I remained in the Navy, I would commit to delivering the most effective and worthwhile service I could render.

I joined the Navy at a time when the RAN aircraft carrier capability was being consigned to history. Plans to replace HMAS *Melbourne* through the purchase of the Royal Navy carrier HMS *Invincible* had been scotched when Argentina invaded the Falkland Islands on 2 April 1982, little more than a month after they were formally announced by the government. The subsequent naval actions – including the British surface ship losses and the sinking of the light cruiser ARA *General Belgrano* by the Churchill-class submarine HMS *Conqueror* on 2 May 1982 – left an indelible impression on me. Accounting for more than half the total fatalities suffered by the Argentinian military, with the loss of 323 lives, and resulting in consignment of the Argentinian Fleet to port for the remainder of the war, it was a compelling example of decisive, contemporary sea power.

After four years in uniform, I knew my 'why', and was increasingly convinced that I knew my 'how.' Against the advice of almost everyone I knew, I decided to serve my country from within the most potent Arm of the Royal Australian Navy. I volunteered for submarines.

This decision was not without professional risk. Although skilled and experienced, lack of time in company with other warships meant that I hadn't qualified as an Officer of the Watch in *Jervis Bay*. If I failed to make the grade in submarines, I would be in an embarrassingly tenuous position – at least a year behind my classmates and starting from scratch to qualify on another class of ship. The Captain encouraged me to stay on board over the coming months to operate with multiple warships, get my ticket and move forward from there. However, given the infrequent intakes, it would mean a delay of at least a year in starting submarine training. Plagued with trepidation, I pushed my career onto a knife edge and took a one-way pass to submarines.

On something of an ego trip, I broke this news to Shaunaugh on her return to Australia. 'You did *what*?' she replied.

Shaunaugh was eventually supportive and encouraging, despite being all too aware of the hazards of submarine service. In August of the previous year, HMAS *Otama* was forced to cancel trials of a new sonar array towed behind the submarine during extremely bad weather. As the submarine pitched violently on the surface, two of the crew were sent into the fin to stow and secure the array. Tragically, they were still outside the pressure hull when *Otama* subsequently dived. Unable to contact the control room, the sailors were swept from the submarine and drowned in the raging sea. Many close Navy friends directly involved in the search would later speak of the painstaking and heartbreaking efforts conducted by the fleet over the next several days and nights. The bodies were never recovered.

Undeterred by doubt or fear, I strode through the main gates of HMAS *Platypus* ready to begin the Submarine Officers Training Course. Taking a winding path past the torpedo maintenance facilities, stores warehouses, battery workshops and the Squadron Headquarters, I finally found my way to the schoolhouse. By design or necessity, all of these buildings, rammed onto the meagre flat gouged into the sandstone between the water's edge and High Street, faced towards or looked down over the submarines berthed alongside. While the agglomeration appeared haphazard, it was interconnected, utilitarian and purposeful. Nestled into the shallows of Neutral Bay, the base contrasted starkly with the open expanses and grand vistas of Garden Island and Fleet Base East on the other side of the harbour.

It soon became apparent that I was barely prepared for this endeavour. My rank as a Sub-Lieutenant meant little here. Apparently, as a Part

One trainee, I was considered a subhuman form of life. The three major phases of initial submarine training had long been known, somewhat unimaginatively, as Parts One, Two and Three. While the length varied depending on whether you were an officer or a sailor, and depending on your specialisation or category, phases were measured in months, not weeks. As a Part One, my sole duty was to acquire submarine platform knowledge – learning the constituent parts of an Oberon-class submarine, the various interconnected systems and how they combine to form a functional seagoing, warfighting vessel.

With only five classmates, we received close and personal attention from our instructors, all highly specialised and experienced senior sailors. A gentlemanly, silver-haired Petty Officer imparted the necessary respect for the lead-acid main batteries that stored immense power and dictated the ebb and flow of our lives at sea more than any other onboard system. Another Petty Officer, with the strut of a pirate who had taken a cannonball to the knee, instructed us daily on the discrete recognition features of regional warships. Everyone wanted us to learn. Our eventual performance at sea would reflect on them and impact their professional standing – and they knew it. We soon appreciated that curiosity and knowledge earned respect, and there was no such thing as a dumb question in submarines.

Although the training was mostly classroom based, we were constantly on and off the boats alongside or in the dock at Cockatoo Island to get our hands on the systems and acclimate to life onboard. With diagrams and sketchbooks always close at hand, my white officers' overalls got a workout. I made my way from forward to aft hundreds of times, crawling into and exploring every accessible space and compartment. Slowly, I built mental layers of the maze of mechanical and electrical systems. I catalogued the location and purpose of every store, tank, bottle, pump, compressor, separator, accumulator, extinguisher, motor, generator, battery, switchboard, converter, resistor, breaker, terminal, cooler, fan, fridge, freezer, fitting, valve, manifold, cross-connection, junction box, strainer, sluice, controller, reducer, vent, relief, meter, gauge, test cock and indicator onboard.

We pushed through a multitude of assignments and examinations to the next phase of our specialist knowledge. Our new course instructor, recently returned to Australia from an overseas posting conducting

Cold War operations as the Navigator in a Royal Navy submarine, had a zeal for submarines that knew no bounds. Notably, *how* we learned was less important than *what* we learned, and *that* we learned. In this school, outcome and effects stood well in front of process and appearances. On a sunny Friday afternoon, he delivered our introductory lesson on 'the attack triangle' – the geometry of launching torpedoes against a target at sea – chalked up on his young son's blackboard in the backyard of their nearby home.

As a seaman officer, Part Two was focused on the navigation and combat systems, masts and periscopes, sensors and weapons, and it included specialist courses, such as submarine escape and periscope photography. Armed with our Canon F-1s, the green and gold Sydney Harbour ferries darting in and out of the bay and the towering palms of nearby Milson Park became our unwitting subjects. Clumsy and ineffectual at first, I developed the negatives and prints in the ridiculously small makeshift darkrooms set up in the showers of the submarines alongside until I reliably produced sharp images worthy of intelligence analysis.

I built an understanding of the watchkeeping orders, routines and standards that eventually enabled me to navigate and operate the submarine safely and effectively. While there were parallels from my surface ship experience, everything we learned had a different, further dimension to it, both literally and metaphorically. With the added complication of depth, the ramifications of operating in three dimensions impacted everything.

CHAPTER 5
STANDBY TO DIVE

By the end of June, we were ready for the next step, and three and a half months in glorious Sydney town came to an end. 'Work really hard, show them how good you are and make me proud of you,' were Shaunaugh's encouraging words as I left to join the sole boat operating out of Western Australia.

The next morning at HMAS *Stirling*, the Navy's fleet base in Perth, my pace slowed to take in the wharf-side scene as I approached HMAS *Oxley*, tied up alongside. The first of six Oberon-class submarines acquired by the RAN, she was launched the year I was born. Her bearded XO, Lieutenant Lachlan King, RAN, beckoned demonically from the fin and ushered us aboard. *The 'black pig' has us, but the 'black pig' will be mine.* In keeping with my Catholic upbringing, I prayed for the courage and conviction to get through this next stage.

Onboard *Oxley*, there were four of us Part Threes. Two of my buddies were engineers, one of whom was a decade my senior, eccentric and had an insatiable appetite for all things submarines. The second made a notably less disruptive companion. The other fellow was a seaman officer. Remarkably, he was not a volunteer, but drafted to boats through a Navy Headquarters program created to bolster submarine recruiting numbers. Constructed on a misguided premise, the scheme was blind to the centrality of volunteer status to submarine service and ultimately proved a dismal failure.

The welcome extended by the crew was decidedly reserved. As Part Threes, we were both the potential future of the Arm and the potential demise of every person onboard. We were the least skilled, least experienced and least proven people onboard, and therefore the most dangerous. Unqualified, we held the greatest prospect of making an error that could cost the life of one or all. Until we knew how to safely live and operate as part of the crew and had proven that ability, we continued to present as a liability. Trust in this environment was hard won.

While it was often heavily disguised under a veil of contempt, I found the encouragement and support the crew provided was directly proportionate to the effort they saw me put into my training. I truly felt I could shape my destiny here.

Within a week, we are letting go lines to deploy. This first day at sea in *Oxley* stretches out beyond imagination: not for tedium, but for the raw concentration of new experience. As we depart in the fierce blow that rips across Cockburn Sound, two sailors securing berthing lines are swept off the aft casing and onto the ballast tanks only moments after I go below. They each find a handhold, saving themselves from washing aft and down into the churning screws, and are hauled back on deck. Not quite a man overboard, but pretty damn close, and a cautionary start to the voyage.

Sailing by the entrance to Fremantle Harbour and past low-lying Rottnest Island, we shape a northerly course. Perched at the front of the fin on the open and windswept bridge for my first surfaced watch, I'm exhilarated. I now have a passion for the majesty and the humility of life at sea, but this is something else. As the long black hull pushes through the approaching seas, which spray away from and then collapse over the egg-shaped sonar dome on the bow, I am tingling with nervous energy. The Torpedo Officer, an old chum from Naval College days, hands me the tannoy to order 'Diving Stations' and report our progress clearing the bridge.

Summoned to the fore-ends, I make my way below and join the XO. Already relaxed into sandals, old shorts and a faded blue work shirt, he moves through the submarine from forward to aft at a rapid and practiced pace as we deliberately check the state of hundreds of valves to ensure the submarine is correctly 'opened up' for diving. Although this has already been proven in each compartment and reported to the control room by the crew, there's no room for doubt as the submarine transitions from the surface to a dived state. And the crew take no offence that their work is checked.

Back in the control room, now packed with more people than I thought possible, every station is manned and then some. The Captain orders the Officer of the Watch and lookout below. They make their way down through the fin and into the cramped conning tower that separates the pressure hull from the outside world. I distinctly hear the clang of the upper lid being shut, banishing the outside world, and the accompanying reports.

'Upper lid shut. Upper lid shut, 2 clips, 2 pins.'

'Diving now, diving now,' crackles over main broadcast.

'Open main vents,' orders the Captain.

Switches are flicked, indicator lights blink. I hear Number 4 main vents, located on either side of the control room, thud open. Outside the submarine, seventeen geysers spray up from the vent holes as air rushes from the ballast tanks, pushed out by the seawater now barging in through free flood holes in the bottom of the tanks. In an instant, our buoyancy is gone and we are on our way.

'1, 2, 4, 6 and 7 main vents open, double indication on 6 starboard,' reports the panel watchkeeper.

'Full dive on the planes, 6 down, 75 feet back to 57,' again from the Captain.

'Full dive on the planes, 6 down, 75 feet back to 57,' acknowledges the Coxswain, *Oxley*'s most senior sailor and experienced planesman. He pushes forward on the single control mechanism, at once manoeuvring the rudder to steer the boat as well as the forward and aft planes to change pitch and depth.

'Report 6 starboard main vent,' orders the engineer on the trim seat.

'6 starboard main vent open,' is the immediate reply over main broadcast.

'Raise forward.'

The panel watchkeeper lifts the short brass lever controlling the attack periscope. The sleek steel of the mast rises swiftly through the deck with a quiet hydraulic hiss. The watchkeeper's gaze is intent on the Captain, a few feet away, to ensure it stops the instant the periscope handles are lowered and his eye meets the monocle.

'Dome under,' reports the Captain, sighting the bow as it slips beneath the surface.

'5 down, 30 feet. 6 down,' says the Coxswain, reporting the keel depth while nursing the down angle on the boat.

'Flooding the masts,' calls the panel watchkeeper as seawater flushes into the induction and exhaust masts above our heads, gurgling past the sight glass.

'35 feet.'

'Blow Q,' orders the Captain, sending high pressure air into this trimming tank and displacing 800 gallons of seawater to lighten the bow.

'40 feet.'

'Upper lid dry,' from the Torpedo Officer – 'Torps' – standing by the tower and ready to climb back to the bridge should we need to surface in emergency.

'50 feet.'

'Shut the lower lid, shut the lower voice pipe cock.'

'Vent Q,' to the rasp of air being released back into the fore-ends.

'Q vented, Q-vent shut.'

'65 feet, Sir.'

'Shut the lower lid, speed for trimming.'

'Stop together, group down, half ahead together,' from the trim seat, swiftly aligning the telegraphs.

'75 feet, Sir. 1 up, 2 up, coming up.'

'60 feet.'

'Raise forward, nothing close, keep 54 feet. Set watch search. Set watch warner. Carry out long post-diving checks.'

'56 feet, 54 feet, on depth. On course, 170.'

'Captain, Sir, sound room. All sonars operating correctly with the exception of PIPRS, two contacts held faint. Sonar 21, bearing 079, held attacker, ranger. Sonar 40 bearing 216, held ranger only.'

'Main vents cycled, all main vents indicating shut.'

'Officer of the Watch. Captain. Pipe the watch "First watch, watch dived, patrol-quiet state".'

With this cacophony of orders and acknowledgements and tightly choreographed actions, the submarine is brought safely beneath the surface. I see the crew, highly attuned to their environment, are at once diligent and relaxed throughout this barrage. Experiencing it for the first time, I know I can make sense of each order and action in isolation, but the rapidity with which the reports come – from every corner of the control room and every compartment of the submarine, in what sounds like a stream of disjointed conversations – is overwhelming. I thought I was prepared for this. My head pounds. It takes a moment to realise that it's all gone quiet. We're under. After five and a half years in the Navy, I am at sea in a dived submarine.

Working with P-3C and P-3K Orion maritime patrol aircraft from the RAAF and RNZAF over the first day or so, I got a sense of what it was like to be hunted as we sought to evade the active and passive sonar buoy patterns they deployed ahead of us. We reduced our speed to a crawl and adopted an 'ultra-quiet state', switching off pumps, fans and other machinery to reduce any noise from the submarine to an absolute minimum. With air-conditioning shut down, the temperature, humidity and CO_2 levels in the boat all rose over several tense hours. Using hushed voices, we moved through the boat with added caution, knowing that something as simple as a spanner dropped on the steel decks would cause a 'transient', sending noise out from the submarine that could be detected by the sonar buoys listening on behalf of the aircraft above.

Eventually surfacing to transit at higher speed, we made our way north past a smouldering Krakatoa early one morning and pushed on through the Sunda Strait and into Southeast Asian waters. Arriving at Sembawang Basin in Singapore for a two-day visit to re-store, I sampled the chilli crab with gusto and got stuck into the Tiger beer at Newton Circus. On Sunday afternoon, my head thick and aching, we sailed for Exercise Starfish – a multi-national exercise conducted in the shallow waters off Malaysia under the waning Five Power Defence Arrangements.

A day later, the confounding sensations of my first dive were replicated and exaggerated as I witnessed the submarine operating at 'Attack Teams' for the first time. Within minutes of closing up, we launched simulated torpedo attacks against our opposing forces. We marked each attack with 'green grenades' – pyrotechnic flares that are fired from our Submerged Signal Ejector (SSE) and soar hundreds of feet into the sky. With a task group of warships manoeuvring aggressively and at speed, the intensity of the work onboard was extreme as the team built the picture of what was happening around us and its rapid evolvement. In the warm tropical waters, the atmosphere within the boat was oppressively thick. The Captain worked himself into a lather, wielding the periscope up and down like a samurai sword as he prosecuted one warship after the next.

'Final target set-up, *Orangeleaf*, raise forward.'

'Bearing that, 176, range that, 7,600 yards, down.'

'Put me 15 port, speed 14 knots.'

'Assign the solution, fire 6 tube.'

'Final target set-up, *Edinburgh*, raise forward.'

I began to realise that we could detect, track, identify and 'attack' these warships at will, seemingly without fear of reprise. Over several days, the combined fleet was unable to locate us and therefore had no response to our provocations. Our own destroyer escort, HMAS *Swan*, the Kiwi escort HMNZS *Waikato* and the Indonesian Kasturi-class corvette KD *Lekir* were identified for early punishment, but there wasn't a ship in the exercise that avoided our lash.

Nonetheless, the attacks took relentless effort. Working in watches, the crew split into three teams with one or more sailors of each specialisation in each watch. I spent two four-hour periods in the control room each day, contributing wherever I could with periscope watches, navigation or trimming the boat on ship control. The control room and adjacent compartments were totally blacked out at night to preserve the night vision of the periscope watchkeepers, so any spare daylight hours were spent working toward sign-off on Part Three tasks. At no stage did I enjoy more than three hours of unbroken sleep. Despite the conditions and the workload, I had found direction.

At the end of the exercise, we steamed through the task group, now assembled at anchor off the Malaysian island of Pulau Tioman. Our Captain, having just returned to the submarine by boat after a final debriefing with the Task Group Commander, decided our successes should be rubbed in a little. He ordered a final green grenade fired into the night as we passed close by the carrier HMS *Ark Royal*.

Part Three or not, I knew the SSE was designed for dived operation. As we yelled a warning to the anchor party standing between the upturned planes, a pyrotechnic shell lobbed out of the launcher with a *poomf*. It carved a slow path about 20 feet into the air, then landed on the forward casing, spinning like a demonic bottle, not 10 feet from the sailor's boots. Moments later, as the time fuse burned out, the grenade fired out of its shell. Pointing aft, it traced an arc directly towards the Navigator and I on the bridge. As we shrivelled to take cover, the grenade struck the fin about three feet below our heads and careened away, spreading a fluorescent green lustre across the night sky.

Having narrowly avoided maiming or killing one of our own, any further fireworks were immediately curtailed. Clearly appointment in command didn't provide complete inoculation against doing something dopey once in a while. It was an early and valuable lesson in the responsibility of the entire crew to back each other up, including through forthright advice to the Captain, to ensure we don't do ourselves a mischief.

A week later, thrilled to be now trusted to keep my own bridge watches, we transited the Gulf of Thailand and drove back into the South China Sea. Others were less comfortable. Within twenty-four hours of departing our last port of Bangkok, one of the junior sailors was laid low by stomach pains. The Coxswain, who had more training in first aid than anyone else onboard, was unable to diagnose the issue, so the Captain decided the young fella needed to be evacuated. We approached the coast of Brunei on the surface, ensuring we didn't close within the limits of their territorial seas. I had the watch and responsibility for the safe conduct and navigation of the boat as we rendezvoused with a patrol boat in the calm seas off Muara, the main base of the fledgling Royal Brunei Navy, in the middle of the night. It brought a curious, almost reckless, feeling to hand off one of the crew to a foreign warship, but our submarine was no place for a sick man right now.

By dawn, the submarine was dived and on a patrol footing executing classified orders, but this was no exercise. Having fully charged the main batteries overnight, we ceased all sonar, radar and radio transmissions. Opening from our last observable position, we intentionally disappeared into the murk and mire of the South China Sea.

In part, I was still trying to make sense of what was going on around me, and I noted little difference in the minute-by-minute or hour-by-hour activity onboard. The orders, reports, drills and procedures were much the same. But the Captain shifted some routines, splitting the crew into two watches, rather than three, and handing over every six hours instead of four. Now we had substantially more manpower and expertise available at any one time. This enabled us to deal with almost any eventuality and stay on the watch, rather than piping 'Attack Teams', which can be far more disruptive.

With the change in routines, there was a decided shift in the feel onboard – an uptick in focus and, at times, intensity compared to when we were training or exercising with friendly warships or submarines. Because of where we go and what we seek to do, there was both more at risk and more to be gained. Consequently, our actions were more considered and our reactions more deliberate.

Within this altered paradigm, these unlikely warriors – meticulously styled in greasy beanies, sweat-stained truckers' singlets and faded uniform shorts – seemed more like a band of pirates than a crew of professional naval officers and sailors. Yet, while there was not a single combat veteran onboard and no state of conflict beyond, they were undeniably living as warriors. Endlessly honing and perfecting their craft to meet the demands of today's mission, the unspoken ethos was one of unceasing preparedness to meet any enemy as and when they might appear.

The better operators relaxed into the patrol environment. Those still mastering their role onboard were a little more stressed. Though in the latter camp, I found the ways and gained enough trust to make a useful contribution. Doing what we have been trained to do, hours, watches, days and weeks passed in a continual rotation of periscope tricks, trimming and navigating the submarine, compiling records and snatching sleep whenever possible.

In time I came to not only belong, but truly comprehend this strange world. I understood that, while technologies evolved, the fundamental characteristics of our submarines throughout the decades remained consistent. Stealth has always underpinned their safety, survivability and tactical effectiveness. Preservation of stealth is what allows operations in otherwise non-permissive or hostile environments. Their long range enables them to sail into areas where the many advantages of a submarine are optimised, and endurance ensures poise and presence on station thousands of miles from our shores over weeks and months.

Total independence allows our submarines to conduct surveillance and intelligence collection in times of tension or offensive operations against an enemy at war without any reliance on direct support from other units. At the same time, interoperability facilitates the sequencing of missions with Allies, such as the United States, to magnify the operational effect across a theatre. With a fearsome payload of highly sophisticated and destructive weapons, these attributes combine to create a devastatingly lethal combatant that is exceptionally difficult and expensive to counter. In essence, we seek to see without being seen, hear without being heard and know without being known, until the day comes when we need to strike.

It is precisely these characteristics, particularly their absolute lethality as a combatant, that generate the true value and potency of our submarines. The ability to consistently achieve credible presence in strategically significant waters creates doubt and shapes the calculus of military and political leaders to deter coercion and aggression by other nation states against us. Simply put, it is the submarines' capacity for destruction that can so powerfully deter a potential adversary.

After three or more full weeks on patrol, I had a new appreciation for the high-level security clearances required to join the Arm. Surfaced again, *Oxley* was now in an altogether different sea and 2,500 nautical miles from her diving position. Having remained entirely undetected throughout that time and with our classified mission accomplished, we were en route back to Sydney.

Despite being smashed with fatigue, my morale was super high – until the XO dropped a bombshell. During our port visit to Bangkok over a month ago, Midshipman Paddy O'Dwyer, RAN joined the boat as a fifth Part Three officer. He and I ran amok for several days and nights, and clearly tested the XO's patience well and truly beyond limits. Having bided his time for effect, he revoked our upcoming shore leave in Sydney just a day before we were due to come alongside. Shattered and forlorn, there was no arguing the toss and, fuming at my own stupidity, there was no-one to blame but myself. It was a total disaster because while in Bangkok I had proposed to Shaunaugh. After a three-month separation, she will be on the wharf as we come alongside, and there's no way to contact her beforehand.

On the day of our arrival, I confidently directed the forward Casing Party as the submarine glided past the moored yachts and eased alongside a wharf packed with welcoming Squadron staff. Heaving and berthing lines were passed in quick succession, a slim gangway was lowered into place and our CO stepped ashore to report to Captain Submarines. Signalling to me from the bridge once we had doubled up, the XO extended the small mercy of allowing me onto the wharf to deliver the news.

I was in a deeper hole than I imagined possible. Our engagement party, hosted by Shaunaugh's mum and dad at their family home, with a hundred friends and relatives in attendance, will be taking place tomorrow night – apparently whether I'm there or not! Returning onboard, a bargain was struck. With scant regard for my feelings, but knowing the importance of family support for submarine service, the XO conceded that I could take leave and attend the party, subject to an invitation extended to every member of the wardroom.

It was no accident that we found ourselves alongside in Sydney at this time of year. *Oxley* was one of the more than fifty warships, including the famed Iowa-class battleship the USS *New Jersey*, and scores of aircraft from fifteen navies, assembled from across the globe for the Bicentennial Naval Salute and Fleet Review. Held on 1 October 1988 to commemorate the arrival of the First Fleet in 1788 and celebrate the nation's maritime heritage, it was the largest such gathering ever seen in Australia, surpassing the Navy's 75th celebrations.

Moored just off Clark Island, the spring sun was beaming down and I proudly paraded with the full strength of *Oxley*'s Ship's Company. Lined up as we were to cheer ship, shoulder to shoulder along the entire length of the boat from forward to aft, I wondered how we could all dissolve back into the hull beneath us. We were among many of the 17,000 sailors who ship-hopped for cheap booze then thundered ashore each night across a week of festivities. The popular adage of 'work hard, play hard' was hammered into my psyche, with a definite 'drink hard' twist reinforced by a lack of real Navy consequence to my excesses. I was well and truly ready for a break when it came time to sail for practice torpedo firings off the coast and our return voyage to Western Australia.

At year's end, with Shaunaugh by my side, my personal life was saturated with passion and promise. Professionally, I had completed a first patrol, a first Southeast Asian deployment and a second circumnavigation of Australia. Crucially, I was wearing 'dolphins', the coveted badge of a qualified submariner. After a gruelling initiation, I was phenomenally proud to be accepted into the tribe. I was a submariner.

CHAPTER 6
SUBMARINER

As I approached the start of my seventh year in the Navy, and with my promotion to Lieutenant imminent, I lost no time joining HMAS *Otway* as Casing Officer, the most junior of the established billets for a seaman officer. She was a taut boat, continually pressed to meet the impeccable standards of her CO. Safety and operational work-ups to prove the state of the submarine and the competency of the crew promptly followed and further deployments ensued, including my sixth voyage to New Zealand.

Otway was home ported out of Sydney, so when I was not out at sea, I lived close by to family and friends. In late April, after developing septicaemia from an infected foot due to a chronic injury, I found myself once again hospitalised at HMAS *Penguin* at Balmoral. Feeling feeble and sorry for myself, I was rattled when the news that some of my classmates, including a great mate, Sean Moles, had been involved in an accident.

Working towards qualification as a clearance diver, Sean had been thriving on the exceedingly difficult course. Humble, charismatic and infectiously happy, Sean was wildly popular. While I spent my youth straining to squeeze every last drop out of life, he had spent his youth simply bursting with it. Out on an early morning training run on Sydney's Northern Peninsula, Sean and two others were hit from behind by a car at speed, and with awful consequences. Hearing that an ambulance was headed for *Penguin*, I made my way down to the ambulance bay. Held away from the scene by grim-faced staff, I realised why I didn't hear any sirens wailing on approach – Sean's injuries were fatal.

My thoughts swung erratically between the certainty that my friend was dead and utter disbelief. Sean was slated to be a groomsman at my upcoming wedding to Shaunaugh. Feeling helpless, miserable and alone, I discharged myself to get away from the hospital and be with friends.

Bracing myself on the drive to the airport to pick up Shaunaugh, returning from a three-week trip overseas, I struggled with delivering the devastating news. Difficult as the day had been, I was wholeheartedly grateful that I wasn't away at sea. We are pierced. We are different. We are vincible.

Journal note, June 1989. *Will I ever captain a submarine?*

To satisfy her love of travel, Shaunaugh put her nursing career aside and became an air hostess with Qantas. The combination of lengthy and volatile submarine deployments and her extended long-haul trips meant we were rarely in each other's company and forever at the mercy of the scheduling gods. On one memorable occasion, halfway through a three-month deployment into Southeast Asia, Shaunaugh lined up her flight bids with a planned stop in Bangkok and we managed to make our two worlds meet, relishing five days together on our first overseas trip.

While we were basking in the lap of luxury at a posh hotel on the banks of the Chao Phraya river, *Otway* was berthed at a small naval pier about twenty minutes from the city by bus along a rough road separating the river from the ever-encroaching jungle. With the onboard galley shut down, the duty watches sent out for meals from a roadside 'restaurant', ordering by number from a scrappy menu pinned to a notice board in the forward mess. Number 16, highly recommended since the first night alongside, quickly became a firm favourite, the hot tip passed at handover to the new duty watch each day. After three days, our Liaison Officer was onboard and spied the menu. A Thai linguist and ever obliging, he scratched a few translations onto the menu. *Number 16 – Stewed monkey brains.* Some were deterred, some were not! It was a difficult week for the local monkeys.

Later in the year, on the return leg, *Otway* operated out of Darwin into the Timor and Arafura Seas during Exercise Kangaroo '89. The Defence White Paper of 1987 placed great emphasis on self-reliance and threats from the north. With 28,000 Australian and US military personnel involved, this was the largest military exercise ever undertaken in Australia during peacetime. So large, it attracted the Prime Minister, Bob Hawke; the Minister for Defence, Kim Beazley; the Chief of the Defence Force and the Chief of Naval Staff, who all embarked in one of the frigates to observe the exercise at sea.

Several hours after sailing from Darwin to join the exercise and conduct our first serial, I was enjoying the tropical sunshine while on the bridge when a pipe came across on main broadcast:

'Casualty, casualty, casualty. Casualty in the after-ends.'

As Officer of the Watch, I was responsible for the submarine and crew. Initial reports were confused, but it soon became clear that the situation was indeed dire. Trevor had been scalped!

Trevor the budgie originally stowed away in our sister boat, HMAS *Orion*, during a port visit to Singapore some years ago. Having come across him in a tiny bamboo cage ashore, the troops decided that an Australian parrot deserved something better than the life of an ex-pat in Asia. They 'acquired' the wayward bird, offering him safe passage home and release on country. Of course, the fine print in our quarantine laws meant that he could never be set free in Australia, so he was named after *Orion*'s XO, Lieutenant Trevor Robertson, RAN, and plied the seas thereafter as ship's mascot. One night years later, immediately before *Orion* docked for an extended refit, Trevor was smuggled across the bow to *Otway*, berthed alongside *Orion* at the time. By sheer happenstance, *Otway* was now under the command of Trevor Senior.

Making a home in the after-ends, Trevor's vocabulary and temperament were shaped by the rough vernacular and less refined humour of the technical rates, which left a lot to be desired. 'Show us your tits' was a common plea and 'Trevor's a … (insert profanity)!' a frequent assertion. To note, Trevor was a wonderful parrot, but no judge of character.

He also learned practical calls, such as 'Budgie on deck!', to alert the sailors to his presence. Regrettably on this day, a Leading Seaman, making his way aft out of the engine room and through the circular bulkhead door, failed to register Trevor's shrill warning. His boot came down on Trevor's head, removing a swatch of skin and feathers and dramatically exposing his little skull.

By uncanny coincidence, the engine room reported a Priority One defect on the oily water separator only minutes after the casualty pipe was heard.

'No, Sir, we don't have the spares onboard. Yes, Sir, they're in our lay-apart store back on the wharf. Sorry, Sir, we'll have to return alongside.'

The local vet was onboard well ahead of any stores. Trevor, and therefore the offending sailor, survived to tell the tale.

Once we are back at sea, the Kangaroo '89 exercise proved exceedingly challenging on a couple of fronts. Working in two watches, I was in the control room from 0100 to 0700 and again from 1300 to 1900 each day. Time off watch through the day was typically spent tending to a raft of essential but tedious jobs, such as managing the contingent account that pays cash allowances to the troops when we come alongside in foreign ports. Time off watch at night was spent catching thirty minutes of whatever video was showing in the wardroom that week – eventually the storyline came together – or else in my cart. In contrast to being on watch or off watch, there was a station and a role for everyone whenever we were at Harbour Stations, Diving Stations, Emergency Stations or Action Stations. Across the weeks of the exercise, we were repeatedly called to Action Stations, adding greatly to the daily workload.

We were most definitely in a 'target rich environment', with up to fifteen warships in area at any one time. Bound by both exercise and environmental constraints, we were often the target, and in much of the areas assigned to us, in 'periscope depth only' water. With 10 fathoms or less between our keel and the bottom, once we were dived there was nowhere to go to escape any potential collision with a surface vessel. This also meant there was absolutely no room for error with trimming the submarine, depth keeping and changing depth. If it were possible to tip the submarine on one end, half the length of the submarine would jut out of the sea into the sky.

With clear waters and a sandy bottom, our black silhouette was also readily visible from the air, and the generally calm seas and good visibility aided visual or radar detection of our masts and periscopes by ships and aircraft. The bathymetric conditions also meant there was nowhere to hide from the active sonar search of the warships. Once detected, we are like the proverbial fish in a barrel; although the steadily escalating rules of engagement meant there was no 'shooting' for most of the exercise.

The Spruance-class destroyer USS *Oldendorf* made a particular nuisance of herself. It became genuinely nerve-wracking and demoralising being tracked day after day, night after night; the haunting whistle of her mainframe AN/SQS53 sonar creeping incessantly through the hull. Sometimes faint, sometimes powerfully loud, it was there when on watch in the control room, while eating a meal in the wardroom or waking from a short, broken sleep in my undersized bunk.

Time and again we thought we had broken contact with her as the range opened and the decibel levels faded, only to find her coming back over the horizon on a steady bearing hours later to nail us down again. We maintained fire control solutions on her continuously, as we did with any warship, so the second the exercise rules of engagement changed and the gloves came off, we let rip with simulated Harpoon missile attacks against her. Though momentarily satisfying, it did nothing to erase the torment and intense discomfort of being hunted during the two-week long experience. Squeezing the exercise for every scrap of training benefit, we came away thoroughly schooled in operating the submarine in particularly shallow water and especially difficult conditions.

Performance report, August 1989. ... *a loyal officer who is consolidating his submarine skills and shows great potential as a submariner.*
– CO HMAS *Otway*

CHAPTER 7
CLUTCHING IN

The following year saw a vastly different deployment as we set sail for the Rim of the Pacific Exercise, known as RIMPAC. This biennial event, the world's largest international maritime warfare exercise – run by the US Navy in Hawaii since the early 1970s – regularly boasted participation, by invitation, of upwards of twenty different nations. The scale and complexity of the exercise scenarios; the number and diversity of warships, submarines and aircraft; and the associated array of sensors and tactics that we needed to recognise, understand and operate against were largely incomprehensible at first blush.

We spent most of February 1990 in simulators ashore conducting weapon employment and command team training. With butterflies in my stomach on the early morning boat ride across Sydney Harbour, we conducted this warfare training in a dedicated classified facility at HMAS *Watson*. The long days were structured to hone and test knowledge, skills and teamwork, and I was acutely aware that the performance of each individual and the team as a whole were on open display, intensely observed and sharply judged.

The next several weeks focused on work-ups: emergency drills and other procedural training practised at first alongside, then at a buoy and eventually while dived at sea. To ensure both the boat and the Ship's Company were ready for whatever challenges lay ahead, we simulated 'fires, floods and famines', seemingly till our heads caved in.

Newly appointed as the Torpedo Officer, I was selected as the subject for an 'at sea' trial as *Otway*'s Weapon Control Console Operator – the button pusher – which had historically been the domain of the Weapons Engineer. Meeting the required standards was a strict precursor for moving forward with the boat's program and eventual weapon certification at sea, enabling us to fire our Mark 48 torpedos and UGM-84 Harpoon missiles. With ample assistance from the senior

Squadron staff, who frequently embarked to steadily ratchet up the degree of difficulty and make final assessments of our performance, we were straining at the leash and ready to go.

Eventually setting sail in *Otway* in mid-March for Exercise RIMPAC '90, Lieutenant Commander Mike Deeks, RAN had assumed command. I first met Mike years earlier at the Naval College. Then a Lieutenant, he was in command of GPV *Banks*, the small training vessel we embarked for Exercise Seatrain. A towering, bearded submariner, Mike might have been intimidating, but for his ever-present humility and compassion for the dozen or so Midshipmen and crew embarked in *Banks*. That short voyage, our initial foray to sea, provided my Midshipman classmates and me with a first practical taste of seamanship, navigation and ship's husbandry. In company with our sister ship GPV *Bass* throughout, I observed early on that pride in your own ship and performance didn't have to come at the expense of another.

Back on the bridge of *Otway*, with a departure fix plotted on the chart and Sydney Heads fading from view over the horizon astern, a young Part Three piped up and said, 'Right, where are we going then, Sir?'

This was Day One of a three-and-a-half-month deployment. Even allowing for the fact that he had probably been absorbed in his own Part Three training, the professional in me was totally riled. *Where the hell have you been for the last two months?* To be fair, we often deliberately obscured the operational details of a deployment from the crew, particularly the more junior sailors. But the fact that we were headed for Hawaii was no secret. However, the explorer in me was absolutely delighted. *What trusting and willing people some of these sailors must be.* Rocking up on the appointed day, kit bag packed and slung over their shoulder, they merrily hopped onboard and made their way below. I would not have been surprised if we turned up in the Antarctic and some of these guys said, 'Ooh, bit chilly. Should have bought my jumper. So … where's the pub?'

It's a long haul to Hawaii in a diesel boat, so we left well ahead of the task group, which comprised of HMAS *Brisbane*, *Darwin*, *Adelaide* and the oiler *Success*. The RAAF Orion maritime patrol aircraft will leave later still to fly across. As such, we were on our own when we suffered a flood two days after departing Sydney. Dived and transiting at 300 feet keel depth, the pressure on the boat was substantial. I marvelled at how readily the training kicked in throughout the boat. Blowing main ballast, we used our speed and rapidly increasing buoyancy to drive to the surface.

Conscious that I had tremendous trust in the skill and expertise of those around me, and particularly those with greater responsibility, I curiously lacked some of the gut fear that usually appeared in an inherently life-threatening incident. I briefly wondered if I was missing something. That said, we had endured worse previously.

Months earlier, we suffered a flood while operating at our maximum operating depth. A failure on the after-services system, which provides cooling to several engine and motor room systems, had us scrambling to get to the roof. Propelling at slow speed at the moment of the flood, the planes and rudder offered remarkably little control over the attitude of the boat. We had been carrying a slight list to starboard and, confusingly, this rapidly increased as we rose towards the surface. The fin, which was open to the sea and heavy with seawater, began to drag just as the bulk of the boat underneath it became more buoyant. The closer we got to the surface, the further over to starboard we came. Knowing the outcome would be catastrophic, I could not quell a rising fear that we would capsize before we got to the roof. We were heeled well over on our side when we finally broke the surface.

By comparison, this more recent flood seems positively tame. We notched it up, shook it off and pressed on across the Pacific towards Hawaii.

Emerging from the engine room hatch into a dazzlingly bright morning, I nearly fell back into the boat when I spied the Rising Sun flying not twenty feet away. A Yūshio-class submarine of the Japanese Maritime Self-Defence Force (JMSDF) had berthed alongside us and her ensign flapped off her stern in the stiff breeze. It was the last thing I expected to see on arrival in Pearl Harbor. Recently invited to participate for the first time, she was here to bring a different dimension and new challenge to RIMPAC. Despite the fall of the Berlin Wall six months earlier, the spectre of the Cold War and the Soviet Fleet still hung heavy in the Pacific, and the importance of democratic alliances across the region was increasingly evident.

Stepping ashore, the troops were delighted to learn that our host boat, the Los Angeles-class submarine USS *Olympia*, was sponsored by a brewery. Accepting their invitation to a picnic day at White Plains Beach, we arrived to find forty cases of beer stacked into a 'mini-Mount Olympia'. Our US Navy colleagues viewed this as an impressive static display. *Otway*'s Ship's Company took it as an amiable challenge, ordered a shed load more ice and proceeded to demolish the Mount over a long afternoon. With an easy rapport between the crews, our American hosts proved generous and hospitable to a fault. Lacking sober judgement towards the end of the day, I accepted an offer of chewing tobacco from one of the *Olympia* crew. Making the rookie error of swallowing more of the vile juice than I spit, I was soon green around the gills and swore off the stuff for life. With a week of harbour briefings and social acclimatisation soon behind us, we were ready to put to sea and get amongst it.

The accumulating seatime brought a string of highlights for me, including steadily adding to my capabilities: first qualifying as a submariner, then keeping Officer of the Day duties alongside, Officer of the Watch on the surface and Assistant Officer of the Watch when dived. Now my qualification as Weapons Controller meant being totally clutched in when we conducted a live firing of a Harpoon missile. It was a ridiculously rare event, particularly in comparison to the endless number of practice torpedoes we fired, and I grasped the opportunity with both hands. Dived on the Barking Sands Missile Range off the island of Kauai, I spent the final hours prior to an early morning firing checking every possible variable on the combat system and adjusting tactics. The range officials would track the missile in flight, ready to cut it down if it behaved erratically or endangered anything other than the target.

'Fire 1 Tube!'

Knowing full well it's coming, I still jumped at the *whoosh*, shake and hiss as high-pressure air forced the missile from the tube. Breaching the surface, the missile broke away from its capsule, launching into the air at over 500 mph to a target more than 60 nautical miles over the horizon.

Stepping up into the role of the Watchleader while dived was an even greater privilege, particularly in the pressure-cooker environment of RIMPAC. It meant building and driving the long-term performance of my own watch of officers and sailors. More immediately, it meant taking responsibility for the conduct of the submarine for the Captain throughout a six-hour watch, twice a day. We were several miles off Diamond Head, tracking a group of warships departing Pearl Harbor, when I first made the report, 'Captain, Sir. Torps has the watch.'

I had been thirsting for this day for years now; and yet I still had to convince myself that I was ready for the challenge. Late that night we found ourselves deep, dodging the towed decoys and variable depth sonars being streamed (contrary to their exercise instructions) by several of the warships. At five tonnes or more, a towed sonar moving at more than 30 knots colliding with a submerged submarine would have a disastrous impact. As the warships above manoeuvred continuously throughout the watch, we relied on our ability to rapidly generate and maintain a clear understanding of their position and movements using only our passive sonar information. Constrained in depth by our own exercise orders, I was operating at the edge of my abilities.

While I was generally content with my life at sea, it was definitely hard graft. Working eighteen-hour days for weeks on end was gruelling – physically, cognitively and emotionally. Staying safe and being effective required continuous attention to detail and unambiguous communication among the team to maintain situational awareness, both within and outside the boat.

Inevitably, there were slip-ups. Handing over to my oppo, Lieutenant Steve Davies, RAN early one morning, we were standing in the middle of the control room between the periscopes. Working our way around each of the stations, I ran through the state of the submarine and its various systems in what was a long and convoluted, but standard and necessary, patter.

'… we are snorting on both, floating the load, steering 240 at half ahead together, grouped up, keeping 54 feet …'

The submarine was just below the surface at periscope depth, with the search periscope, a snorkel mast and an exhaust mast raised. The boat was effectively breathing air, enabling us to run our massive diesel generators and charge the main storage batteries that are the lifeblood of a diesel-electric submarine. Having just taken over on the trim seat, the oncoming Watch Engineer was responsible for ship control. After weeks at sea and not long out of his cart, he was, like all of us, fatigued and possibly not fully awake yet. However, he was alert enough to hear me say 'half ahead together' to Steve.

Mistaking it for a propulsion order, the Watch Engineer leaned forward and rotated the main motor telegraphs. Thinking he was changing them from slow ahead to half ahead, he unwittingly ordered both main motors to full power. The submarine surged forward and the planesman lost control of the depth, dragging the snorkel mast beneath the sea surface. As flap valves slammed shut, cutting off the supply of air, the diesels rapidly drew a massive vacuum inside the entire submarine and we 'flamed out'.

'Stop snorting!'

All masts and periscopes were lowered, and the diesel generators were crash stopped. The snorkel system was flooded, dramatically altering the trim of the boat. While there's no damage done, Steve and his crew will spend the next twenty minutes sorting it out.

'It's all yours, mate, I'm off to brekkie!'

We were still at sea on the penultimate day of the month-long RIMPAC exercise when we received signal advice that HMAS *Darwin*, the senior Australian ship at RIMPAC, had run aground. Conducting an overnight passage around the coast of Oahu at relatively high speed, she found a charted rock off Makahoa Point. Leaving her bow sonar array and all five blades of her single propellor behind, she was later docked for extensive and lengthy repairs. They were fortunate no-one was seriously injured, but I shuddered at the thought of how it might have ended up. Most unusually, it was her second grounding in recent times, having come to grief off Hayman Island a year earlier. Happily, our RIMPAC concluded in much less dramatic fashion and we shaped course for home.

CHAPTER 8
STEPPING UP

By January 1991 I had posted to my third boat, HMAS *Orion*, which was finalising a major refit in Sutherland Dock at Cockatoo Island – the last for a submarine at that yard. Joining as Navigator after passing an intensive three-month course, things were stepping up a level. She was one of the two newer submarines in the fleet of six. Mike Deeks, now a full Commander, was embarking on his second command and had been deliberately sent to *Orion*. We knew she would attract more than her fair share of demanding operational deployments, and we were committed to setting the operating standards accordingly.

While the work-ups out of Sydney progressed unremarkably, when we got to New Zealand for our Operational Readiness Evaluation – a final week-long, at-sea assessment of the whole submarine's performance – the heat came on.

The trip across the Tasman was memorable for two reasons. My life off the submarine had changed rapidly over the past two years. In 1989, Shaunaugh and I married in the chapel of my old school during a mass celebrated by my Uncle David. Our daughter, Laura, was born early one morning in October 1990 at Manly Hospital on North Head. And exactly one year later, I was on the bridge of *Orion* headed east. As the sun rose brightly, my thoughts drifted toward home, remembering the terrible pain Shaunaugh suffered during childbirth, my total helplessness and the unbounded joy of hearing Laura's first cry and holding her in my arms.

Moving through the day, I conjured up images of what Laura and her mum might be doing, which grandparent was making an extra fuss, which present was being opened. At times, I was surprised to find that I didn't feel that sad; as though I was there, in a way, sharing in the day as the hours went along. But in the evening, again on the bridge as the sun set and darkness grew astern, it hit me hard that her bedtime had passed. My daughter was one year old. She was likely asleep, the day gone and I had missed it. I brought my binoculars to my eyes to hide the tears.

Twenty-four hours later, adrift in the middle of the Tasman Sea, both our diesel generators were down with defects. The main storage batteries that powered our onboard equipment and propelled the submarine have immense capacity, but without the ability to recharge, it was finite and could be rapidly expended. No matter how we did the sums, we did not have enough battery to make landfall – in either direction. I signalled Fleet Headquarters twice in twelve hours with changes to our planned progress.

With a darkened boat, propelling intermittently and as slowly as need be to hold the ship's head into the sea, we tried to buy the engineers time to rectify the defects. Unable to dive and bumbling along on the surface – with the ignominy of a sovereign warship calling for rescue and being towed into port playing increasingly on our minds – the engineers eventually came through and we celebrated the reassuring rumblings of a big V-16 marine diesel engine bursting back to life.

On arrival in New Zealand there was some stiff opposition lined up against us. Our own destroyer, HMAS *Hobart*; the Kiwis' Leander-class frigate, HMNZS *Canterbury*; and the Canadian Mackenzie-class destroyer, HMCS *Saskatchewan,* operated against us throughout the next fortnight. Having embarked Captain Submarines – Captain John Dikkenberg, RAN – for the duration, we knew that they would be frequently cued onto our location to generate interaction, keep the pressure on us throughout and ensure a rigorous assessment.

As Navigator, I was one rung further up the ladder as an integral member of the wider command team. The inshore operations were mine to orchestrate. Designed to severely test every facet of our ability to operate the submarine dived and within tight navigational bounds, our lack of familiarity with the land features, bathymetric conditions, tidal streams and currents added a further dimension of complexity. With a dozen inshore operations planned well in advance, we knew we would also receive short-notice tasking. And despite spending weeks poring over charts, studying the bottom contours and fixing points to best understand where we might operate and with what level of risk, one tasked operation in particular had me stumped: a simulated minelay on Port Abercrombie on the western coast of Great Barrier Island. Working with the known dived turning circles and other manoeuvring data of the submarine, I was at a loss as to how I could safely penetrate this tiny horseshoe bay, lay our mines in precise locations and retire safely back to sea, all the while avoiding counter-detection by the warships or grounding the submarine.

I became increasingly certain this was a stitch-up – an unachievable run thrown in to add pressure by chewing up time and a critical test of my judgement. I determined there was a single approach plan that might work, but it relied on absolute precision in execution. If the CO was up for it, we would go.

On the day of the race, we closed up at Action Stations and approached from the north. I guided the Captain close by Green Rock, the northernmost limit of the bay, leaving it to port and straight at Nelson Island, the southernmost limit, directly ahead. He raised the attack periscope intermittently to take bearings and fix the position of the submarine. Otherwise, we were blind and running on dead reckoning – our best estimated position given our ordered course and speed. At precisely the right moment, he ordered the Coxswain to wheel over hard to port and commenced a continuous turn into the mouth of the bay.

For much of our time inside the bay, we knew that the steep to shores were only a couple of hundred yards away on our starboard side. Halfway through the turn, with the high peaks of Kaikōura Island on the southern shore towering 400 metres above us, the Captain took an all-round look for safety and a single bearing to fix our position.

'I'm glad you can't see where you are, 'Swain!' was his only remark.

With minimal speed rung on to reduce the feather and wake of the periscope, the Coxswain deftly handled the submarine's depth and change of course. We fired watershots from the torpedo tubes to mark the position of the 'mines', turned through 240 degrees and shaped course to escape to the west.

Unbeknown to us, and totally unexpected, Captain Dikkenberg had tasked an opposing frigate with penetrating the sound from the east to force us deep at the exact time we were to be farthest within the bay. The only available passage was narrow, shallow and barely navigable for a frigate, much as the westerly entry had been barely navigable for us. The warship failed to appear, scotching the cunning plan. With the opportunity to test us further lost, his displeasure with the frigate CO was palpable and best vented once he was off the submarine.

With the relentless activity of the evaluation behind us, and coming through with flying colours, we spent some quiet time in the wardroom with Captain Dikkenberg. He offered a maxim, which I readily adopted: 'When you go to sea, you go to war!'

It was his philosophy on the required attitude and preparedness of a submarine crew, and it could bind and unite a crew at every level. Assuming this attitude meant nothing was left to chance, with the problems and the potentials thought through in advance. It ensured that you were as prepared as possible and that your people were ready in all respects: fit, trained, cohesive and motivated. Assuming this attitude, the step up to operations and combat wouldn't be insurmountable – it's just another step up. It was simply a different mission, with different objectives, limitations and constraints and a different adversary to know and understand. Assuming this attitude would give you the best possible chance of mission success, whatever that mission might be.

> Performance report, February 1992. *A most accomplished and competent Navigator ... a dedicated and loyal officer who is determined to succeed and who has every reason to be confident that he will do so.*
> – CO HMAS *Orion*

Leaving *Orion* the following year, my resolve to command one of Australia's submarines was stronger than ever. I was inspired by Mike Deeks' leadership – a man ever willing to seek and take advice to complement his own competence, and never scared to admit a mistake or another's correctness. For that, he was rewarded with a happy and able crew who always put in the hard yards. In Captain Dikkenberg, I had a view of what might lie beyond. He positioned himself to foster habits of tenacity in the face of adversity and built resilience into the character and culture of the entire Squadron.

While enjoying a sense of deep belonging as I crafted a reputation as a submariner 'worth his salt', command was still a long way off. Passing the Submarine Warfare Officers Course – a four-month course to consolidate and build on our knowledge and experience, preparing us to serve in more senior roles at sea – was the next obligatory step. Two Canadian officers made up our small cohort of six. Born to be submariners and richly gregarious, they each added more than their fair share of character to the mix. Travelling both interstate and overseas, we studied communications, sonar, electronic warfare, weapon employment and tactics under the best experts available, then put it all to practice in a final assessed phase at sea off Western Australia. Safely passing was the objective, but the chance to test and hone skills and leadership with a live submarine crew was an opportunity not to be missed.

After five and a half years of seagoing postings in ships and submarines, I savoured my second short posting to a job ashore. A couple of years earlier, in 1990, I took up the role of lead instructor for the Submarine Officers Training Course. Still relatively short on submarine time back then, it was a daunting prospect but an amazing opportunity to make sense of what I had experienced thus far, consolidate what I had learned and impart a little wisdom. That course, comprised of a handful of Australian officers, included a future Commodore and a future Admiral.

Posting back to the same role in mid-1992 as a qualified Submarine Warfare Officer and with more seatime under my belt, there was an additional challenge. The Malays, who were contemplating establishing a submarine service, dispatched five Royal Malaysian Navy officers to qualify in Australian submarines. Perhaps because of, rather than in spite of, the cultural differences they were an absolute delight to teach. One of their number would later rise to be their Submarine Force Commander and eventually their Deputy Chief of Navy. Throughout this time, I discovered the intrinsic rewards and satisfaction of teaching something you love and helping people grow and develop. I even decided I might have some talent for it.

By year's end, I was ready to be tested anew.

CHAPTER 9
ST PATRICK'S DAY

Thrilled with the news that I had been selected for a prized exchange posting with the Royal Navy as the Sonar Officer of HMS *Unicorn* – an Upholder-class submarine in the final stages of build at the historic Cammell Laird shipyards in Birkenhead, Liverpool – we prepared to move as a family to the United Kingdom. The Wirral, a picturesque peninsula on the northern border of England and Wales, appeared postcard perfect from afar. With enchanting villages, lush farms and endless seascapes, it would be our home for the first six months of a two-year adventure.

However, life in the birthplace of The Beatles was not as we imagined. Arriving in the depths of a Northwest English winter, we discovered a severely depressed economy, record unemployment, appalling crime rates and an openly fractured society. On our first short trip through the Mersey Tunnels we encountered a Liverpool falling to ruins, with empty buildings and boarded up shops everywhere. Within weeks of our arrival, the nation was shocked and outraged by the abduction, torture and murder of youngster James Bulger by two ten-year-old boys. Occurring only a few short miles from our new home, this did nothing to help us settle us into our surroundings.

A fortnight later, the launch of an Irish Republican Army (IRA) bombing campaign, targeting infrastructure and shopping centres in nearby Warrington, ratcheted up our growing sense of displacement and threat. I learned that something I had always taken for granted at home – wearing uniform in public, including to and from work – was prohibited for the risk it brings of becoming an IRA target.

Within days of our arrival in Birkenhead, I was unexpectedly dispatched to Portsmouth, then Plymouth and back to Portsmouth for three weeks of training with the crew in various onshore simulators. A mountain of examinations on the submarine, its systems and procedures stood before me, and it was a peak that took nine months to summit. Even then, the learning didn't stop. I was there to do a job, but also to gain experience and develop as a submariner. Acutely conscious of the 'Australia' flashes on my shoulder boards, I was also desperate to uphold the reputation and standing of my Navy and Submarine Squadron.

My purpose in the UK was straightforward – qualify on this most modern of submarines and prove myself within a new Navy. But for Shaunaugh, left to care for Laura and establish a new home on her own, the logic wasn't as evident and the question began to build: 'What the hell have we done?'

Journal note, January 1993. *You can slump or shine here, Scotty.*

By mid-February 1993, the boat is ready for seven weeks of builders' sea trials to test and prove the submarine. Not yet commissioned into the Royal Navy, we fly the Red Ensign as we back quickly out of the graving dock, tugs connected, into the strong tidal stream of the River Mersey. As we exit the main channel and fall out from Harbour Stations, I am in the wardroom and ready to tuck into lunch when we hear a dreaded pipe.

'Fire. Fire. Fire. Fire in the Engine Room!'

The submarine immediately goes to Emergency Stations. We soon realise that it is not a fire, but an 'engine run-on'. One of the dockyard workers, embarked to support the various trials, had a suspicion that the port diesel might continue to run once the external exhaust valve was shut. Incredulously, without warning the Captain, he shut the valve to see if the engine would 'diesel'. With the valve shut, and nowhere else for the exhaust to go, the diesel engine started belching toxic black smoke back through the engine drains and into the submarine.

The civilian Harbour Pilot, sitting in the wardroom and awaiting a safety brief as the run-on happens, has a handful of plastic and rubber hosing flung at him.

'Here, shove this on!' says the Weapons Engineer as he turns and races to the control room. There endeth the lesson.

A saving grace is that we are on the surface, substantially reducing the potential hazards and simplifying any emergency procedures. Nonetheless, for the next three and a half hours, we suck on rubber masks on long hoses fed by the emergency breathing system (EBS) until we get the atmosphere back within habitable specifications. With smoke permeating every porous surface onboard, including our uniforms, the acrid sting in our nostrils lingers for much longer. The foul taste of a near disaster is with us even longer still. As night falls on Liverpool Bay, it's been a tough first day in command at sea for the Captain, Lieutenant Commander John Gower, RN.

The hazards of an engine run-on were drummed into me during my earliest days in the Squadron. A twenty-year-old sailor, Able Seaman Christopher Passlow, lost his life onboard HMAS *Onslow* in 1981 during an engine run-on. Exercising off Sydney Heads with an RNZN frigate, the submarine crash stopped the diesels to go deep and avoid detection by an Orion maritime patrol aircraft. The starboard diesel continued to run and blew toxic exhaust, heavily laden with carbon monoxide and carbon dioxide, into the submarine. Passlow died of asphyxiation, while nearly one-third of the Ship's Company were rendered unconscious or suffered carbon monoxide poisoning. Emergency breathing air systems were later introduced into the control room and subsequently extended throughout the submarine. They become an essential element of damage control training and procedures moving forward.

Journal note, March 1993. *Don't concern yourself with what people think of you, just do your job.*

As a hybrid design, the front half of Upholder-class submarines effectively resembled a Trafalgar-class nuclear-powered submarine, with similar combat system, sensors and weapons. The back half differed substantially in that it had a diesel–electric, rather than nuclear, propulsion system but shared multiple systems, equipment and fittings in common with the Trafalgars.

The Ship's Company of *Unicorn* also had a mixed pedigree. While many had Oberon-class experience like myself, others were nuclear attack sailors, having served on the Swiftsure- and Trafalgar-classes, and there were some who had only ever served on the Resolution-class ballistic missile submarines. As each of these submarine types had unique roles, so the officers and sailors brought distinct experience and expectations. Professionally, the interactions across these divides made for intriguing viewing. The diversity extended well beyond their professional experience; what differed massively from home was the impact of the various nationalities of the crew.

The English, Scots, Welsh and Irish each brought their own distinct history, language, politics, allegiances, religious beliefs, sports and sense of humour onboard. It was months before I could penetrate this social maze and crack a joke that reliably got a laugh rather than a quizzical sideways glance. Seemingly the only things they had in common was their shared obsession with fried potatoes and the all-important saving grace that none of them were 'bloody colonials'!

Then again, better to be a lone colonial than the sole Part Three officer onboard. Sensing that we were both partial misfits, I made a special effort to offer a helping hand to a young trainee. A fresh-faced Sub-Lieutenant from Blackpool, he was willing to learn from anyone, but also naïve enough to be taken for a ride by all and sundry. His character and talents eventually shone through, but not before he endured some rugged months.

The environment, both onboard and ashore, was substantially 'stiffer' than at home. The rigidity of rank hierarchy and the separation of officer and sailor in *Unicorn* was more like being in a senior destroyer at home than within the close-knit professional fabric of an Australian submarine. From the earliest days, my efforts to engage with my sailors socially, including inviting them to our home, was welcomed warily by the troops.

'Thanks, Sir ... if you're sure the missus won't mind.'

The officers simply recoiled at the notion.

Journal note, March 1993. *Rule Number One: keep the water out of the people tank!*

On St Patrick's Day 1993, we are at sea in *Unicorn* out in the Atlantic several hundred miles west of the Hebrides coast. It is just after midnight and the end of a long watch is drawing near. We are dived and at periscope depth, so the control room is pitch black, with only the most essential gauges dimly lit by red backlights. We're snorting to charge the batteries ahead of the next day's trials.

We're also in a Force 10 gale, with 40 foot seas and 50 knot winds. The sea above us is thrashing wildly, so visibility through the periscopes is poor and our other sensors are severely degraded. Just keeping depth is a massive challenge for the watchkeepers. The induction and exhaust masts are continually washed over by waves, automatically shutting and opening the flap valve that lets air into the submarine to feed the diesels. As they shut, the diesels continue to pump exhaust out of the boat and into the sea and air above us, drawing a vacuum inside the boat that is released when the flap valve is open. So, it's difficult but manageable … until we flame out. The vacuum is too strong and both diesels are shut down.

Putting the snort back on, both diesels trip and we get some exhaust back in the boat. Trying the diesels a second time, in order to clear that smoke from the atmosphere, the port diesel suffers a full run-on and rapidly fills the submarine with thick, black, highly toxic diesel exhaust. The oncoming watch get a rude awakening as I pipe the submarine to Emergency Stations and we don emergency breathing masks throughout the boat. Critically, the bulkhead doors are shut, isolating a third of the Ship's Company in the accommodation spaces forward, and drastically reducing our ability to deal with the growing crisis.

Notwithstanding the sea state, the Captain determines that we need to surface the submarine to properly ventilate the boat. He decides to run the submarine 'opened up', with both the upper and lower hatches open, to best clear the toxic atmosphere within. Driving the boat to the surface, we put a short blow on all the ballast tanks. Our ever-chipper Scots Navigator is first through the conning tower and up to the bridge. One of my lads, a young sonar rating, goes with him as lookout. Another follows them with safety harnesses and to act as a sentry on the upper hatch, ready to shut it if required.

Within a minute of the Navigator reaching the bridge, the submarine is pooped; a massive wave picks us up by the stern, overruns us and drives us back beneath the surface. Now bows down, at speed, with minimal buoyancy, we are effectively diving again, but with a full bore of exceedingly cold Atlantic Ocean flooding through the conning tower.

For one incredulous moment, I am standing by the chart table peering forward through the gloom past the diving console and the periscopes to the torrent of water obscenely invading our home. Every eye in the control room is fixed on the mortifying scene before us. The reality of the situation is brutally stark. If the hatches stay open and the water keeps coming, we will never get up again.

I race forward to the base of the tower, nearly losing my head as the hose on my EBS mask comes short and rips away from my face. Moving upward through the deluge, the cold is stunning and the noise astounding. I make it to the top rung but cannot reach past the hatch coaming. Glimpsing the sentry, awash in the dark fin, he's struggling valiantly to reach and shut the upper lid.

The Captain below roars through his mask and above the din, 'Shut the upper lid! Shut the lower lid! Shut any fucking lid!'

I let go. The torrent grabs me and shoots me back down through the tower towards the control room deck twenty-five feet below. I grasp desperately for the 'Jesus rope', the short stiff lanyard secured to the underside of the lower hatch. *I have it!* It's ripping through my grip as I fly past. *The Turk's head; it's my last chance.* There is an almighty clang as the hatch is driven shut above me by the waterfall now filling the conning tower. The ingress stops, but there are still three of our number outside the pressure hull.

Picking myself up off the deck and regathering my senses, the state of the control room is astonishing – smoke-filled but also awash with tonnes of seawater. Languishing on the surface, the submarine is smashed from port to starboard and back again. We lose our sonar, fire control, navigation and internal communications systems. The search periscope, only partially raised, is jammed by the impact of the seas. The Weapons Engineer furiously buckets water down the mast wells to the bilges. As the briny stuff forces its way below decks, hydraulic pumps and gyrocompasses are lost, fires break out and the main storage batteries are threatened. Salt water and lead acid batteries make a disastrously explosive combination.

Unable to establish communications with the bridge, the Captain and I acknowledge that the Navigator and lookout are quite possibly gone; either washed from the submarine and adrift, or trapped within the fin and drowned. There is nothing we can do for them. With pandemonium below, we are in a battle to save the submarine from total loss. Facing the grim reality of our worsening situation, I advise the Captain to send out a distress message, an immense call for any sovereign warship. He summons the Radio Supervisor out of the comms shack to the plot, and says, 'Talk to anyone, give them our position.'

The mayday call is sent out repeatedly. It goes unacknowledged.

The Petty Officer on the diving safety console, following standard procedures with the utmost discipline, calls out ship system failures as they light up on the alarm panel above his head and initiates the emergency procedures for each.

'Hydraulic failure.'

'Electrical failure.'

'Gyro failure.'

'Propulsion failure.'

Ordinarily any one of these would be enough to send the submarine to Emergency Stations. Within minutes, every single indicator on the ships alarm panel is lit up.

'Fuck it, Full House!' he calls.

When we eventually establish comms with the bridge, we learn that the Nav and lookout are still with us, and the upper lid is shut. We drain down and empty the flooded conning tower. I open the lower lid from below, uncertain of what I will find inside. The sentry is propped up at the top of the tower. Having done his duty, shutting the upper lid above him, he had thereby trapped himself in the tower, up to his neck in frigid seawater with a mere headspace of air to breathe. Isolated for over an hour, he had had no way of knowing whether we were winning or losing our damage control battles below, other than sensing that we were still somewhere near the surface. He beams the widest, most appreciative grin at me and clambers down.

At 0530, after a long and dreadful night, we fall out from Emergency Stations and I pipe the watch, 'Patrol routine'. On the bridge, having relieved the Nav an hour or more ago, sunrise is an hour away still, but the day creeps over the grey and indeterminate horizon as we slog east. The seas are less tempestuous by now, but they still carry some of the menace from the previous night. A Royal Air Force Nimrod maritime patrol aircraft flies overhead, responding to our mayday, but it is only mildly reassuring. We had survived some of the wildest seas and the most dangerous situation I had ever encountered. The fight to save our lives and our submarine lasted four and a half hours. I am beyond exhaustion and beyond emotion. My body and my mind feel as though they have been through a forge – blasted and hammered into something and someone that I was not before.

Later that day we brought ourselves alongside the NATO fuelling berth at desolate Loch Ewe in Scotland. The crew spent the week repairing damage, testing equipment and drying out the boat. Taking turns to get away in small groups, the crew would drive two hours down to the Kyle of Lochalsh for a couple of days off the boat. Needing some time and space, I took a day by myself on the Isle of Skye, climbing hills and wandering the streets of the quaint fishing village of Portree. Overcast but calm and peaceful, it was a day of difficult reflection.

There is nothing natural about taking submarines to sea. Built of high-tensile steel to withstand the forces of the sea at depth, they are tightly packed with high-pressure air, high-pressure hydraulics and high-voltage electrical power systems, not to mention high explosives. They are the alien invaders of nature's depths. On St Patrick's Day, during the hours of grim, desperate effort to control the damage, it seemed as though the ocean was hell-bent to either repel or devour our boat. Without doubt, it nearly pounded us to death.

Astounded at the rapidity with which the situation had spiralled out of control as the consequences of lost and damaged systems unfolded exponentially, I was equally amazed by the fact that, in the end, we dealt with it all and recovered. At times, I seriously doubted our ability to prevail. Certainly, there was nothing in my previous training or experience that compared with the gravity, intensity and chaos of those hours, or guaranteed our survival. But the Ship's Company responded magnificently to the challenge. Not just because our lives depended on it, but because we had been taught, trained and had a duty to do so. Determined to persevere, we knew our boat, our shipmates and the sea well enough to not only survive, but save the submarine. The two went hand in hand.

As the sun set over the sharp peaks of Skye, I embraced once more the notion that the sovereign value inherent in a strong and effective submarine force was worth the sacrifice and risks of submarine service. I had seen what they could do and what they meant for a nation. Three days later, we set sail again.

CHAPTER 10
SEATIME

Our time in the UK was punctuated by attendance at some superbly British events. Shaunaugh and I enjoyed days in the Royal Enclosure at Ascot and Trooping the Colour in London. Though decidedly less high profile, none was more memorable than the commissioning ceremony for HMS *Unicorn*. Notwithstanding the fact that submariners prefer to be known for their operational prowess over their ceremonial precision, we proudly paraded in our Number 1 dress uniforms with swords and medals. Marching to the resounding beat of 'Heart of Oak', we welcomed *Unicorn* into the Royal Navy with all the pomp and ceremony we could muster.

The occasion was particularly impactful for the local community. Cammell Laird had delivered hundreds of ships for the Royal Navy over the previous 170 years, including the battleship HMS *Prince of Wales* and two of the four carriers named HMS *Ark Royal*. Paradoxically, the successful delivery of *Unicorn* also marked the final demise of the last Merseyside shipyard in operation. For *Unicorn*, it was licence to redeploy to her new home port of Plymouth and a place in the 2nd Submarine Squadron under the command of Captain Chris Wreford-Brown, the erstwhile Commanding Officer of the famed HMS *Conqueror* who sank the *Belgrano*.

Making the day a personal highlight was the fact that I shared it not only with Shaunaugh and Laura, but also Mum and Dad, out from Australia, and my brother Mark and his wife, Aileen, down from Scotland. Submarines are such a distant way to serve those you love, so sharing the occasion with family was especially poignant, particularly so far from our Australian homeland.

At sea again, dived and hugging the bottom, we slowly crept away from Orsay Island, steadily opening the distance from two Sea King HAS 6 helicopters. It was a Saturday night in November, and the final night of a week-long evaluation to certify us as ready to deploy operationally early in the new year. One of the helos hovered 40 feet above the sea surface, as his dipping sonar pinged relentlessly. They were looking for a return displaying the tell-tale Doppler effect to indicate an evading submarine.

The Rhinns of Islay Light, flashing white every five seconds, blinked through the helicopter's side door window at the sonar operator. As the winchman reeled the sonar body back into the belly of the aircraft and the pilot prepared to reposition, the second helo came into the dip. It pitched up, hitting the sea with its tail rotor and breaking off the tailcone. The cab crashed into the sea several miles astern of us in the blind-arcs of our sonar, then sank in 90 metres of water. Three were rescued from the water by the first helo, but one crewman didn't escape the cab and perished in the cold, dark sea.

When we finally came to periscope depth to read signal traffic hours later, we returned to the scene at best speed. We established a datum on the wreck by plotting the emergency locator beacon that automatically activated when the aircraft sank. With nothing more to offer, we surfaced and shaped course for home just as daylight broke. The crewman was in our feeble prayers as the Captain conducted the regular Sunday Service. I couldn't help but feel some sense of responsibility for this man's death, his life taken as he worked to ready us for operations.

As 1994 opened before us, I took on an additional role in *Unicorn* as the Operations Officer, with responsibility for planning our exercises and operations. The year saw us traverse the Irish Sea, the North Sea, the English Channel, the Atlantic, the Mediterranean, the Suez Canal, the Red Sea, the Gulf of Oman and the Indian Ocean. We made port as far north as Stavanger, Norway and as far south as Diego Garcia, in the middle of the Indian Ocean.

Early on in the year, I had my first chance to dive the submarine, traditionally the sole purview of the Captain. A technically brilliant submariner and intensely focused warrior, he set impeccable standards and put the wind up most of his officers, although I had a strong and straightforward relationship with him. Seeking to give his officers every opportunity to develop, he came to the bridge during the afternoon to sit and quietly walk me through his expectations.

'If you're ever in doubt,' he stipulated, 'shut main vents and blow.'

Later that night, heading south into the Hebrides by Neist Point, I took a final all round look on the periscope and called for shipping, navigation and ship control reports from around the control room. Knees wobbling, but satisfied that we are safe to dive, I ordered, 'Open main vents. 6 down, 25 metres back to 19.'

Twenty minutes later, after passing through the myriad of orders, acknowledgements and actions required to safely dive the boat, I ordered, 'Pipe the watch, second watch, watch dived.'

One of the tactical systems sailors, not one to mince his words, found my ear and softly said, 'Shit, Sonics, I was impressed to fuck. Do you do that back at home?'

A typically affable Welshman, this sailor often burst into song on the bridge to while away his hour as lookout. Although the youngest, he was, like every other sailor onboard, a keen observer of his officers. And, like most others, he was quick to learn. Months earlier while trialling our electronic warfare gear close off the port of Campbelltown and amid a fleet of fishing vessels skippered by petulant Scotsmen, I lost my patience trying to get a response from him as track manager.

'Ops. Search. Are you awake?' I queried.

'Yes, Sir, are you?' was the quick and chirpy reply.

It's the sort of crack he might have gotten away with on the bridge, if it was only he and I. But dived and in the strictly naval atmospherics of John Gower's control room, it was asking for trouble. The Captain flew out of his cabin, passed me on the periscope and barked down the young sailor's throat before I uttered a word in reply. Threatened charges of insubordination were tempered by the senior sonar rate who offered to take him aft and 'fill him in' – a still common and less administratively burdensome form of discipline. Perhaps unrealised by the Captain, the sonar supervisor, a fellow Welshman, probably took the youngster aft and ran through a few Tom Jones hits.

Journal note, January 1994. *I am often fearful for my life.*

While I have never been claustrophobic while awake, I had long suffered from 'coffin dreams' at sea, and this continued in *Unicorn*. The officers shared a six-berth run athwartships, with a narrow single doorway at the entrance and three slim racks stacked on either side. You need to decide how you will sleep as you get in because they lack the height to roll over in the night. Uncommonly, I chose to lie with my head away from the small reading light, because that end was boxed in to shield the light and for privacy. Nonetheless, I frequently woke in fright, scratching and scrambling to get free from the coffin within which I was 'buried'. Regaining my senses, it was with much relief that I would realise I was not underground in a box but under the sea in a submarine.

My coping mechanisms ashore were more destructive, particularly away from the girls. Knowing my limits on the grog full well, I continually exceeded them. Stavanger–Plymouth–Gibraltar–Souda Bay–Muscat–Diego Garcia sounded like the itinerary of a short first-class passenger cruise (with the possible exception of Diego Garcia), but it was actually the ports where I destroyed myself over several days and nights. It's also every port we visited. There were no missed opportunities to push my limits to breaking point and beyond, all in the name of having a wild time. When the unquenchable thirst for alcohol and for liberty from loneliness, stress and trauma took hold, the consequences barely seemed to matter.

One afternoon, eight pints in, my inner punk broke out. I challenged the junior sailors to a head-butting competition at The Horseshoe on Main Street in Gibraltar. I did pretty well for a while, until one particularly burly Leading Seaman stoker put me out of my misery. The clash was at an end, but the night went on. It seemed much of the tension from the previous year lingered within me.

Journal note, June 1994. *Near death experience No. ???*

An average day at sea in a submarine can be pretty routine, mundane even. A less than average day, pretty exciting. Operating in the Gulf of Oman in the middle of the year, we nearly came undone again. Having transited through the Red Sea a month earlier and operated here for weeks with the Carrier Battle Group of the USS *Carl Vinson*, we had grown accustomed to the adverse sonar conditions in the region. The combination of excessive salinity and intense thermal layers had the effect of bending the sound waves of a ship's propellors sharply down into the ocean depths, rather than out near and along the surface. This dramatically reduced the range at which we could detect a ship on sonar. More than once during the Red Sea transit we came up from deep to find a merchant ship within visual range ahead and steaming towards us, but not yet held on sonar – the sound of its engines and propellor blanked by its own massive bulk and the sonar conditions.

After manoeuvring to clear our stern arcs and making all the usual preparations to return to periscope depth, I ordered the boat up. Closing the surface, I raised the periscope into position to breach the surface. As we neared the ordered depth, sonar reported a 'faint rise in background noise' on our port beam. Designated Sonar 7, it was our only, and therefore most dangerous, contact. Training the periscope handles to begin my first quick all-round look there, bubbles breezed past the periscope window as it neared the surface, then disappeared as it broke into open air.

'Go deep, go deep, go deep!'

HMS *Exeter*, a Type 42-class destroyer, was racing towards us, close enough to fill my periscope view and send a shot of adrenalin coursing through my veins. Sonar finally gained her on our port bow as she went screaming by at 22 knots. We were barely deep enough to avoid collision as her thrashing props passed mere yards ahead of our fin.

'I knew she must have been close to drain the colour from your face!' said the Captain as we levelled out at safe depth.

Transiting the Indian Ocean on the surface early one evening, my heart skipped a beat when I sighted the familiar stars of Crux. Our scheduled port visit to Pakistan was cancelled in the wake of the escalating violence of the Karachi riots, so we were southward bound for the British Protectorate of Diego Garcia to berth for a two-week maintenance period. The shining lights of the Southern Cross were low in the sky but right ahead. Even though I'd been looking forward to it for a long time,

I was surprised at just how happy it made me; this simple vision was a constant feature of all my previous years at sea and of my homeland.

I also felt a pang of guilt for being in a place where I could see and enjoy the Southern Cross, while my girls were stuck in faraway England. There was never any question that we would not move as a family to the UK for the duration of this posting. For us, it was part of the shared adventure of a naval life. But I had asked the girls to leave the support and connection of family and friends far behind them.

Thankfully, I was not cursed with seasickness, but homesickness was another miserable story. The heartache of separation was rarely far beneath the surface of my emotions. While the heavy emotional pain of missing my parents and siblings when I first joined the Navy had softened over the years, the anguish of being away from Shaunaugh and Laura never did. At sea, typically I boxed it up under lock and key. Not infrequently, I pulled a small photo album from under my pillow or re-read a letter in the quiet of night to reminisce, appreciate and preserve connection. Occasionally, tears came when I lay my head down at day's end. As the long deployments and years at sea inexorably racked up, I came to accept that I was powerless over the immovable object of time and learned to endure the physical separation with a little more grace.

My stuffy, but fiercely loyal, friend deserves an honourable mention here. He was sent my way by Shaunaugh when I was still a Midshipman in HMAS *Bendigo*. I knew instinctively that it was not the done thing for a grown man to take his teddy bear to sea in a warship, but had little choice really.

Over the years, I learned – through a series of tough ransom negotiations – that Horatio and I were both better off if his presence onboard was not widely known. Amazingly, I was in my final weeks of service in *Unicorn* before he was discovered. When a sailor ripped the bedding off my bunk to contain a nearby hydraulic burst, Horatio tumbled out and onto the deck, exposed as a stowaway and naked as a bear. The inherent prize value in the Aussie's mascot was immediately apparent and, not for the first time in our seagoing careers, he was swiftly spirited away. The best kidnappers would wait at least a week before posting a ransom note or offering proof of life. The Brits were impatient for their fun; I had him back before we made landfall. Eventually a veteran of Iraq and Afghanistan, Horatio was my mute companion in every ship and submarine I served in across nearly three decades.

Returning to England later that year, my ultimate duty in the UK was to navigate one of *Unicorn*'s sisters, HMS *Unseen*, from Plymouth to Barrow-in-Furness. Following a severe miscalculation by the Admiralty, the government of the day had announced in July 1993 that the Upholder-class build program was to be cut and the entire class paid off. As the curtain drew on 1994, all four submarines were eventually brought alongside and put into preservation. It would be a decade before they sailed again under the ensign of the Royal Canadian Navy.

For me, it meant an early return to Australia to attend the Submarine Executive Officers Course and qualify as an Attack Coordinator, licensed to lead the tactical team for the CO at Action Stations and to assume responsibilities as second-in-command. I survived all that had been thrown at me during a highly rewarding exchange with the Royal Navy, albeit with a few fresh psychological scars, but I would need every ounce of experience gained to deal with what was to come in the years ahead.

CHAPTER 11
BREAK IN AN EMERGENCY

Returning to Australia as second-in-command of HMAS *Otama*, I rejoined a Submarine Arm stretched to breaking point. With no more than six hundred qualified officers and sailors, there were barely enough submariners to effectively operate the Oberons in a stable situation. Yet the meagre strength of the Arm was scattered across the country. The continued presence at HMAS *Platypus*, substantially defrayed when Squadron Headquarters relocated to HMAS *Stirling* in Western Australia earlier that year, left only a small cohort of officers and staff to try and hold the strategic fort in Navy Headquarters in Canberra. Necessarily, a growing proportion of qualified officers and sailors were being posted to conversion training in Perth, then on to Adelaide to stand by the first of the Collins-class submarines in build.

The promise of new submarines was having some positive impact on recruitment. However, the decision to base the entire class in Western Australia, as the lead element of the government's 'Two Ocean Navy' policy, throttled the flow of volunteers from a service that historically drew most heavily on the populated states of the Eastern seaboard. The strain of introducing a new class of submarine brought the Navy's proclivity to chronically under-resource the submarine workforce into sharp relief.

Throughout the 1950s and 1960s, the Royal Navy had operated submarines out of Sydney as targets to support anti-submarine warfare training of Australian and New Zealand warships. During the 1980s, as the Oberon-class submarines became increasingly operational, successive epochs of Navy senior leadership perpetuated the paradigm of Australian submarines as a discretionary training asset. To be fair, the vast majority of the officers and sailors in the RAN had no knowledge of the secret operations our Oberons conducted over this time period. Many were oblivious to the full capabilities of the submarines or did not comprehend the deterrent effect they have on the calculus of regional navies and governments.

Others in our Navy, some much better informed, were simply ruthless in denigrating the capability. They purposely discouraged officers and sailors from volunteering for submarines and withheld transfers in deference to crewing the surface fleet. Worse yet, our submarines and submariners were characterised as 'the enemy', an attitude that leached across from the exercise domain into the general mindset of other arms of the Navy.

The changing character of the Navy added pressure to this dynamic. As the aircraft carrier HMAS *Melbourne* was decommissioned in 1982, a previously task group–focused Navy devolved to a more destroyer-centric one. With the subsequent loss of the Perth-class destroyers in the late 1990s, the stage was set for a further devolution to single ship deployments drawn from a frigate-centric Navy. Ongoing myopic fascination with surface ships meant that fully resourcing the submarine capability became a perennial problem. The consequence was chronic organisational fragility, leaving the Arm susceptible to failure and levying a disproportionate strain on those serving within it.

Workforce pressures aside, with the ageing Oberons being paid off through the 1990s, *Otama* was set to become the nucleus of our high-end submarine capability through the next half decade as the Collins-class submarines entered service and became operational. We had a clear mission to not only deliver as much strategic effect as possible for a single submarine, but also attain and preserve the highest standards of the operational art within the Squadron.

The difficulty from the outset was that *Otama* was in pieces. Deep in the throes of the last full refit for an Oberon, she was laid up in the Captain Cook Graving Dock at Garden Island in Sydney. Cockatoo Island Dockyard, the traditional home of this highly invasive and intensive work, was shut down in anticipation of the Squadron's eventual move to the West. A two-year project at the best of times, the refit was now in the hands of Australian Defence Industries (ADI). Conducting their first submarine refit, ADI had minimal submarine experience or expertise and a workforce highly distracted by extensive commitments elsewhere. Compounded by waning spares support worldwide for an ageing class of submarine and a lack of industrial leverage, the schedule was under immense and continual pressure throughout the year.

Journal note. September 1995. *Seen today – 'The XO licks dead dog's arse!'*

While the dockyard workers rebuilt the submarine, as the XO, I set about establishing the organisation and building the crew that would see a bare and sterile boat brought back to sea as a living, breathing warship. Full of the complexities and necessary drudgeries of administration, months were spent establishing and embedding safety, security, correspondence, medical, logistics and victualling systems and routines. I oversaw training programs for the ten officers and fifty-five crew across specialist skills as distinct as firefighting and submarine escape drills, as diverse as helicopter transfer teams and ship's diving teams, and as disparate as small arms and heavyweight torpedo qualifications.

The challenges I felt most keenly were around my responsibility for effectiveness and cohesion across an entire Ship's Company in both the short- and long-term. The groundwork required – establishing the standards of professionalism and the onboard culture that would determine our eventual performance at sea – and breadth and depth of my responsibilities accelerated the shift in my mindset and approach to work. More so than in any other role to date, I noticed that any need or desire for acceptance took a deliberate back seat to the execution of my responsibilities and leadership. Beyond their expertise and experience, the assembled crew were trustworthy, courageous and patriotic to a man, but hardly timid or docile, and I occasionally needed to bang a few heads. Slanderous graffiti painted on the dock wall told me that my efforts and approach were not always appreciated, but I had obviously made my presence felt somewhere.

During this time, I joined RAAF Base *Williamtown* in the Hunter Valley for a two-week course. In the Officers' Mess one night, I asked after my old primary school mate Mark Cairns-Cowan, or 'CC' as he was known to his flying chums. Mark had followed through with our childhood pact to head 'to the skies'. Joining the Air Force in 1984, he qualified as a navigator in 1985 and flew in C-130 Hercules transport aircraft with No. 37 Squadron. While our paths rarely crossed over the following decade, I knew he later navigated the supersonic F-111s with No.1 Squadron out of RAAF Base *Amberley*. As a long-range strategic bomber, these aircraft were the only capability in the ADF inventory other than our submarines that presented as a strategic deterrent to would-be adversaries.

'CC is dead,' was the muted reply from one of the Air Force officers.

Reeling from shock, I am told that he died in September 1993. At twenty-seven years old, having accumulated nearly four thousand hours in the air and nearly three hundred hours in F-111s, Mark was a highly experienced and capable airman. He and the pilot were only twenty-three minutes into a night time land-strike training sortie when the F-111 he was navigating crashed into a field in Northern NSW and disintegrated. Both Mark and the pilot were killed in a mission designed to reinstate squadron proficiency in night operations.

While the tragedy made headlines at home, this sad news failed to reach my ears while at sea on overseas exchange. As I placed my drunk head on my pillow late that night, ruminating on the abrupt and brutal end of a boyhood dream, I was filled with respect and admiration for his achievements and his sacrifices. *Here's to you, mate.*

Journal note, March 1995. *Be a grown up, Scotty for at least the second half of your life.*

As my professional competence and confidence grew, I placed myself under increasingly intolerable pressure to prove my worth. Having propelled myself through a decade of alcohol abuse, dressed up in bravado and revelry, the extremes of my drinking were frequently fuelled by self-doubt, loneliness or fear.

Over time, I became a key protagonist in a Squadron culture that, in every practical sense, celebrated heavy binge-drinking. Alcohol was seemingly the exclusive avenue for bonding with each other, airing shared experience and coping with trauma, stress and anxiety.

'One beer is too many and a hundred not enough!' was a common refrain in the Mess – however, no longer a joke for me, but rather a visceral truth. I developed a perverse pride in outlasting any drinking competitor. Friday lunchtime beers in the wardroom at HMAS *Platypus* routinely slid into afternoon sculling sessions in the Senior Rates bar that rolled out of control into sleep-deprived crawls on the town.

Late one evening, having quaffed whatever was at hand for untold hours after a mess dinner, it seemed like a good idea to scale the high barbed wire fence of the base perimeter to avoid scrutiny at the main gate. Momentarily holding a shaky balance astride the fence top, I launched myself off, catching my hand on the wire as I fell to the ground. It opened the full inside length of a finger, flesh and tendon erupting like a raw sausage. I stumbled home. Shaunaugh, rudely awoken and exasperated but ever patient, hauled me off to the hospital in my blood-soaked uniform. The Emergency Department staff produced some deft work and fine stitching. Careful not to draw attention to the injury at work over the following weeks, I eventually regained the use of my finger.

In a classic misadventure, my plan to 'knock over the Christmas shopping' one year turned into a lost weekend. Three and a half days passed before I returned to our apartment. At a time when mobile phones were well beyond our means, Shaunaugh was beside herself with worry and justifiably angry; not the least because she was once again left caring for young Laura at a time when I should have been doing my bit. Despite her demands to know where I had been, I couldn't tell her. No matter how hard I tried, I only gathered together the sketchiest recollection of the days and nights that had rolled by. My only saving grace, which had its own detracting possibilities, was that I returned with more cash in my wallet than when I left.

At sea on the O-boats, the common lore for beer issues for the sailors was 'Two cans, per man, per day, perhaps!' However, officers rarely drank at sea, and typically only ever on the surface with the same 'two-can' rule. Out on the briny, for whatever reason, I didn't need it and I didn't miss it. But locked into an extended refit with no seatime to break the daily and weekly cycles of habitual, dangerously excessive drinking, I was headed for disaster. And I was increasingly alarmed at the escalating risks I was taking and the hardening impacts on everything I valued.

Out of desperation, and in a deliberate circumvention of the Navy health system, I took myself off to the family doctor to seek help. On her referral, I found myself, eyes downcast, at the locked front door of the Herbert Street Clinic – the drug and alcohol addiction treatment centre attached to the Royal North Shore Hospital. I had passed the brown bricks and barred windows of this non-descript building a hundred times without ever wondering its purpose.

In time, I celebrated a week without alcohol. Then two. Then more. Then a week without a cigarette. Then two. The counselling and treatment enabled me to establish some limits and curb some of the excesses that might otherwise end my submarine career, destroy my health and break my family.

Herbert Street didn't fix me. Nor did it normalise my relationship with alcohol. But as a place and a point in time, it marked my decision to accept that alcohol was not my friend and probably never would be. I needed to find other ways to cope with stress, hold my life together and perform.

We managed to wrest *Otama* out of dockyard hands before Christmas, so as the calendar ticked over into 1996 and I was promoted Lieutenant Commander, we were seagoing once more. Stuffed into the front of the fin one glorious morning with our highly personable Captain – Lieutenant Commander Mark Merrifield, RAN – and our budding Navigator, it was an absolute delight to let go lines, silently back out of Neutral Bay and glide through the aquatic wonder of Sydney Harbour.

As we rounded Bradleys Head and shaped course for the Western Channel, the Navigator ordered the diesels started. The sharp-eyed lookout sent a friendly wave towards the skipper and passengers on MV *Freshwater* as she ferried her passengers towards the Quay. I ordered most of the Casing Party below, their job securing the berthing lines now complete. The spell of the morning broke when we heard the muffled report of an engine run-on coming through to the control room below.

In pilotage waters, the Captain's place was on the bridge and mine below. *Bugger!* With a wink and a snappy salute, I shimmied down the conning tower ladders, towards a potentially toxic and deathly scene. Memories of *Unicorn*'s first day at sea came rushing back. With a thumping heart, I took a good deep breath and descended into the control room.

A guff of exhaust had plumed into the submarine when one of the diesels failed to start properly. The team did exactly the right thing going to Emergency Stations immediately, and we soon had the atmosphere back within specification and continued through the Heads and out to sea. The situation was not so bad.

We spent months running in and out of Sydney, up and down the east coast, and across to New Zealand for one more work-up. It was entirely pleasant to realise that that life as the XO at sea is completely different to life in refit. Mark Merrifield, the consummate professional with an engaging charm that carried all the boys along with him, was well and truly in command. We had an eager Ship's Company, focused on the full program set before us, and a dependable boat in which to live and work. We were at home, and it was time to get down to business.

CHAPTER 12
ARCHIMEDES' PRINCIPLE

In my earliest days at the submarine school, we received a refresher on 'Archimedes' principle'. The famed mathematician of ancient Greece taught us that buoyancy depended on the density of the water in which an object, such as a submarine, floated and the weight of the water that it displaced.

For years now I had been trimming submarines on the watch: balancing the boat's overall weight by pumping water out or flooding water into various internal tanks, to ensure it is neutrally buoyant at the ordered depth. The weight of the submarine, and distribution of that weight, changed continuously as fuel was burned, fresh water used, food and stores expended, and torpedoes fired. The density of the water also changed as we opened from the coast, moved from one ocean eddy or current to another or changed depth.

Now, as XO in *Otama*, I had additional responsibilities as the Trimming Officer and needed to set the trim on the boat prior to the initial dive after leaving any port. There's both a science and an art to safely diving a submarine, bringing it from floating on the sea to floating within the sea. Before we sailed, I used the draught marks forward and aft as a guide, and seasonal changes in the density of seawater as a benchmark. But I soon learned that every change in the overall weight of the submarine needed to be forensically tracked, down to the number of spuds onboard.

In our first week at sea, as we dramatically and expectantly opened main vents, surprisingly little happened. Air pushed skywards from the vents as seawater partially filled the ballast tanks, but we remained languishing near the surface, the fin and masts stubbornly proud of the sea. The senior panel watchkeeper in the control room, a Petty Officer with the build of a bulldog and a mask of scrappy facial hair, sat three feet from me and accused me of setting 'a married man's trim'.

'Scared a' goin' under, are ya, Sir?' he quipped, as I ordered hundreds, then thousands, of gallons flooded into the trim tanks to bring us beneath the waves. He demanded crates of beer for his watchkeepers manning the ballast pump as recompense for their extra efforts.

In the following weeks, my 'Tanky', one of the Leading Seaman stokers, tirelessly and precisely kept track of the contents of every tank onboard for my refined calculations. If the forward dome wasn't going under sixty seconds after we opened main vents, there was work to be done. Although diving light wasn't ideal, there could be a more dramatic outcome from diving too heavy and plummeting out of control to the bottom. The troops would be on my case either way, so there was a strong incentive to get it right.

Journal note, March 1996. *Dived today, didn't move a drop!*

Submarines can be fickle things at the best of times and a dived submarine can be a particularly fickle beast indeed. At higher speeds, they fly through the water much like an aircraft does through the air, smoothly banking into turns and readily changing depth by pointing the bows up or down. At lower speeds, submarines are more sluggish and require skilful handling and teamwork to keep the boat on the ordered course and depth while minimising the movement of water over the planes, either of which can create noise and offer opportunities for an adversary to counter-detect the submarine. An advantage of being at depth while at slow speed is that some leeway can be granted with the ordered depth or course.

Operating at periscope depth takes even greater skill. Patrolling at minimal speed reduces the visible wake caused by periscopes and masts slicing through the sea surface, but makes depth keeping substantially more difficult. Particularly for surveillance or intelligence collection patrols, sensors such as the periscope windows or electronic warfare antennae need to be exposed to the air and not washed over, but the total length of the periscopes or other masts that can be seen or detected on radar also needs to be minimised. The balance demands an ability to maintain depth precisely, within inches of the ordered keel depth, and often for hours, if not days or weeks, on end.

If a submarine needs to stop while dived, generally for tactical reasons to reduce the noise or sonar signature of the boat to an absolute minimum, the planes and rudder become totally ineffective. Unlike some submarines, Australian boats have no hovering system, so absolute precision with the trim of the boat is required. Too much or too little weight overall and the submarine will continue to sink or rise. Too much weight forward or aft and the submarine could tip on its head or stern like a half-empty shampoo bottle in a bath.

The initial sea trials of the ASRV *Remora* tested our submarine handling and ship control skills like nothing else. Named for the suckerfish that cling to a larger host animal, such as a whale or shark, *Remora* was our first dedicated and crewed submarine rescue vehicle. Weighing in at more than 16 tonnes, she was designed to mate with the escape hatch of a distressed submarine at depths of up to 500 metres while tethered to a mother ship for communications and power, and then bring survivors to the surface.

Tasked with supporting the first transfer of personnel from a dived submarine to *Remora*, we made our way to Jervis Bay and joined HMAS *Tobruk*, the amphibious landing ship acting as mother ship. Moored within the bay in an area surveyed clear of obstructions and designated a safe bottoming area for submarines, we made a surfaced approach at right angles to *Tobruk* to avoid her mooring cables. We dived within 600 yards of her starboard beam, working briskly to catch the trim and continued to close her at slow speed. With the Captain on the periscope, calling down the range to *Tobruk*, we caught a stopped trim at periscope depth within yards of the ship.

'Have a look at this, XO,' said the Captain.

Even ignoring the magnification afforded by the periscope optics, she was close.

'Captain, Sir. *Tobruk* reports our bows have drifted under her ship's side,' came the urgent report from the Radio Supervisor.

The whole area being exceedingly shallow, there were mere feet between our keel and the bottom, and mere feet again between our relatively fragile bow sonar dome and *Tobruk*'s hardened keel. We were so precariously balanced that the weight of one sailor moving through a compartment was enough to alter the trim of our 2,500-tonne submarine. Ordering two sailors forward as a 'trimming party' to keep our bows down, we backed out marginally, then rapidly flooded a forward tank to make us heavy and put us on the bottom.

Later in the day, after several successful cycles of *Remora* diving, mating with our escape hatch, transferring personnel into the rescue vehicle and up to the surface, we delicately reversed the procedure. Pumping from forward, we became progressively lighter, lifted off the bottom, backed away gingerly, came up to periscope depth, then finally surfaced – mentally exhausted but much relieved to be unscathed.

In early July, we embarked ten Australian soldiers from the Water Troop of one of the SAS squadrons to re-certify them in dived swimmer release. Their young Troop Captain was shown to the wardroom and introduced himself.

'Call me Joe,' he said.

'Righto, Joe, here's the program, what do you need?'

It seems to us a lot of these guys were called 'Joe'. None of them were wearing rank, and they apparently had an even flatter professional hierarchy than we did in boats. They certainly worked in much smaller teams and were as specialised, in their own way, as our sailors. We turned the fore-ends over to them and they made themselves at home among the torpedoes, bringing all manner of gear and weapons with them. We embarked extra rations – having had US Navy SEALs onboard *Otway* out of Pearl Harbor previously, I knew these guys could eat. With their equipment checked, familiarisation tours of the boat conducted and dry runs complete, we set sail for the exercise areas to the south.

We had worked with the New Zealand SAS earlier in the year, drilling them and ourselves in procedures to launch zodiac inflatable boats from the submarine to insert their patrols onto foreign coastlines. They launched (typically at night) by positioning the zodiac on the forward casing, then diving the submarine beneath them, enabling them to propel away once in the water. It did not always proceed smoothly.

Recovery was no easier. Signalling the submarine by light, the zodiac would match the speed of the submarine as we surfaced beneath them, guided by a taut line running at an angle from the top of the fin onto the front of the casing. Given that the forward casing was no wider than the breadth of a zodiac, sticking the landing was no mean feat, particularly with any sort of a sea running. The first several runs, the zodiac swung off the side of the casing and bashed against the ballast tanks, sending soldiers scrabbling to get back onboard. Eventually, we all got the hang of it.

This work with the Australian SAS was different. Our objective was to achieve dived launch and recovery. Having completed dry runs while surfaced at sea, we were forced into Jervis Bay by weather that totally prohibited moving onto the dived serials. With his keen foresight, Mark ensured that one of the safe bottoming areas was reserved for us. The area was tiny (at a mile long and half a mile wide), shallow and generally used for static dives to sit on the bottom and do mast timing trials or calibrate electronic warfare sensors. While authorised to be dived in that area, we had no licence to be dived anywhere else in the bay. I couldn't see how this was going to help, so Mark talked me through it.

'We line up on the surface, pre-position the SAS troops in the fin, open main vents precisely as we cross into one end of the dived area. Catch the trim, signal the divers to release, surface before we exit the area. Dive, release, surface, repeat.'

Risk was everywhere. If the trim wasn't spot on, we'd be through the area before we got under, or aground and bashing against the bottom. Worse still, any excursion beyond periscope depth carried a severe risk of the divers developing deadly embolisms. The use of speed to control depth was not an option, as it risked the divers losing their grip on the submarine and washed astern into turning propellors. Once under, any delay in release meant staying dived to propel clear of the troops in the water. In the submarine world, the principle of 'dived water' is sacrosanct. Running beyond the area boundary would be a grievous transgression of dived safety orders that could see the Captain removed from command.

'Scotty, you can do it. Let's go!'

We had a particular determination to see this exercise through. A few days earlier, on the Wednesday night, tragedy had struck. A formation of six Black Hawk helicopters, conducting a live-fire exercise near Townsville and flying using night vision goggles, were on approach to the landing zone when two of the helicopters collided, bringing both aircraft to the ground. Eighteen soldiers were killed. Three of those men were from the 5th Aviation Regiment and fifteen from the SASR, making it the worst accident in the history of the SASR.

I asked Joe to come to the wardroom and showed him the signal we had received, which included the names of the dead. Without doubt, he knew many of the those who had died, and some of them well.

'What do you need, Joe?'

'I need some time.'

He went forward to speak with his troops, signal in hand. I shut the bulkhead door behind him and began to make contingency arrangements for their return travel. Thirty minutes later, Joe was at the door of the wardroom.

'We're good, let's go,' he said.

Given the immensity of the disaster, it was entirely reasonable to cancel the remaining exercise serials and get them ashore. Instead, they chose to put their grief on hold and crack on. Joe and his troops knew the value of the exceedingly rare time they had with the submarine – which would be rarer still in coming years with the boats being retired – and they would not forego the professional opportunity they had before them. I was indelibly impressed and humbled to witness the willingness of these soldiers to place mission before self.

Journal note, September 1996. *My girls are champions.*

A circumnavigation of Australia made for plenty of extra seatime in the back half of the year. Now, with a decade of submarine experience in addition to my less formative earlier years in the wider Navy, I had proved myself at every level up to XO. Garnering approval from my superiors, I achieved selection for the toughest military command course in the world – the Submarine Command Qualifying Course.

But there was one more adventure lined up before Christmas leave. After just a few short days at home with the girls, I flew out to Canada to join HMCS *Ojibwa* for a final opportunity to hone my skills before embarking on the Command Course early the next year.

A frozen, mid-winter Halifax, Nova Scotia was the first stop, to work-up in the Canadian Navy's submarine control room simulator. Over a couple of weeks, we established some solid teamwork across the half dozen students, who encompassed a wide range of experience. The senior

Canadian on course, and undisputed leader of the pack, was a quirky but affable fellow also readying himself for the Command Course.

Once finished with the simulator and drills, we drove the nine hours from Halifax down to Portland, Maine to join the boat and set sail. Scott McVicar, one of my Warfare Officer Course classmates, was the XO of the boat. Known onboard, a little unfairly, as 'Newman', after the *Seinfeld* character, he ran a tight ship and it was great to be back at sea with him. The CO was a tall French Canadian who addressed people as 'man' when chatting and 'mister' when he was not. Helpful and encouraging, he gave us free rein and plenty of rope with his submarine.

The crew were immediately impressive; surprisingly so given they were one of only four submarines in the Canadian Navy, meaning theirs was an even smaller and intrinsically more fragile squadron than our own. Our cohort needed all the help we could get, because the Canadians arranged for plenty of opposition. HMCS *Nipigon*, an ageing but capable Annapolis-class destroyer, and two Halifax-class ships, HMCS *Halifax and Montreal*, were our tormentors. The Halifax were modern, purpose-built, anti-submarine warfare frigates. Faster than any ship I had previously worked against, they offered a new challenge, particularly operating along the fog-bound eastern seaboard. More than once, I retired to the fore-ends to lick my wounds after getting shown up by the frigates.

It wasn't a total disaster, but by the time *Ojibwa* returned alongside, the supreme confidence I carried stepping off *Otama* was shot. I came away rattled, and it was a timely shake. If I was to bring the thousands of days and nights of struggle and effort to full fruition, and to turn the years of heartache and separation endured by my family into something truly worthwhile, I still had work to do.

PART II

MASTER AND COMMANDER

CHAPTER 13
THEY CALL IT 'PERISHER'

Journal note, 24 February 1997. *Pass Perisher, Scotty.*

In the new year, Paddy – my long-time submarine buddy – and I fly to the Netherlands for the Submarine Command Qualifying Course. I am utterly determined to see it through, realise my dream and assume command of an Australian submarine.

Originally developed by the Royal Navy as the 'Periscope School' during the First World War, the course is now known universally by the grim contraction 'Perisher'. And for good reason. Despite the rigorous preparation and selection process, many aspirants who start the course do not make the grade. As the ultimate test for a submarine specialist, it is also known as a 'Dagger' course. There are only two possible outcomes: pass and achieve qualification to command a submarine, or fail. Crucially, Perisher is a once in a lifetime opportunity; failure is absolute and irrevocable, leaving a seagoing submarine career extinguished. Unique to submarines, there is no comparable prerequisite for command of a warship, air squadron or establishment.

For decades, our submarine officers have travelled first to the United Kingdom and later, since the late 1990s, to the Netherlands to undertake Perisher courses conducted by their navies. A deployment in itself, the course is about four and a half months long and runs through safety and tactical phases ashore, then at sea. Widely acclaimed as the toughest military command course in the world, Perisher offers an opportunity to do anything and everything a warfighting submarine can do. Inshore operations, opposed transits, underwater looks, trailing nuclear submarines and attacking carrier task groups are daily fare.

For an avid submariner, Perisher is rife with opportunity: to observe and learn; to practise, refine and demonstrate; to err, correct and succeed; to thrive and excel; to lead and command; or to fail. Going in, I know that the ships, rocks and people are hard, the intensity and pressures are real, the margins for error slim. I also know that 'Teacher' will frame the question that only I can answer: *Am I enough?*

Our arrival at the main naval base of the Royal Netherlands Navy (Koninklijke Marine) at Den Helder – occupying the northernmost tip of the North Holland Peninsula – is decidedly anti-climactic. The weeks and months stretch before us, cold and bleak. Mercifully, we are at sea within days, joining the Dutch Walrus-class submarine HNLMS *Zeeleuw* (Sea Lion) to transit the North Sea past Denmark to Kristiansand, Norway. Here we transfer to HNLMS *Bruinvis* (Brown Fish) – our Perisher boat to be – for an at-sea familiarisation before the course proper begins in a few weeks' time. On the bridge of this new submarine, I draw an easy confidence from my comfort levels and ready understanding of all things submarine.

The towed array is streamed and we depart for the shipwreck-strewn Skagerrak, the strait separating the North Sea and the Baltic. The week passes quickly, beginning with dived high-speed planing and manoeuvres. Reaching a 34 degree bow up angle as we rocket upwards, the Dutch are more than happy to throw the boat around at speed. Submarine-on-submarine tracking and torpedo firing exercises against the *Zeeleuw* follow, supported by the submarine tender HNLMS *Mercuur*. The anticipated intra-squadron competitiveness is readily apparent as the two crews fight for bragging rights in this most difficult of tactical environments.

Unlike our Oberons at home, the Walrus-class are a 'not-to-hit' target for the Mark 48 exercise torpedo. For the first time, I am on the receiving end of a heavyweight torpedo attack. Witnessing *Zeeleuw*'s torpedo discharge on our sonar screens, we soon hear the weapon running and the active sonar searching for us.

'Torpedo, torpedo, torpedo bearing 166, 170, 174,' calls the sonar operator.

The pinging grows more rapid and fervent. The torpedo accelerates as it detects then locks onto us. The guidance wire linking the torpedo with *Zeeleuw* can be heard to pay out – *phlat, phlat, phlat* – and the control vanes actuate – *tscht, tscht, tscht* – as it manoeuvres aggressively. Knowing the destructive power of a warshot torpedo, the sights and sounds bring on an involuntary sense of dread, rising up from my toes and rapidly spreading through my body. I make a conscious effort to recall the torpedo pre-sets that will ensure it skims safely underneath us.

A real benefit of this time at sea is having one of my main fears substantially allayed. How do I command a Dutch submarine when my vocabulary doesn't extend beyond *aardappel* (potato) and *frietjes* (fries)? It becomes apparent that I don't need to understand precisely what is being said around me to know where and when to pay attention. Chat between comfortable and confident Dutch sonar operators looks and sounds remarkably similar to that of Australian sonar operators. Importantly, the tell-tales of confusion or concern – rising pitch, a forward lean, hands to headphones – are also similar and just as discernible. I listen in a different way as we get to know the Captain and crew, looking less for what is being conveyed and more for *how* it is being conveyed. I see that they, too, have their sensors trained upon us.

It is 10 March, and our Perisher class musters at Den Helder. Paddy and I are joined by two Dutchmen, Herman and Michel. A South African, Kristian, and a Dane, Thagaard, make up the six-pack. Herman and Michel are particularly sharp operators; they each have the distinction of being a known entity to Teacher, seemingly a good thing for Michel, perhaps not so for Herman. Kristian, humble and charismatic, is deflated early by the periscope safety drills, which are entirely foreign to him. Thagaard, all red beard and gruff exterior, is our resident Viking. Armed with determination and will, we each shield our own particular fears and doubts.

The following day we meet Teacher, Commander Jan Wibrands, RNLN. I know him by reputation thanks to those few colleagues who preceded me on the course. Jan is hard: a highly experienced submarine commander, a Cold War veteran and a Feyenoord football fanatic. Highly attuned to the potential consequences of his judgements, he has a particularly solemn regard for his responsibilities as Teacher. While he alone does not determine our fate as submariners, he presides over the chapter of our lives that does.

Lunch that day is shared with Teacher and hosted by the Dutch Squadron Commander, Captain van Beek, RNLN – a rare treat. Making it all the more remarkable, we are joined by Rear Admiral Perowne, RN, the Commander Operations and Flag Officer Submarines – a man who will become Deputy Supreme Allied Commander Atlantic the following year. Perhaps to make us feel at home, the Admiral spins a yarn about a lunch he shared with Alan Bond in jail in Western Australia. Both their wives attended what was a decidedly pleasant affair, with the jail staff apparently wrapped around Bondy's little finger. Teacher doesn't share his personal stories.

The first full month of Perisher is spent ashore in the 'Gipsy Trainer' – a simulated submarine control room, replete with computer-generated graphics of ships projected into the periscope view. Open, spacious and well lit, the trainer is fitted with the inboard section of a periscope, a small handful of operator's consoles and an instructor's desk. It bears no resemblance to the closely packed confines of an actual control room, but the pressure that Teacher and his committed staff continuously generate within these four walls is astonishing.

Notwithstanding the ultimate prize of command qualification, Perisher is first and foremost a teaching course, and submarine periscope safety training forms a large and integral part of it. It raises the knowledge and skills taught to periscope watchkeepers from their earliest days in the Arm to an art form and engrains them to the point of instinct. These skills are absolutely critical to the effective operation and, in extremis, to the survival of submarines executing their various missions.

At periscope depth, a shallow depth that allows use of the periscopes and other masts, a submarine is vulnerable to collision with surface ships – by accident or design. The risk is necessarily accepted and managed to make use of these sensors. Periscopes can be used to assess the surface picture quickly and effectively, and it is routine procedure to maintain a continuous watch on one when at this depth. The basic premise of periscope safety training derives from the requirement of old for submarines to remain safe from collision while manoeuvring to launch a spread of torpedoes at close range from the target.

With modern weapons, the original requirement of dramatically closing a defended target to launch is no longer as valid. There are, however, many occasions when the skill of handling a submarine in close proximity to shipping is still required. The most common is returning to periscope depth from deep. There is a period where the submarine moves through the surface ship stratum, but still can't see ships through the periscope. When it clears, the Captain can find himself surrounded by contacts and needs to be capable of instantly assessing the situation and taking appropriate action. Visual, acoustic and electronic intelligence can often only be achieved at shallow depth and close range. For these reasons, our submarines spend a great deal of time at periscope depth.

The methods around periscope safety training were refined by Commander Sandy Woodward, RN during his years as Teacher. Woodward famously went on to command the British Forces during the Falklands War as a Rear Admiral. He developed the mathematical approach to the speed, time and distance problem of keeping a submarine safe from collision with surface ships while minimising mast exposure and achieving its aims, such as avoiding counter-detection and attacking the ships. Essentially this was to assess the range of a given ship and, knowing it's maximum available speed, calculate how long it might take to be 'on top' of the submarine. Keeping in hand the required time for the submarine to go deep and get under the ship, you can calculate a 'look interval'. As the look interval expires, the periscope is raised again to check the range of the ship. If it is within the 'Go Deep Circle' the submarine must take evasive action. If not, another look interval is calculated.

This is quite straightforward, but can be further complicated by sailing boats, fishing vessels, ferries or other traffic. Navigational boundaries, such as the shoreline or the bottom, don't simplify the problem. Life becomes exciting with two, three, four or more warships, each manoeuvring at speed and requiring constantly updated ranges and look intervals. A warship that begins as a speck on the horizon can fill the periscope view within minutes. The look interval on a charging warship can be timed down to about five seconds. If you get it right, he thunders overhead at 30-plus knots, passing with about 15 feet of clearance above the top of the fin. Get it wrong and you destroy one submarine with crew, and probably one warship.

Wegduiken is Dutch for 'dive away'. *Wegduiken* shouted from the diaphragm, as periscope handles are flung up and stopwatches are started translates to 'Take this submarine deep right now, this very second, or be rammed and sliced open by the 5,000-tonne warship charging us at full speed!'

Cycling through one student after another in the trainer, Teacher launches pre-programmed scenarios at us to test our periscope safety skills. We support the Duty Captain by filling various roles, such as Attack Coordinator or Periscope Assistant. Importantly, we learn from every run, not just our own. We begin with the simplest of single ship attacks, which we all botch for various reasons, and progressively build to scenarios of greater complexity and length.

The staff record the details of each attack. While these consist mostly of bearing, range, course, speed and time data, jocularity does find its place. 'I would give you more speed, Captain, but I don't have the powerrrr!' appears on one of my run sheets a few weeks in (apparently there are Trekkies the world over). The pace of advance and expectation of performance is steady but relentless. Single degrees, yards and seconds matter, and determine the success or otherwise of a run. The days are a seemingly endless pattern of run, analyse, digest, reset, repeat.

Though we are all highly capable, the small variations in our skill become apparent and amplified. Teacher doesn't hesitate to publicly correct shortcomings and we are each on the receiving end on a regular basis. Working with the tension as we move from week to week, I take the absence of any scathing remarks from Teacher as positive reinforcement. Still, I continually battle to remain positive and confident, and deliberately preserve three minutes alone in the heads at the start of each day to set my determination.

As the days become weeks, temperament and character are revealed alongside technical ability. Brash to the point of contempt, but with an abundance of talent, Paddy is Teacher's kind of student. Herman, on the other hand, needs to push from the front and doesn't endear himself. Michel, a man of precision and order, is seemingly unflappable. Kristian, an excellent student, draws himself up from a slow start and gains momentum. Thagaard is taking knocks. At times, he seems unable to lift himself; at others, staunchly resolved.

'They will have to throw me off this course. I am not leaving,' he asserts.

At the end of the ashore phase and seven weeks into our odyssey, I am in a good place and choose to be confident. Teacher offers me this verbal debrief: 'Thoroughly prepared – usual for Australians. Don't see any problems.' Translation: I haven't failed yet.

We are preparing to take command of strategic assets. The strictures imposed by the preservation of stealth will often mean that we are operating in complete isolation from higher authority, guidance or direction. Despite many magnificent advances in technology, submarines are not fitted with 'how am I doing in command today?' barometers. So, while he is ready and willing to point out our multitude of tactical errors and failings, Teacher feels no obligation to provide assurance on our overall performance or trajectory. Tummy rubs are not in Teacher's repertoire.

'Klaarmaken voor onderwater, klaarmaken voor onderwater!' Prepare to dive!

We use the transit north to drill ourselves and the *Bruinvis* crew on 'go deep' routines in readiness for the real shift from training in a simulator to driving a dived submarine. Five miles off the coast of Norway, we are into it, conducting single ship attacks with a Danish Niels Juel-class corvette, the HDMS *Olfert Fischer*, and a Karel Doorman-class frigate, the HNLMS *Van Nes*. I conduct four short runs, including two heart-stopping 'Q runs' with the warship charging directly over the top, deafening us and rattling the boat, as we duck under and come up astern of her. Off to a decidedly steady start, I'm at ease within this high-octane excitement.

Day Two is a little different; we are into two ship attacks. The sea is up, making the handling of the ships more erratic as they manoeuvre to comply with Teacher's pre-ordained run plans and impacting on the accuracy of our ranging. On one early run, with the *Van Nes* racing past us on the port side, the *Olfert Fischer* is also at speed, but on our starboard beam. Fully expecting her to continue skirting past as well, she makes a small alteration of course towards us. I see it, but make a bad call and turn my attention back to *Van Nes*. Teacher's response is swift: *'Wegduiken!'* The submarine is going deep, out of my hands. *This is how you fail, Scotty.*

Back at periscope depth, with a heavy sea still running and visibility closing in, the pressure is on. On the last run of the day, I track two merchant ships inshore. I know from sonar that the warships have been closing for ten minutes, but I don't get them visual until they are already in at around 3,000 yards. I get a first accurate range on *Van Nes* at 2,400 yards – only 60 seconds from sending us deep. She is right ahead and charging straight at us, sea spray erupting from her bows as she cleaves her way through the opposing seas. *Olfert Fischer* is on my starboard bow – closer than *Van Nes* and also carving up the seas, but definitely altering away. I make a call, 'Skirting.'

A range on the most dangerous – *Van Nes* – puts her at 1,600 yards, 20 seconds. But I sense that something is wrong with the sonar bearings of *Olfert Fischer* – she should be moving faster to the right. I go up on the attack periscope to check her course. The *Olfert Fischer*, already approaching my beam, is now under hard wheel and turning directly towards us. You bastard!

Unseen by me, Teacher has gone up on the other periscope to check *Olfert Fischer* – the run plan he ordered had her continuing away. The control room get it with both barrels as Teacher and I scream out in unison, '*Wegduiken!*'

She is at 900 yards, well inside our Go Deep Circle, and heading directly towards us. Our bow is driven down sharply and the planesman levels out at 30 metres as the warship thunders past, immediately astern. We are safe and I am in control. *This is how you pass, Scotty.*

The second week of at-sea safety training is something else. The weather in the North Sea worsens, so Teacher decides to conduct the runs within the Norwegian fjords. Bjornafjorden (White Bear Sound) will be our playground. Exceptionally tight navigationally, and with traffic crossing from half a dozen different directions, the fjord is frantic with fishing boats, ferries and small merchantmen. More often than not, it is cloaked in fog, snowstorms or both. During my first run on the second day, the weather changes rapidly and dramatically. Initially, the visibility closes in to 1,200 yards with passing snowstorms. This is followed by a distorting haze – blurring the image of contacts as they pass between 5,000 and

6,000 yards – then by the brightest sunlight and clearest visibility I have ever encountered through a periscope, all in the space of a five-minute run.

To up the ante even more, a Norwegian Oslo-class frigate, the HNoMS *Trondheim*, joins us. With a small fleet of warships charging around at full speed in this busy little pond, the concentration and teamwork required to stay safe is phenomenal. The opportunity to get it badly wrong is ever present. On one run, I stay at periscope depth searching for *Van Nes* and *Trondheim* as they steam in, getting steadily louder and louder on sonar. I don't actually know how far through the swirling snowstorm I can see. My sole indication is that I have seen the *Olfert Fischer* come though on the beam at 2,500 yards. I hold my nerve. Teacher holds his tongue. I prepare the boat for an immediate depth change. Ghostlike with masts covered in snow, the ships appear – too close – and pass us by.

'You should have gone deep,' Teacher says softly into my straining ear.

Both in the moment and on reviewing each run, I unfailingly find some fine detail needs improvement. I'm yearning for the perfect run, but repeatedly disappointed. Apparently, mastery is not perfection. As the week progresses, I get fewer and fewer opportunities. Paddy, Kristian and I come through clean; Teacher will take us forward to the next phase. With others, he is less convinced as Michel and Herman are put through any number of extra runs, more than I would have expected. By the end of the week, Thagaard is gone.

Another month in the trainer at Den Helder awaits. The emphasis shifts from safe operation to tactical employment of the submarine as we plan and conduct inshore operations, and hone our skills in open ocean tracking of warships and submarines. Most days, these runs seem satisfactory until Teacher gets stuck in with his debrief. He can make you feel like a flying fish that's landed on the casing of a submarine overnight – washed up, dried up and kicked back overboard. Even though the whole adventure is more about what you learn than how you feel, after three months the sustained pressure and effort is punishing.

I distract myself from work with letters to and from home, and a running program designed to get me ready for a first marathon somewhere down track. The other main distraction, which helps nothing, is the rubbish Dutch beer. Working till midnight most days of the week, we hit the local bars on Friday nights and make a practice of taking 'stress relief' to ridiculous extremes.

In early June, before we sail once more, I call home. For months, conversations with Shaunaugh have been punctuated by loneliness and sadness. We are fed up with being on our own, enduring one extended separation after another. Intensely conscious of some impacts, one of my journal entries captures some of the loss: *I will never know my little girl as a five- or six-year-old. I missed it.*

But this chat is a little different. 'I've already organised your congratulations party, that's how confident I am! Just get out there, get it done and get home,' says Shaunaugh.

And from Laura, 'Good luck on your course, Daddy.'

I take them both to sea with me for courage.

The days of the tactical phase are chock-full of adventure. Ranged against the combined might of a massive NATO exercise, every anti-submarine warfare platform that can be brought to bear is on a mission to ruin our day. In turn, we search for and exploit every discoverable advantage. We have earned a licence from Teacher to operate the submarine to its absolute limits – I feel ready, but there are no guarantees.

On one occasion, under cover of darkness, I drive the submarine into the lee of Garron Point on the north-east coast of Ireland. Having completed an inshore operation off the approaches to Belfast earlier in the day, we are evading the searching sensors of maritime patrol aircraft, anti-submarine helicopters and frigates. The battery is running low, and we have places to be. We snort there at full power, less than 300 yards from shore, while stemming a 2–3 knot tidal stream. The lights of cars passing high overhead along the cliff tops add an eerie spectre to the scene. It is a wicked hideout. Demanding immense concentration from the watch and particularly skilful shiphandling, we press limits like I have never done before. Paddy, typically bold as brass, refuses to take over as Duty Captain when he sees where we are. I back off from the coast a little and coax him into taking the boat, and he edges back in. Undetected throughout the night, we proceed to our next tasking at dawn with a full battery.

The following day, I successfully drive *Bruinvis* through a dived 10-mile transit of Kilbrannan Sound relying solely on bottom contour navigation, using discrete and sparse transmissions on the echo sounder. Meeting suspiciously little opposition along the way, I am unsurprised to detect HMS *Manchester*, on patrol and closing from the north, just as we return to periscope depth. A modern British Type 23 anti-submarine frigate, her powerful active sonar flashes up. Transmitting various search patterns at different frequencies, she is combing the water for the submarine they know is out there. The sound bangs through our hull with absolute menace. We are directly in her path, but there is nowhere to run. Teacher, who has written the score and is conducting the orchestra, is a first-class prick!

With the active transmissions getting more intense by the minute, I turn to starboard and close the coast, coming in over the exceedingly shallow water south of Catacol Bay. We parallel *Manchester*'s course and drift along the shoreline at the barest of speeds, minimising the Doppler effect that her sonar is tuned to detect. Hugging the coast at 200–300 yards, we are hopefully hidden among the reverberations as their sonar transmissions bounce off the steep face of the Isle of Arran.

I stay safe navigationally using sonar bearings taken on the faint rippling noise of a small but charted stream running into the sound. I have never done this, or seen this done, before or since. If we are forced deep, there will be mere feet to spare between ourselves, the ship's propellor blades above and the unyielding bottom below. Breaking every periscope safety rule, I keep our masts lowered and track *Manchester* on our sonar as she creeps past at 1,000 yards. My heart is in my mouth as she continues on and we are clear.

'*Ein uit!*' Time for the crew to light up a smoke.

In late June, we pull into Loch Fyne alongside our Perisher playmate, HMS *Triumph*. Becoming disoriented during an inshore operation earlier in the week, Michel has been landed, his Perisher course now over. Herman, now the sole Dutch student, is in torment and despair after overhearing a Teacher-to-Teacher conversation regarding his performance.

We sit in a corner bar. Herman talks and I listen as we drink whiskey, weep for his dying father and make crude jokes at Teacher's expense. At 2 am, his head lifts. He shakes my hand, stands and takes the next step.

Journal note, 27 June 1997. *Less than 48 hours to go. Be safe, be safe, be safe.*

At sunrise we are onboard and heading back to sea, leaning in. Over the final days and nights, Teacher has Herman doing every other inshore operation, with the Dutch, Australian and South African Squadron Commanders embarked to add just a little extra pressure. The ultimate run is a penetration of the Clyde estuary against exceedingly tough competition, a classic finale. It is his to win or lose.

'*Klaarmaken om leeg te maken.*' Prepare to surface.

During the month, *Bruinvis*, *Triumph* and the Norwegian submarine HNoMS *Ula* were all at sea with their respective Perishers embarked. Of the six British students, one passed. Of the six aboard the Norwegian boat, one passed. In sum, only six of the eighteen highly experienced and talented submariners embarked on the course emerge as Submarine Daggers.

Over the following decades, Herman goes on to successfully command both *Bruinvis* and HNLMS *Walrus*, and the fleet oiler HNLMS *Zuiderkruis*. He serves as Teacher for many years and rises to command the entire Dutch Submarine Service. When you are on the edge of both success and failure every day, the way you lean matters.

From a hotel room on the banks of the Gareloch, I call home, buzzing. *Yes, I am.*

CHAPTER 14
THE VORTEX

Our little navy blue Mondeo sedan was packed tight for the long drive ahead. Stretched out before us was a month-long holiday driving south through New South Wales and Victoria, then across the vast expanse of Australia, to mark our move to 'the West'. Shaunaugh and Laura were stoic as we separated ourselves from work, school and family once again. Two weeks in, and before setting out across the Nullarbor, we splashed out and treated Laura to a Nintendo Game Boy. Endlessly flipping the Backstreet Boys cassette in the car stereo had left us desperate for alternative entertainment.

With a week's accommodation lined up in Fremantle, we were on the hunt for a new home. Obliged to start down near the Garden Island base, where Navy had one or two unoccupied married quarters, we headed along Cockburn Road, past the industrial grime of Henderson and Kwinana, to sleepy Rockingham. The married quarters were empty for a reason – they were run down and uninhabitable.

We drove around in search of a coffee. With Sunday trading not yet part of WA's economic plan, the yawning shopping mall was empty apart from yesterday's trash and last night's track-suited drunks. Finally, the tears came.

'Where have you brought me this time?' Shaunaugh sobbed.

We trekked back up the Kwinana Freeway and soon settled into shady Willetton, south of the Swan River.

After several months of Collins-class conversion training in the school, I was primed to join in command. With my duffle bag packed and ticket in hand to fly to Adelaide and pick up the boat, I called on Captain Peter Clarke, RAN before departing. Our highly polished and exceedingly capable Squadron Commander, he had made a clean transition over recent years from a stellar submarine career with the Royal Navy into our own. Tea consumed and guidance received, I stood to take my leave as Peter ambled over to his desk.

'Come and have a look at these,' he beckoned.

I detected only the slightest hint of amusement as he lay a series of photos on his large timber desk. My eyes widened as I took in half a dozen shots taken at the Perisher breakfast, held at Admiral Perowne's Faslane home to celebrate our success a year earlier. Splashing around in the Admiral's sizeable backyard pond, I was totally starkers. It was quite a party for a formal naval gathering! Wordlessly, Captain Clarke gathered them up. I extended a hand forward to collect them just as he opened the top draw of his desk and they disappeared. My outstretched hand carried awkwardly up into a salute.

'Thank you for your time, Sir.' I was on notice. Still.

HMAS *Collins*, commissioned into the Navy in mid-1996 and subsequently home ported in Perth, was back in Adelaide for a 'Post-Delivery Availability' docking – the nonsensical name used by the Australian Submarine Corporation (ASC) for a warranty service. Despite all the preparation, there was more than a little apprehension as I took the reins in mid-October, joining in command with minimal experience of the class.

More importantly, the responsibility I shouldered was at the forefront of my mind. The potential destructive power of the weapons embarked in these submarines – and the scale of national investment and resultant dollar value of each platform and sea day – was immense. The strategic deterrent value was incalculable, but nonetheless real. We were scheduled to be home before Christmas, ready for a full two-year cycle of operations to deliver on our collective potential.

Quite directly, I was responsible for the lives and wellbeing of my Ship's Company, and in some measure, the welfare of those who depended on them. I set about getting to know the crew, the lifeblood of my submarine. Having sailed in *Collins* for the Perth to Adelaide passage a few weeks earlier, I was conscious that many of the Ship's Company were onboard as commissioning crew, ushering it out of build and into full service. Their submarine experience over the past several years had consisted of interminable delays, incessant trials and the lashing tongues of a malicious press. Seemingly denied a sense of ownership of their submarine, a few remained marked with the stain of a 'build culture' – obsessed with process and eyes averted from the sea. Some had known little else.

I envisaged a more purposeful future for these sailors; a day when they would be ready in all respects to deploy on meaningful tasking, unencumbered by trials officers and independent of sea training units, and doing the work and providing the service they had joined and trained to do. I earnestly looked forward to leading them towards this, in quick time. By Remembrance Day, I had my first sign of things to come.

'They're talking about a delay, Sir,' said my ground-truthing and straight-shooting XO, JJ Cupples.

'Who's talking?'

'The ASC guys on the floor. Two months – they reckon it's a done deal.'

While the submarine had been largely built in Australia, two major sections were constructed by Kockums in the Swedish yard at Malmö. Complicated by the weapons discharge system and the escape tower, these sections were deemed too technically complex for the Australian workforce, but they had arrived riddled with welding defects. While more than a thousand of these defects were repaired years ago, and before *Collins* was launched, a decision was made to substantially progress the invasive repair of hundreds more while she was in Adelaide. Christmas came and went.

Early in 1999, further delays were introduced with the requirement to fit modifications to the fin and casing. Drawing on expertise from within the United States Navy, the composite fibreglass 'spoiler kit' was designed to ameliorate deficiencies in the original Kockums design and improve the acoustic signature of the boats. A four-month docking had blown out to ten long months, and it suited ASC down to the ground.

The submarine's program, and our fate, was being driven by highly politicised and industrialised strategic level decision-making over which I had little influence and no control. Despite being a commissioned Fleet unit, we were enveloped by a dockyard that continued to evince a proprietary attitude towards the submarine and were entirely ambivalent to Navy's needs, which included a timely progression to sea and return to home port.

Among the submariners, this yard was known as 'the Vortex' – an industrial whirlpool dragging submarines alongside and pulling them under. Despite having multiple submarines on the hardstand or alongside, ASC were unwilling and unable to effectively progress work on more than one boat at a time. With the gross profits already syphoned out of the project, their priorities were driven by the remaining build program. Schedule impact was the preferred solution for a board and executive team that was collectively happy to retain submarines in the yard in perpetuity, spreading work out across the boats as they saw fit. The earnest goodwill of those occasionally engaged in actual work onboard was no match for this paradigm.

'She's our tail-end Charlie,' confided the ASC manager responsible for progress on *Collins*' docking.

Through this time, a report on the state of the Collins-class was compiled for the Minister of Defence. When released in June, Rear Admiral Peter Briggs, RAN was appointed as Head of a new Submarine Capability Team in the Defence Materiel Organisation (DMO) to implement its recommendations and realise the potential of the class. A man who did not include the word 'failure' in his lexicon, he was easy to follow … if you could keep up. Peter visited us shortly after taking up his appointment and his energy and direction made an immediate difference, and we needed all the help we could get.

Journal note, 18 July 1999. *Yeah, at least I can grow up with my mum.*
– Laura, age eight

Many of the Ship's Company, myself included, suffered extensive separation from their families during this time. I knew from experience that separation could be painful during long deployments at sea, but much more readily endured by all concerned because we achieved a recognisable effect for Navy. Given the expected short duration of the initial docking, the officers and sailors were sent to Adelaide while their families remained in Perth. Two reunion travel permits a year – Navy's standard entitlement for sailors posted interstate from their hometown – wasn't going to cut it for these guys, particularly when their next door neighbours in Perth flew in and out of the mines once a week on FIFO swings.

As the months rolled on, and consecutive delays built an air of uncertainty, the strain became increasingly apparent. When a further delay was announced, the morale of the crew, and that of their families, slumped dramatically. An ABC *Four Corners* report raising 'safety concerns' with the boats did nothing to ease collective tensions. Requests for compassionate travel to send sailors home to families under stress were on the rise. The sailors tried to keep it from my ears, but threats of and requests for divorce started to emerge, and a number of de facto marriages collapsed. The requests for discharge from the Navy stacked up in my office.

I wasn't immune to these effects. I worked out pretty early that there was a trap for me in Adelaide, renowned as the City of Churches but actually the City of Pubs. Setting my sights on a marathon in four months' time, I got stuck into a strict regime of training to occupy my time off the boat and away from family. But this was only a part solution, and by May I was under distinct pressure. Shaunaugh drew a line in the sand, stating that if I was not in Perth by October, she and Laura were going back to Sydney.

Journal note, August 1999. *It happened. Dived, in command of my submarine.*

Finally undocking in late June, I enjoyed a first, memorable meal in my cabin, a pastie and a sausage roll on paper towel. *We're on the way up!* We had a wet hull and the Australian White Ensign was flying once again, but it was early August before we finally broke free of the yard in Adelaide and sailed the few dredged miles of the River Torrens to berth at Outer Harbour. Replete with fin and casing modifications, the press finally had an opportunity to make some positive comment. Thankfully, they weren't aware of the thirty-eight urgent defects that we discovered and rectified over the subsequent four weeks of Navy-led harbour acceptance trials.

At sea and closing our diving position, I released the Next of Kin signal for the fifty-one souls onboard. After witnessing, checking and standing by every piece of work done on the submarine, we thought we knew what we were taking to sea, but we needed to prove it to its limits. Internally, my own limits were being pushed as I fought back the increasing tension, and worked hard to maintain outward composure and lead.

'Officer of the Watch, Captain. Pipe Diving Stations,' I ordered for the first time.

After four and a quarter hours underwater conducting post-diving inspections and functionality checks, I felt cautiously settled. The weather off Kangaroo Island was clear, the sea glassy. At 0100 we surfaced, just to be sure that we could do that too. The number of dives equalled the number of surfacings – tick. Day One was done. Seven weeks of progressively testing and proving the submarine and re-training the crew had begun.

Late one morning in September, working our way through a series of evolutions and drills as part of our safety work-up, our objective for the day was to achieve a licence to operate all three diesels at once. This was a routine progression but involved major changes to the line-up of systems and rapid alterations in ballast, with associated challenges for ship control and depth keeping. The Sea Training Group were onboard to put us through our paces. Simulating a risk of collision with a ship, they caused us to go deep in emergency while snorting on all three diesels, and the watch swung into action. The planesman, joining us as an operational relief just the day before, pushed the bows down. Momentarily distracted as he donned his emergency breathing mask, he lost control of the boat and it pitched down wildly. With speed coming on, we shot through the ordered depth.

We were in 95 metres of water. While the initial 'risk of collision' that forced us deep was simulated, the risk of an actual grounding was now real.

'Depth 50 metres, 6 down,' reported the planesman.

'Sounding 43 meters,' from the sonar operator.

The Squadron Engineer raced into the control room. Quick to pick up on the situation, the colour drained dramatically from his usually tawny and cheerful face. The Officer of the Watch took charge, ordering weight pumped from the submarine, more speed and a bow up angle. I tracked his actions and the descent rate. Collectively, it was not enough. Taking command of the submarine, I ripped off my own mask and ordered even more speed, but less bow up.

'Depth 65 metres.'

'Sounding 28 metres,' came in reply.

Although we were still going down, I was confident we had regained control of the boat. Steve Davies, my former shipmate from *Otway*, was now a full Commander and onboard as the Commander Sea Training. He was less certain and grabbed main broadcast.

'Safeguard, safeguard. Standby grounding, brace for shock!'

'Depth 76 metres.'

'Sounding 17 metres.'

Alone in my cabin that night, I listened to the 'Big Brother' recording of the incident, drew out the geometry and reflected. At our deepest point, the bow was up and well clear of the bottom, but we came within 5 metres and mere moments of slamming our stern in. Lessons all round.

Most days blended together in a steady stream of scheduled and deliberate activity, training the team and pressing the boat deeper and deeper. Every day we built on the skill and experience of the crew. Every day we discovered limits on the systems and equipment, with something new threatening to pull us back in to the yards.

Despite the grinding work, there was no doubt the troops were in their element and happy to be living seagoing routines once more. After two weeks at sea, an experienced sailor, embarked as a trainee for his Part Three, dropped a small canvas bag in my cabin with my clean laundry.

'Been away from the missus for a while, eh Sir?'

'Why's that, mate?'

'Jocks are getting a bit tardy. My missus buys all mine, too.'

It wasn't a comment on the wear and tear of my jocks, but an understated acknowledgement of the separation and strain we all faced as we struggled to get this boat and her people back to where they belonged.

A week later, we are closing the coast to embark Rick Shalders, my former CO in *Oxley* and now Captain Submarines, for a safety assessment ahead of the planned Deep Dive later in the week. I surface with a big Southern Ocean front closing in from the west and push into Memory Cove, north-west of Kangaroo Island, for the transfer. Pressing back out to sea through Thorny Passage, we pass the ominously named Cape Catastrophe. As the weather builds, we contend with wind gusts exceeding 50 knots and waves growing to 6 metres.

Driving south on the surface, I am increasingly impatient to reach the 100 metre contour and water deep enough to dive. With the submarine pitching and rolling violently, and our options limited by submerged banks on either side, I decide to cut the margins for error and bring forward the diving position into shallower water.

Whack! We are over on our starboard side. Right over, 70 degrees over. I start a watch. *Whack!* Thirteen seconds later, we are on our port side. *Whack!* Over again.

The Collins-class is known to suffer from snap rolls induced by a certain combination of sea and swell direction and ship's speed. This is the first time I'm experiencing it, and it's frightening. There's a heart-stopping sense of imminent capsize as the submarine leans further and further over. The complete absence of control as the whole 3,300-tonne submarine is flung from side to side terrifies me.

It's not long before casualty reports come in. The galley is awash with hot cooking oil and food covers the bulkheads of the adjacent junior sailors' mess. Up top, the Officer of the Watch and lookout are lashed to the submarine, but repeatedly dragged beneath the sea surface as waves roll over the bridge. Standing with my feet planted on either side of my cabin doorway, which is directly beneath me instead of directly in front of me, I grab my tannoy and pipe 'Diving Stations.' *We have to get under.*

Finally in a position to alter to the west, we drive directly into the storm and dive. Once under, we steady at a depth of 30 metres even as we continually lift and drop with the massive swells piling up in the relatively shallow water. With minimal clearance under the keel, we grope for deeper, calmer water to lick our wounds.

Successfully completing the safety assessment over that night and the following day, I land three of the crew for full medical assessment and treatment. The irony of suffering casualties during a safety assessment is far from lost on me. While we brought ourselves through a difficult situation, the guilt jabs sharply within my chest as we turn our head to sea once more.

Journal note, 21 September 1999. *What a friggin' day!*

Seated at my fold-out cabin desk, I read the latest signal broadcast. Three and a half thousand kilometres to our north, Major General Peter Cosgrove had landed in Dili and the number of the International Forces East Timor (INTERFET) coalition troops on the ground was swelling rapidly. 'Real world' operations, including submarine operations, seemed a whole world away.

Suddenly, the wild shriek of expanding gas burst around my head. 'What the fuck is that?' I cried to no-one in particular, as a dense fog of white vapour swirled around my cabin.

'It's the halon, Boss!' was the quick-shouted reply from somewhere up the passageway.

A connection failed on one of the main halon storage bottles immediately outside my cabin. Taught to understand that halon extinguished fires by displacing the oxygen in the air, I held my breath and raced for the control room. We spent the next several hours at Emergency Stations running the diesels for toxic gas clearance.

In the seven weeks since leaving the dockyard, we had logged over seventy urgent defects. While many of these were rectified by the crew at sea, this was a massive number. None of the crew had taken more than twenty-four hours off in all that time, and we suffered a staggering twenty safeguard incidents – real, life-threatening emergencies – in the past three weeks. While we made huge inroads preparing the submarine for operations, the torrid nature of the whole period totally exceeded any previous experience.

Highlighting the state of play, in recent days I had received a personal letter written by one of the most knowledgeable, respected and loyal sailors onboard. Over several pages, it calmly and respectfully spelled out what he thought were the risks of continuing to operate the submarine, including the risk that the Ship's Company might lose confidence in my ability to safely command them. I read that as some of them were already there. It hit like a punch to the guts. Still, I was immensely appreciative of this sailor's honesty and willingness to expose his fears and reservations to me. Feedback like that was so rare as to be priceless. I was confident in my abilities, but knew that command authority wouldn't last long without command credibility.

I signalled an incident report to alert Fleet Headquarters to the latest catastrophe and followed it up with a status report and intentions. Releasing the RAAF Orion aircraft that joined us for our ultimate series of trials, we hit the roof and shaped course for Adelaide. The trials would wait, and the relief in the crew was palpable and immediate.

The response from Squadron wasn't long coming. When it arrived, it wasn't directive but I was reminded of 'the strategic importance of the outstanding trials', and it was proffered that my 'signal may have been drafted in haste'. I ordered passage routine, pressed on towards port and retired to my cabin to fume, and then to think.

I'd long had visibility of our intended operations. Successive objectives were progressively foregone as we lost more and more time in Adelaide, but our remaining tasking was bold, dramatic and still stood before us. Conscious that I needed to command these people throughout the next year and beyond, and that we would together face immense challenges in waters and situations that many of them could not yet envisage, I wondered if there was an opportunity before me. Thirty minutes later, I called the command team together.

'I intend returning to allocated dived water and resuming the conduct of the final trials,' I said matter-of-factly, noticing the mixed response. 'Brief me in an hour on what is required to achieve this.'

Precisely one hour later, we reconvened and the XO led off. JJ was backing me, although I suspected he was in two minds as to whether I would actually take them out again or not. I was genuinely fearful that I might be about to precipitate a mutiny. After explaining the importance of the program and, more importantly, my confidence in their ability to safely execute it, I stepped into my cabin and picked up the tannoy.

'Officer of the Watch, Captain. Reverse course. Make preps to dive on the watch.'

To my substantial relief, my cabin curtain remained undisturbed and the aft control surfaces came over. They took up the challenge and once again I was humbled by the commitment and resilience of the little tribe of people gathered in this boat. This was a crew to take to the edge and beyond.

Going for a run in the Adelaide hills, I reflected on what had been achieved over the recent weeks at sea. Notwithstanding the challenges, morale onboard was high and a real sense of satisfaction pervaded, despite being up on the hardstand once again. And we had reconciled ourselves to the latest delay in returning to home port: a series of dockings and sea trials to change out and test new propellers. The Swedish propellors suffered cracking across the class and we had been treating them with kid gloves to prevent the loss of blades at sea. Once again, the US Navy came through for us and provided their latest propellor, which not only removed that massive risk but also made the boat faster and quieter. We took particular care to protect it from the prying eyes of foreign nationals, including some of the senior executives in the dockyard.

But we were in for another shock. The replacement of HMAS *Collins'* now ageing main batteries had been looming for some time and the argument to have this work done in Western Australia had not carried. When repairs to corroding hull valve forgings became the next excuse to hold the submarine in Adelaide for further months, my ambition to have the submarine worked up and ready for operations by the end of the year evaporated. Observing the damage being done to the fabric of the Squadron for the sake of parochial and commercial interests, I was increasingly bitter and resentful. My pervading sense was that we were fighting an enemy on our own shores. *This was not the command challenge for which I had undertaken Perisher!*

When I reached out to an already stretched Squadron for help, volunteers willingly flew in to Adelaide to form a cadre crew, foregoing their own Christmas leave. I abandoned the boat to their care and sent the Ship's Company home for extended leave with their families.

Arriving home at year's end, I was completely spent. While I enjoyed the dedicated support and leadership of several key officers and senior sailors onboard, and a highly responsive Ship's Company, the weight of command in these circumstances was immense. Despite projecting calm determination and quiet optimism day by day, the intellectual and emotional effort of responding to seemingly never-ending setbacks took its toll on my own morale and mental health.

Emotionally drained and fragile after fifteen months in command, I felt inadequate, increasingly paranoid and totally isolated from friends and peers. As my defences came down, desperation and frailty coursed through me. Suffering from depression, I struggled to rebuild the shattered connection with my family, grateful beyond words that they were still with me.

Journal note, 31 January 2000. *Manage your stress. Lead your people.*

In January 1999, shortly after joining in command, I travelled to the US to explore options to replace the submarines' combat system. Overly ambitious and unnecessarily complicated from the start, it failed to live up to expectations and severely limited the operational effectiveness of the boats. We were on a mission to find a solution, and it came from the experts at the Naval Undersea Warfare Centre (NUWC) in Newport, Rhode Island.

As I returned to the boat in early January 2000, we had an augmented combat system being readied for sea trials. Rising attention and successive visits by senior Defence leadership and, just as importantly, the Commander in Chief of the US Pacific Fleet, built the necessary momentum to break the shackles of the yard. Public commitments were made on our scheduled program for the remainder of the year, including participation in Exercise RIMPAC and acoustic ranging at a USN facility in faraway Alaska to map the noise signature of the submarine.

In early April, we departed the South Australian Exercise Areas and left the Vortex in our wake. Settling back into our at-sea rhythm, I knew the crew were happy because the banter was incessant. Rounding Albany, we had an opportunity to go up against *Waller*, heading in the opposite direction on her own deployment to Hawaii. She had enjoyed a great deal more seatime recently, and I expected to get kicked. A patient approach won out and we detected her coming shallow through a sound layer, firing watershots to signal our attack. There was only time for one interaction and it went our way. Our embarked specialist advisor from NUWC was delighted. The USN combat system, originally envisaged as an add-on and back-up for the legacy system, didn't miss a beat and was now at the heart of our tactical efforts. It was further tested as we headed north and found more playmates in HMAS *Canberra* and HMNZS *Te Mana.* We were back in the game!

One by one, often in the quietest hours of the night, the papers to revoke discharges were slipped onto my desk.

We arrived alongside the newly constructed Diamantina Wharf at HMAS *Stirling* in WA after eighteen straight days at sea. This set a new class record for at-sea endurance, but was hardly an impressive number. And it wasn't the real measure of tenacity; eighteen months after HMAS *Collins* left for a four-month docking, she was home once more – and ready for sea.

CHAPTER 15
NORTH TO ALASKA

Journal note, 6 May 2000. ... *my worst and best day in command.*

Early in the year I write to the families, outlining the program and the challenges of what the Admirals were calling 'Australia's most significant submarine deployment for many years.' While RIMPAC in Hawaii is a routine commitment, only one of our submarines has ever sailed to the west coast of North America, and none as far as Alaska. I explain that precisely capturing and analysing the noises that the submarine makes underwater will allow us to optimise the stealth of the entire class, and we simply don't have a facility in Australia to match the acoustic range available in Alaska. And while the detailed results will be highly classified, I hope the outcome will also silence some of our critics. Worth the effort, but another year of extensive separation and often profound isolation.

With the negative impacts of minimal seatime last year readily apparent, there is substantial pressure on the program. To get away from Perth, and to close the distance on *Waller* now crossing the Pacific, we need to achieve our torpedo and missile weapon certifications and pass an exacting operational evaluation. With weeks of this work-up now behind us, the whole final period out at sea is set up to simulate a hostile environment. And we are on track to succeed as we head into the ultimate night of the final operational assessment.

Working with a maritime patrol aircraft, we locate the opposing task group of warships over the horizon and at 0315 'launch' a three-weapon salvo of missiles. Operating in more than 1,000 metres of water, I alter course, change depth and increase speed to evade the anticipated counter-attack from the fleet. Running deep, we shape course to close the coast for the last task – an inshore operation off Rottnest Island – set to take place at daybreak.

Huddled over the plot, I walk through my Night Orders with the Watchleader, laying out the detailed plan for crossing the continental shelf and positioning ourselves for the next event. Checking my watch, I go to my cabin to lay down and catch some zeds. I can get nine minutes sleep out of ten minutes in the rack, and there's a chance here to snatch thirty or forty.

My slumber is broken by the merest fluttering sensation, unlike anything I have ever felt, faintly rising through the slim mattress of my bunk and up into my bones. Instinct tells me the submarine is 'smelling the ground'. Sick to my stomach, I leap to my feet and race to the control room.

Sailing at speed and at depth, we have driven ourselves onto the continental shelf. We are screaming along the bottom, thankfully meeting a shoaling slope of brittle shale rock rather than a sheer cliff face. The watch-keepers, entirely confident of the submarine's position only moments before and intending to remain at that ordered depth for at least another half hour, simply cannot comprehend what is happening ... or do not want to.

I announce, 'We are aground!' I don't take the submarine, nor give any order or direction, but the response is immediate.

The Watchleader orders, 'Full rise on the planes, stop main motor, man the echo sounder.'

Springing into action, they regain their situational awareness and bring the submarine to a safe depth. Closing up at Emergency Stations to check for damage and account for personnel, we eventually return to periscope depth, surface and return alongside to *Stirling* to face the music. Disappointingly, the media are alerted by someone ashore and onto it even before we berth.

Divers from Clearance Diving Team Four get under the boat and video the results. Starting from the bow and running down two-thirds of the submarine's length, I have taken layers of paint off the bottom right back to bare metal. At over 40 metres long and up to 2 metres wide, it's quite a scar. Critically, the engineers' circularity test shows no deformation of the hull whatsoever, despite the shabby treatment.

Stepping off the submarine to go inboard and appear before the subsequent Board of Inquiry, dressed in my best uniform and cap, as I cross the rickety brow I am at pains to ensure that the trepidation I feel in my heart does not appear on my face. I am still their Captain, though for how long I do not know. The Board, which runs over nine days, finds that the continental shelf lay precisely where the Hydrographer had forecast it would be. It was our own navigational errors that brought us undone. While I brought clarity to the situation at the time of the grounding, I did so all too late.

In a personal letter, the Fleet Commander pointed to an error of judgement in my decision to proceed deep while closing the coast – a tactically valid decision, but not appropriate given the experience and tiredness of those on watch. At the back end of a long work-up and an intense evaluation, I had set up my people to fail. I wrongly assumed that if I had the wits and energy to conceive and draw up the plan to approach the coast, balancing tactical expedience with navigational safety, then they had the wits and experience to execute it.

In fact, many of my people were substantially more fatigued than I was, in no small measure because they had been working harder than me. To varying degrees, they lacked both the depth of experience – including experience in managing fatigue during work-ups – and the physical and mental reserve I took for granted. Ultimately, the Board decided I would retain command of *Collins,* but I felt that I transgressed my own dictum to 'know your people' and Teacher's dictum to 'never risk your pressure hull' – and endangered both.

A month on from the grounding, we deployed. USS *Jefferson City*, a Los Angeles-class fast attack submarine conducting an Indian Ocean deployment, was tasked as our opposition for the re-scrub on the operational evaluation. Ordered to act as a renegade submarine, she offered a substantially greater challenge than the forces originally arraigned against us a month ago. Over the next two days, we searched the depths for each other. She had free rein while we were also contending with the embarked Sea Training Group staff and Captain Submarines who looked to test us anew; their focus on generating dived navigation challenges for us was deliberate and concentrated.

Over the first night, we successfully closed and attacked *Jefferson City* three times. Our control room drills were far from the slickest I had seen; regardless, we gave her CO pause. Collins-class submarines were still an unknown entity for much of the US Navy, and there were serious bragging rights on offer. Severely limited in our ability to snort for fear of counter-detection, we contended with a slowly draining main battery and a steadily worsening atmosphere on board. Eventually, Captain Submarines tired of the inaction and we were finally betrayed to the American sonar operators by the ruckus of an onboard evolution initiated by the Sea Trainers. *Jefferson City*, bringing her immense speed advantage into play, was onto us immediately and struck. But with a 'standard achieved' deemed by the Sea Training Group, HMAS *Collins* was released for tasking.

The initial transit is far from uneventful, and by the time we reach the Bass Strait I am holding onto a fistful of defect signals. Rounding Wilsons Promontory and entering the Tasman Sea, we cross the halfway mark between Adelaide, our purgatory, and Sydney, our destination. Happy that the risk of being sucked back into the Vortex for defect rectification is passed, we let the signals fly. After a four-day stop at Fleet Base East in Sydney, repairing and re-storing the boat, it's a magnificent feeling as we drive close by Bradleys Head, with Mum and Dad standing under the HMAS *Sydney* memorial waving me off. We push the submarine through the heads into the Pacific and away from the Australian station.

Early the next day, 170 nautical miles out to sea, we prepare to pull the plug on the ballast tanks. Seized by my responsibility for what we are undertaking, the hollow, watery sensation in my gut is standard for any day before sailing, but most foreboding in the hours immediately before diving. I spend some time in my cabin, away from the watchful eyes of the crew, to control my nerves.

I breathe. *Calm down. You're bloody good at this, and you've got a first-rate crew with you. One step at a time.*

I focus. *Safety of the submarine. Avoid counter-detection. Achieve the aim.*

And I pray. *Dear Lord, give me the strength and the wisdom to keep my submarine and my people safe.* No longer a churchgoer, but still happy to seek help from above, I run through this one twice.

Half an hour later, we're under, and I am enjoying the periscope view of a low rolling swell on a sunlit day. But not everything is calm in the Pacific. As we cruise dived past Suva on 4 July, shots are fired in their Parliament. George Speight, leader of the latest military coup, remains in-situ with Prime Minister Mahendra Chaudry and the thirty-five other parliamentarians that he is holding hostage. With unrest in the neighbouring Solomon Islands, Papua New Guinea, the Moluccas and the Philippines, it occurs to me that we may be heading the wrong way.

Journal note, July 2000. *A good day. I can still smell it!*

'Crossing the Line' ceremonies have been a part of Navy life for centuries. Heavy on myth and lore, they celebrated the occasion a sailor first traverses the equator at sea. Invariably in submarines, the festivities happened on the surface, the forward casing setting the stage for King Neptune's throne and his court of 'Sheriffs' and 'Bears'.

Breaking some of the monotony of our transit, the lads in particular took great delight in dressing up for the occasion. Already in the Western Hemisphere, we steadily closed on the equator and the Northern Hemisphere. Sailors emerged from the fin barely clad in alfoil sheeting, cotton gash bags and cheesecloth, all scrounged from around the submarine and artfully fashioned into ragged costume. Given the temperature and the tailoring skills of the crew, the couture gave way to folds of sweating, hairy male flesh. Old mop heads were worn as wigs, fishnet stockings and high heels appeared on the legs of some, and bright red lipstick embellished more than one pig.

For days now, a large empty cooking oil drum set aside in a bilge was filled with various offcuts, scraps and fluids from the galley and surrounds. Stewing in its own juices for days on end, the resultant mustard-coloured broth was heavy with textural surprise and carried a foul, acrid stench. Carefully hoisted through the hatch and onto the casing, the cauldron was dragged to the foot of Neptune's throne. The uninitiated 'Turtles' cowered together as they were herded forward, anointed with the putrid chrism and admitted to Neptune's realm.

Despite being a veteran of these ceremonies many times over, I was not spared and, in fact, the first one generously daubed. Their excuse – my promotion to Commander. The annual promotion signal came in days earlier. I knew I was in with a chance of selection for promotion from the following January but didn't expect it this early.

A week later, the Commander of Submarine Squadron 3, a USN Captain, joined us as we steamed into Pearl Harbor. Replete with an oversized Hawaiian lei to drape over the front of the fin, and a set of Australian Commander's boards and brass hat so I wasn't caught 'out of rig', he also did me the honour of presiding over a snappy promotion ceremony. I was now ready to come alongside.

We were met on the Submarine Base wharf by the CO of USS *Louisville*, our 'host boat' for the visit. *Louisville* famously carried out the first war patrol conducted by an American submarine since the Second World War. Sprinting 14,000 miles dived across the Pacific and Indian Oceans to take up station in the Red Sea, she fired Tomahawk missiles against Iraq during Operation Desert Storm. The *Louisville* officers proved a great sounding board for our initial task, a live Harpoon missile firing on the instrumented range off Kauai Island.

Our preparations for this firing, a first for the class, had begun back in Australia. Our Harpoon certification off Perth went fairly smoothly, but coincided with an exceedingly rare overnight ride by news media. Embarking a *60 Minutes* film crew of four, including journalist Ellen Fanning, it was impossible to escape the microphones and cameras. Experience with the media in recent years did nothing to engender trust and we were highly sceptical of their motives. While it proved to be one of my more difficult days at sea, the Ship's Company predictably won them over in their own inimitable way. When the program eventually aired months later, and five days after our successful live firing off Hawaii, we got a fair shake.

With no rest between taskings, our next venture was to support the at-sea phase of the USN Potential Commanding Officers (PCO) course – America's version of Perisher. We were pitted against our sister boat, HMAS *Waller*, and two Los Angeles-class submarines. The USS *Chicago* and *Sante Fe* carried a dozen American officers slated to assume command of Pacific Fleet submarines, and the complex, fast-paced exercise scenarios were set to test their tactical acumen.

Patrolling through and around choke points created by the islands, we hunted each other day and night. While we generated opportunities to fire practice weapons against the other submarines, it was the USN boats firing their latest weapon, the Mark 48 'ADCAP', that got my attention. With upgrades to the guidance, control and propulsion systems, those torpedoes simply gobbled us up. They were a promise of things to come, as we would soon have these fearsome weapons in our own inventory. In all, we got a phenomenal opportunity to lift our anti-submarine warfare skills and experience across the entire crew.

Throughout this period at sea the Squadron Psychology Officer, one of five women embarked, was building a database using motion tracking watches to record our sleep cycles. While the results varied substantially across the crew, depending largely on the particular role of a sailor or officer, we were evidently getting more than a fair day's work out of everyone onboard. My own data quantified astonishingly poor patterns of insufficient and disrupted sleep, especially during tactically intense periods. With the scars of the grounding and the Board of Inquiry still fresh, I took it as a further warning to do things differently and stay ahead of the fatigue curve.

Lockwood Hall, the Officers' Mess at Pearl Harbor Submarine Base, offered welcome respite when we finally got alongside. Most happily, I joined Shaunaugh and Laura for a two-week holiday while the submarine was alongside for scheduled maintenance. But a dark shadow came over our otherwise idyllic holiday when we heard news of the *Kursk*.

An Oscar II-class nuclear-powered cruise missile submarine, she was dived in the Barents Sea on 12 August, participating in the largest Russian naval exercise since the fall of the Soviet Union a decade earlier. A practice torpedo being loaded into the tubes exploded, sinking the submarine. When the resulting fire triggered the detonation of multiple warshot torpedoes two minutes later, further massive damage was inflicted throughout the boat.

In any submarine rescue operation where there is a chance of saving lives, time is of the essence. While most of the 118 souls inboard perished in the first catastrophic explosions, twenty-three found refuge in the aftmost section of the submarine. They survived long enough to scrawl letters to loved ones in the dark. Hours, and then days, were lost in the hesitant response of the Russian Northern Fleet command, failed early attempts by a Russian Priz-class rescue submersible and President Putin's rejection of offers of assistance from foreign navies. By the time British and Norwegian forces gained access to the submarine a week after the sinking, all hope of recovering any survivors was lost.

Watching the saga unfold over the days and weeks after the accident was painful. I needed no reminders of the dangers inherent in submarine operations, but this was professionally captivating. In one sense, the Russian determination to keep their Cold War adversaries at arm's length from one of their most prized naval warships was understandable. In another, the rejection of the extensive specialist escape and rescue capabilities being offered, in good faith, by other navies was unfathomable. The end result – loss of life in a potentially rescuable situation during a peacetime exercise – was a travesty.

The torment of the Russian sailors' families, searching for knowledge of the fate of their husbands, sons and brothers, grew in intensity by the day. Their anguish over the outcome was overwhelming and broadcast internationally. More intimately, I was with Shaunaugh and Laura as they grappled with their own worst fears unfolding for the families of another submarine in another navy. Our shared heartache, grief and sorrow were intense and hard to contain.

'Fire, fire, fire. Fire in the MGR.'

It's 1203. We are less than a day out of Pearl Harbor and into the two-week trek to the west coast of North America when the guttural voice of the Petty Officer on watch in the engine room barks out over main broadcast. I can feel my heart crash stop along with the diesels.

As the submarine closes up at Emergency Stations, I take post in the Captain's chair. Two of the control room watchkeepers are dressing for fire just a few feet away. They are the designated Attack Party, a role that rotates through the junior watchkeepers, effectively the 'first responders' at the scene of any emergency. I see their eyes, intensely alive to the moment, through the full-face masks of the breathing apparatus they have strapped to their backs. This is not an exercise on a training day. We are on our own, and we are on fire. Air tank pressures are recorded and time is marked.

Sixty seconds after the initial Emergency Stations pipe, the Officer of the Watch orders them aft: 'Attack Party, fight the fire!' And they are gone.

One deck below us, the off-watch sailors who are not yet up for lunch scramble out of their bunks to muster in the junior rates mess. Two are designated as Support Party and dress rapidly in full firefighting gear. With the added protection of their 'Fear Fuckall Suits', they too are dispatched to aft.

Stories of the tragedy onboard the fleet oiler HMAS *Westralia* two years earlier remain fresh in the minds of our crew. A fuel fire that raged in the engine room of that ship for nearly two hours resulted in the death of a Midshipman and four sailors. We know what it can mean if a fire gets hold in the generator room of a submarine.

'The fire is out. The fire is out!' It's 1205. The fire, which erupted on the exhaust manifold of the midships diesel, has been rapidly extinguished by the quick action of the team. It's a dramatic start to this leg of our journey, especially for the small batch of fresh trainees who joined a few short days ago.

A week later, we are making solid progress down track and spend most of each day focusing on training. One of the senior electronic warfare sailors onboard, responsible for small arms and pyrotechnics, is at my door.

'Sir, can I give the Part Threes some instruction on the SSE while we're deep?'

Our Submerged Signal Ejectors – one forward and one aft – are used to discharge flares, communications buoys and other stores from the submarine, including the green grenades that signal exercise attacks against ships and the red grenades that signal distress.

'No worries, Mac.' I grab the tannoy. 'Watchleader, Captain. Load the aft SSE with a bubble decoy.'

Returning to my reading, I expect to hear the faint but distinct crump of a discharge sometime in the next five to ten minutes. Six minutes later … *whoom-pah!* The boat shudders with a short explosion, sounding like a loud discharge. *That ain't right!*

'Watchleader, Captain. Take the submarine to safe depth, make preps to return to periscope depth.'

Twenty seconds later, as I enter the control room, there is a second, much louder explosion.

'Watchleader, Captain. Pipe Emergency Stations, Pyro Actuation.'

Back in the engine room, six Part Three trainees had been huddled together on a small platform, listening intently as Mac demonstrated how to prepare, load and fire a bubble decoy. A metal cylinder the length of a cricket bat, each decoy is packed with lithium hydride pellets that generate a violent chemical reaction when exposed to salt water. Once the decoy is fired into the open ocean, the rapidly expanding hydrogen gas creates an acoustic barrage designed to mask the signature of a submarine and distract incoming torpedoes.

Unbeknownst to the sailors crowded around the signal ejector, the decoy had been incorrectly prepared for loading. As a result, lithium hydride had been trapped within the now flooded ejector as the decoy left the submarine. This reacted with the seawater in the ejector, creating severe over-pressurisation until pipework failed, and it exploded into the submarine. The hydrogen gas lit off as it vented under pressure, resulting in a fierce fireball that blew over the sailors, sending them flying for cover.

As the ejectors form a major hull penetration and are an essential element of the escape and rescue suite onboard, we are obliged to stay on the surface for the remainder of the transit. I wrestle with my frustration and a sense of vulnerability for the boat as we help our Part Threes contend with a hell of a fright.

Journal note, 6 September 2000. *Distance. I call it independence, they feel isolated.*

A week later, we were much relieved to make landfall at Cape Flattery on the Washington State coast, with our arrival welcomed by a pod of six magnificent orcas who accompanied us through the Strait of Juan de Fuca towards our next port of Esquimalt, British Columbia. Without doubt, morale was wearing thin. Two-thirds of the way through the deployment, we still had much to achieve, but some had reached their limit. I flew two of my junior sailors home – one qualified, the other under training, but both suffering from anxiety. I lost another sailor who took a beating ashore in Esquimalt and had his eye socket fractured.

I felt these losses deeply. I was intensely committed to bringing my sailors home from this deployment better for the experience, rather than damaged by it. Some of the more experienced crew were also on edge with the daily strain of operating and maintaining the submarine and the steady accumulation of traumatic incidents. Nonetheless, they continued to muster the courage to press on.

Upon crossing into Alaskan waters, I sent a locator report to Captain Submarines and the other boats. It was a significant moment for the Squadron and I wanted them to share in it. *'Position: Alaska. Course: North. Speed: Enough.'*

CHAPTER 16
PACIFIC ALLIES

The US Navy was ready and waiting at Back Island in Behm Canal, the location of their awkwardly named Southeast Alaska Acoustic Measurement Facility (SEAFAC for short). Given the sensitivity of the work they do here, I was unsurprised to learn that we were the first foreign submarine and the first diesel boat ever permitted to operate at the site. There were two ranges, one for measurements with the submarine underway and one for static measurements, with the submarine motionless in the water. Together they mapped the acoustic signature of their boats, including their ballistic missile submarines, on build and on completion of major refits. The location was specifically selected for the deep, quiet and isolated waters of the canal.

The program would be intensive, with 150 laps completed over and through the arrays of hydrophones on and above the seabed. The onboard Test Director detailed the machinery line-up, speed and depth required for each run. Before long, the Range Hut staff, who control the whole evolution and collect the recordings, got a sense of our manoeuvrability and the substantially shortened run-up we needed. Day after day, we chewed through the work at a great rate.

Switching focus to the 'static' recordings, we surfaced and connected the submarine to massive buoys forward and aft. Diving in position, we were steadily winched down to the required depth and collapsed to a 'dead boat'. Everything was switched off and isolated: air conditioning, refrigeration, generators, power converters, lighting, emergency lighting – everything. Condensation formed and dripped down on our already clammy heads. The troops monitored the oxygen, carbon dioxide and pressure levels closely and continuously. Moving through the boat by torchlight and talking in whispers, we spent four days in a perfectly dark, bone-chillingly cold and eerily quiet submarine.

We communicated with the Range Hut through secure umbilical lines, our only contact with the outside world. One by one, each piece of onboard equipment was turned on, run up, recorded and shut down again. The Range Director, who first briefed me on SEAFAC a year and a half earlier back in Australia, got on the line.

'Switch on Item 136,' he directed.

'Item 136 is running,' we replied.

'Roger, nothing seen or heard.'

It's a frequent refrain as we steadily worked through the hundreds of pieces of equipment and machinery onboard and built a comprehensive picture of our incredibly quiet submarine.

After ten days on the range, we came alongside the Coast Guard station at Ketchikan, the frontier salmon and timber town turned cruise-ship tourist trap. Most of the troops had managed to get ashore at some stage, cycling off the submarine every couple of days to make room onboard for the SEAFAC test staff. Apparently, they made quite an impression on the townsfolk, as the moment I walked into a diner and opened my mouth to order a burger, the waitress picked the accent. Knowing I'm one of the few she had not yet met, she hollered to all and sundry, 'It's the Caaaptain! Yours is on the house, Sir!'

'Ready to go, Nav?'

'Ready, Sir.'

We were at the front end of an eighteen-hour transit of the Inside Passage, on the east coast of Vancouver Island, Canada, and Scott McVicar, my old Canadian mate, was waiting for us at the far end. He was in charge of our next commitment – a week of tactical development and weapons firings at the Canadian Forces Maritime Experimental and Test Ranges (CFMETR) out of Nanoose Bay. Six months earlier, the Navigator had pitched this particular route, rather than the lengthier westabout circumnavigation of Vancouver Island. 'We'll buy an extra day and a half this way, and it will be a great challenge for the pilotage teams,' was his argument.

We set off with the night and weather closing in around us, disconcertingly dark and brittle winds blowing a bastard. Zipped up in our red 'Mustang' survival suits, my exposed face felt the sting as sweeping rains hit and visibility closed in. Pushing into Christie Passage in British

Columbia, the steep granite foreshore and Lodgepole pines of Balaklava Island were close aboard while immensely powerful tidal currents swirled around us. They played havoc with the helmsman below, who struggled to hold course and keep us on track. Finding a patch of water that was marginally and momentarily tolerable for a boat transfer, we picked up two Canadian pilots. Aghast at the conditions, they took turnabout through the night, keeping us company on our cramped and open bridge.

'This is not what you sold me, Nav!' I shouted into his ear to get above the din of the howling wind.

Johnstone Strait, the narrow channel that forms most of the passage, was navigable but tight and long. Tugs strained to control their tows – huge barges piled high with timber– as they shimmied past us. After an exhausting night on the bridge, the passage culminated with Seymour Narrows, a hair-raising, fast-flowing chicane. Judging the rips we saw ahead, we commenced our wheel overs to port and then to starboard three cables early and were swept around on track. Making good over 16 knots, twice our regular surfaced speed, we were flushed through and out into more open waters. I later discovered we were the first submarine to complete the passage since a Japanese boat during the Second World War.

Nanoose Bay gave us a chance to focus on our warfighting skills once more. Shaking off the lingering sting of the Nanaimo nightclubs, we sailed out of harbour each morning, dived and immediately went to Attack Teams. The Canadians provided us with a belly full of practice torpedoes, which we fired off at our playmates, the destroyers HMCS *Regina* and USS *David R Ray*. They were supported by maritime patrol aircraft and helicopters, so we dealt with ship- and air-launched counterfire torpedoes and decoys, making for an electrifying week. Though the warships manoeuvred desperately to avoid our weapons, we repeatedly brought them under their bows. Running shallow, but just beneath keel depth, the rippling, menacing wakes of the torpedoes were visible from the air and from the ship.

Having recently retired the last of their Oberons, the Canadians were eagerly awaiting the arrival of HMCS *Victoria*, the first of the British

Jack Scott, AIF, 1917 (Boyd's Studio, The Strand, London)

Right: Family portrait taken at Grandma and Grandad's golden wedding anniversary, 1973. I'm front left, sporting a tie.

Below: One of many family holidays with my four siblings; Warrumbungle National Park, 1978.

Above: On the dais with the Governor-General, Sir Ninian Stephen, AK, GCMG, GCVO, KBE, QC at my Passing Out parade, December 1985.

Right: Celebrating a new year and promotion to Sub-Lieutenant with shipmate James McCormack, Melbourne, 1987.

Above: Our wedding day with our parents Kevin and Sonja (left), and Michael and Margaret (right), October 1989.

Left: HMAS Orion, *departing Cockatoo Island Dockyard, Sydney Harbour, on completion of her last major refit, 1991. [Image courtesy of DoD]*

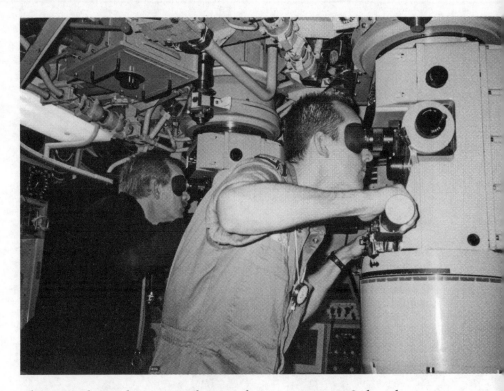

Above: Teacher and I go up on the most dangerous contact. Onboard HNLMS Bruinvis *during Perisher, 1997.*

Left: HMAS Sydney *charging and at the go deep range. Pre-Perisher training off the east coast of Australia, 1996.*

Above: Perisher celebrations. Me (left), Captain Peter Clarke (centre), and Lieutenant Sean (Paddy) O'Dwyer (right). Faslane, Scotland, 1997.

Below: Crossing the Line ceremony, HMAS Collins, 2000.

Above: Homecoming. Laura welcomes me back from deployment.

Below: Together again. [Image courtesy of DoD]

Conning the submarine alongside, with XO JJ Cupples. [Image courtesy of DoD]

Above: With Shaunaugh on the bridge, HMAS Collins' *family day, December 2000.*

Below: With Mum on the occasion of my Conspicuous Service Cross investiture.

Right: The 'Chief Tiff' (Chief Petty Officer John Ryan, SM) and crew in the lower motor room of HMAS Dechaineux, *during the aftermath of the flood, February 2003. [Image courtesy of Geoff Wadley]*

Below: HMAS Dechaineux *departs Kuantan, Malaysia, disappearing into the murk and mire of the South China Sea once more, in 2002.*

On the plot, HMAS Dechaineux, *working up a cunning plan with the Ops team. [Image courtesy of Frances Andrijich]*

On patrol. The search periscope viewed through the attack periscope.

HMAS Stuart *in the sights. We could often detect, track, identify and 'attack' warships at will. [Image courtesy of Frances Andrijich]*

In my cabin at sea in HMAS Dechaineux. *The only single berth on the boat, it was a rare privilege as Captain to have this much private space. [Image courtesy of Frances Andrijich]*

HMAS Dechaineux *officers, post patrol, July 2003.*

Left: HMAS Dechaineux Ship's Company, post deployment, July 2003.

Right: HMAS Dechaineux arrives Fleet Base West, 29 July 2003. [Image courtesy of DoD]

Below: Three at sea. Exercise Pacific Reach, 2007. [Image courtesy of DoD]

At Government House, Sydney, with Laura and Shaunaugh on the occasion of my Commendation for Distinguished Service (CDS) investiture, May 2008.

With then Rear Admiral Bill Merz, USN (centre) and Rear Admiral Youn Jeong Sang, ROKN (right) onboard ROKS Dokdo, with HMAS Waller and MV Swift Rescue in the background. Exercise Pacific Reach, 2016.

On my promotion to Commodore, 2013. [Image courtesy of DoD]

Above: My mugshot, 2021. [Image courtesy of Joshua Dasey]

Previous page top: HMAS AE2, at 72 metres, Sea of Marmara, Turkey. [Image courtesy of Dr Mark Spencer]

Previous page bottom: Five alongside HMAS Stirling, *Fleet Base West, December 2016. [Image courtesy of DoD]*

Upholders to be commissioned into the Royal Canadian Navy later in the year. There were lessons here in how other navies managed their submarine forces, including those who failed to ensure continuity of capability. Our 'attacks' on *Regina* were a graphic reminder of what they currently lacked in their force structure.

The Americans, by contrast, had scores of submarines operating from more than half a dozen bases. Bangor Naval Base, in Puget Sound, Washington, was the home of Submarine Group 9 and the Pacific-based Ohio-class ballistic missile submarines designed for extended strategic deterrent patrols. Bangor was our next destination and it was not lost on me that the offer of a berth there was a notable exception for a foreign submarine. The welcome was warm, genuine and loaded with curiosity about our boat and crew. The CO of USS *Alaska* signalled me weeks earlier requesting a list of every sailor onboard and their hobbies. Whether it was riding Harleys or flying kites, he found someone in his crew to match. Assigned individual host families, it made for a fascinating couple of days in and around Seattle.

Unfortunately, an official welcome function on 12 October was over-shadowed by breaking news of a terrorist attack on the USS *Cole*. An Arleigh Burke-class destroyer alongside and refuelling in Aden, Yemen, she was struck by a boat packed with explosives in an al-Qaeda suicide attack. Opening a massive gash in the ship's port side, the explosion killed seventeen sailors and injured another thirty-seven.

With the gravity of the attack apparent, the Commander of Submarine Squadron 17 made an emotive address to his people. Emphasising that 'we want peace and tolerance in the Middle East', he also made it abundantly clear that, with six Trident missile–armed submarines under his command, they had the means and the will to bring wholesale retribution against the perpetrators if called upon to do so.

With tensions this high, it probably wasn't the time for a couple of our stokers to wander the vast base at night looking for their next beer. Armed Marines, patrolling the perimeter and the underground Trident missile magazines, shouted, 'Halt, or I will shoot!'

Turning to look down the barrel of an assault rifle, one of our guys responded with an insistent 'Don't point that thing at me!'

'Oh shit, it's the Ossies. Christ, boys, we were just about to take you down!'

Never one to miss an opportunity to searide a diesel boat, the rangy, kind-eyed Commander of Submarine Group 9 joined us as we departed Bangor several days later. His smile widened as we dived in an area within Puget Sound where his 18,000-tonne submarines, the largest ever built for the US Navy, were strictly confined to the surface. For the next hour and a half, we flung the submarine around in a sporty display. What we lacked in top speed, we made up for with agility and he marvelled at our ability to operate this close inshore – a definite tactical advantage in some circumstances and something that was beyond the US boats. Trading dolphins with the Admiral before he disembarked, I knew we had another ally.

Three uneventful weeks later, we depart Pearl Harbor once more, this time to commence our passage home. And we have one more distinguished visitor to welcome: Rear Admiral Al Konetzni, Jr. USN, the Commander Submarine Force Pacific. Known from Davy Jones's Locker in Waikiki to The Capitol in Washington, D.C. as 'Big Al, the sailor's pal', the enigmatic Admiral was down below, moving through the submarine and talking with the sailors. We first came under his operational control three and a half months ago and spent most days since then at sea. Yet somehow, he knew nearly every one of my sailors by name, and they all knew him. Coming to the bridge, he lit a cigar for me and wished us well. Still puffing on his stogie as he stepped aboard the pilot boat, he returned my salute.

'See you Down Under, shipmate,' he pledged.

We were not done yet. Although less eventful, the return passage was another trans-Pacific marathon. It passed no more quickly as we nursed the diesels and the battery over the last several thousand miles. One clear difference was that for the first time in more than a year, we regressed to an all-male crew.

While the women onboard were integrated in every other sense since first joining *Collins* in late 1998, government policy of the day insisted on segregated accommodation with one of the six berth cabins designated for 'females only', and a minimum number of women onboard. In a submarine, where every bunk is allocated against the experience and expertise needed to form a proficient crew, the policy was a source of substantial frustration for all onboard and a nightmare to manage. It meant, for example, qualified officers were excluded from the wardroom cabin and bunked with junior unqualified sailors. When, for whatever reason, a woman was posted off the submarine without a female relief, it meant another empty bunk and a hole in the capability of the submarine.

Conventional privacy was hard to come by in a submarine where living cheek by jowl was more a matter of fact than a metaphor. Within a tight crew of professional submariners, personal space – physical and emotional – was offered and honoured wherever possible. In later years, we got the licence to manage our people at sea without the misplaced constraint of segregated accommodation, making for happier and more effective submarines.

For now, and for several days after sailing from Hawaii, I heard the more boisterous lads celebrating being back at sea in 'Chick Free 73'.[2] It didn't last. Whether qualified or under training, officer or sailor, the women who had sailed to Alaska delivered talent and passion and brought a fresh dimension to life onboard the submarine and ashore. They were shipmates, and they were missed.

Rounding Albany, Western Australia and heading into the Indian Ocean once more, we launched into our final week at sea. Pencilling the programmed exercises onto the weekly template, there was no white space across any twenty-four hour period. Tasked with embarking the Submarine Executive Officers Course for the students' final assessment, as well as joining forces with HMAS *Darwin* and *Anzac* and HMNZS *Te Mana* to work up HMAS *Melbourne,* it was a stark and welcome contrast to the solitary transit of recent weeks. The fact that our forward hydroplanes were out of action, a defect which would have brought us alongside six months ago, merely added spice to the challenge for this now seasoned and confident crew.

The final few miles running between the channel markers down Cockburn Sound were at once too long and too short. We left Australia

---

2   73 is the pennant number of HMAS *Collins.*

under a dark cloud of reliability and performance issues, with the national reputation of the class in tatters. But at 185 days and 21,000 nautical miles steamed, mostly dived, it was the longest deployment in the history of the Australian submarine service.[3] Proving the endurance so vital to submarine operations restored the confidence of the government, and parts of the Navy, in the capability and potential of the class. And with HMAS *Farncomb* and *Waller* deployed and the upgraded *Dechaineux* and *Sheean* soon to commission, it had been a good year all around.

Looking upward from the bridge as we wheel over into Careening Bay on our final approach, I could see that the last fix had been plotted on the chart. The periscope now scanned the wharf as sailors in the control room lined up to search for a long yearned-for glimpse of loved ones. Family and friends thronged the wharf, dressed up just a little and excited to welcome us home after a six-month absence. True to his word, Al Konetzni was there too, deep in animated conversation with the children of the crew. It was a great day to be part of the submarine family. And it was great to be home.

Less than a week after coming alongside, I was told that *Collins* would be sent back to Adelaide early in the new year to conduct a Full-Cycle Docking. I was flabbergasted and morale onboard slumped. Although the submarine had only spent a total of six weeks alongside in her home port over the previous two and a half years, we had been relishing the promise of a full year of seagoing operations out of Perth during 2001. The Fleet Commander was quick to reassure me that we wouldn't face a repeat of our previous experience in the Adelaide yards. *Collins* would be decommissioned and her ensign struck. Total responsibility for the submarine would be handed to the DMO, with material and operating control contracted to ASC, negating the need for the Ship's Company to stand by her throughout this next docking.

Departing *Stirling* in early February 2001, probably for the last time in command, I was on the bridge with Lieutenant Commander Lachlan King, RAN. Still finding ways to support the Squadron, he relieved JJ as

---

3   Two decades on, it is still the farthest!

XO when he headed off to Perisher. Lachlan and I happily reminisced about the first time we sailed together in *Oxley* many years ago. Over the forenoon we disembarked *Collins'* warshot torpedoes for storage at the Ammunition Wharf, rendering the boat impotent, then headed out to sea and traversed the South Australian Basin. Surfacing north of Cape Borda Lighthouse on Kangaroo Island, our trusty Sonar Officer piped up with, 'Last time you do that for a while, eh Sir!' I appreciated the underlying vote of confidence.

With *Collins* docked again in Adelaide, I stepped ashore, head filled with pride and a large hole in my heart. It was hard not to be envious of the Ship's Company, who would transfer to *Farncomb* operating out of Western Australia and head back out to sea. *Collins* didn't emerge from that yard and commission back into Naval service for a further four and a half years.

CHAPTER 17
DARKER SKIES

After *Collins,* in April 2001 I joined the submarine school at *Stirling* to establish a new Commander's position as Head of Submarine Warfare Training. The job: to lead the thirty-strong team of senior specialists and warriors at the Warfare Faculty and train the Australian submarine force ashore for war at sea. It was the best of both worlds – time ashore to recuperate from command and reconnect with my family, but with direct connection to the seagoing submarines and submariners. It was also a terrific opportunity to fold some hard-won experience back into the Squadron.

Leaving the platform and technical training to others, half of the role was to deliver specialist individual training to the acoustic and electronic warfare analysts and warfare officers at every level up to command. The other half was delivering combined training ashore to the watches and command teams of the submarines, preparing them for at-sea training and exercises and for operational tasking.

Beyond the various classrooms, the SCTT – Submarine Command Team Trainer – was our main work shed and the Nissan hut-style roof and red lighting provided a crude enough imitation of the confines of a control room. Submarine watchkeepers manned the various consoles connected to sonar, weapon and combat system simulators, with dummy periscopes served by computer graphics. My staff were a world away behind glass panels, like the technicians in a recording studio, controlling the game, the tempo and the tension. Preparing a boat for an 'up top' deployment, we steadily ratcheted up the degree of difficulty, replicating the navigational, shipping and tactical conditions they were likely to encounter.

When the crew of HMAS *Dechaineux* failed to avoid the attention of a 'patrolling warship', we turned it towards and brought it in over their heads. They were no longer playing a game on base. They were 'at sea' –

dived off a foreign coastline, counter-detected by a potential enemy and facing a possible attack.

'Zig towards, Master Contact 3, bearing rate steady,' reported sonar.

'All compartments assume the ultra-quiet state,' the Watchleader ordered.

'Revolution increase, Master Contact 3. Very loud, getting louder,' from sonar.

'Splashes heard on the bearing, possible weapon launch,' again from sonar.

'Ahead revolutions 110, port 30 steer 270, 10 down keep 100 metres, fire the bubble decoy!' barked the Watchleader in response.

Unnoticed by the crew, I positioned one of my team outboard of the Nissan hut. She swung a cricket bat down against the 'hull' of the submarine, hard! A monstrous thunderclap reverberated throughout the control room. We got a chuckle; the crew jolted and shrank with fright.

Laughs aside, it was serious business. The good submarine practice and lessons learned in the dedicated platform, weapon and control room simulators while ashore saved lives at sea. We deliberately built the scenarios around the submarine's intended tasking and lessons learned from experience, our own and others.

The recent tragedy of the USS *Greeneville,* which resulted in the dismissal of her skipper, was topical. A highly charismatic officer, whom I had met in Hawaii the previous year, he was operating south of Oahu with a group of distinguished visitors onboard for a tour. Conducting a demonstration emergency surface, he failed to properly clear himself of surface traffic and brought the submarine up under the Japanese fishing vessel MV *Ehime Maru. Greeneville*'s rudder sliced the hull of the fishing vessel clean open, and the *Ehime Maru* was lost, sinking within minutes and taking nine lives with her. Rich in lessons on priorities, teamwork and leadership, we picked the bones of the reports provided by our USN allies.

Our partnership with the USN, and specifically with the Pacific Fleet submarines, continued to deepen. Charged with a review of our preparations for command, including any shortfalls in Perisher, I developed and implemented a complementary Command Skills Course. Securing agreement for our officers to join the at-sea phase of the USN PCO course was a critical component and a major windfall.

The great thrill of this was that our submarine COs could ride the US nuclear attack submarines as Duty Commanding Officer – operating their boats tactically, firing practice weapons and exploiting the speed and unlimited endurance of their nuclear reactors. It was a unique arrangement, not offered to any other Allied Navy. The quid pro quo was the opportunity for the USN officers to experience the less exhilarating but highly intriguing sport of poking around in an Australian diesel boat, tracking and attacking their own submarines. Both sides gained invaluable experience, and an enduring basis for close professional relationships across the forces was established.

Contrasting the professional highlights in creating the Head of Submarine Warfare Training role, my time in the school brought the fragility of the Arm into sharp relief. Previously well aware of the shortfall of qualified submariners around me, I was now face to face with the inadequacy from an organisational perspective. And it was plain to see the cumulative effects of perennial shortfalls in numbers commencing submarine training, the challenges of introducing the Collins-class, and the resultant dearth of seatime and experience. A prime example was that despite our best efforts to train, there simply were not enough qualified and experienced Watchleaders to crew the submarines and fill the specialist support billets ashore. With only one eligible candidate, I begrudgingly cancelled the Submarine Executive Officers Course for the year. It was a dire omen; the wire was stretched to breaking and the Squadron headed for a fall.

Work challenges aside, the shore time offered the chance to reconnect with Shaunaugh and Laura. We spent some time creating memories: travelling east together for family weddings; exploring Western Australia; taking road trips north to Exmouth and south to Margaret River; discovering Bunnings; renovating the kitchen of our small home. Our evenings were short, but they were ours. Our weekends were full, but they were ours.

But at times the urge to make up for lost time became a little desperate, and I worked hard to fit in, pushing away the occasional sensation of isolation and strangeness in my own home. It was my home, but not my ship. Someone else was in command and running the routines, which were well established and slick! While I was delighted by the bond that Shaunaugh and Laura shared, it occasionally sparked a pathetic jealousy. They were such a tight pair by now that conversations happened around me, such as when I mistook a reference to 'Big Brother' as a comment on George Orwell's novel.

'It's his "popular culture void" again, Mum,' Laura sighed.

When I took a Friday off to attend Laura's school athletics carnival – a first – I was amazed and ashamed by the number of fathers I saw there. With time, I realised just how spent I was coming off the boat, and how tenuous some of our connection had become. We each leaned in and, with shared experience and time together, regained some of the strength and the tenderness of our relationships.

It certainly wasn't all smooth sailing. I took the students on the Submarine Warfare Officers Course up to Darwin to put them through their paces onboard HMAS *Waller*. Returning alongside after a week at sea, they had passed the final assessment of a four-month course and had something to celebrate. For me, away from home and thirsty, a few quiet lagers in a beer garden descended into a fierce overnight binge. Checking in late and obviously drunk for the return flight home to Perth, I was refused permission to board. With the next flight a day away, Shaunaugh was ropable when she was left to host a social event that I had organised with people she didn't know. Instead of topping up the 'goodwill bucket', I kicked it a mile.

Though I was no longer continually plagued by drink, I remained susceptible to its lure as a ready veil for loneliness and fear, and a lamentable excuse for poor judgement and carelessness. *Honour what you value, Scotty.*

As the strategic sands in our region and beyond began to shift, the Global War on Terror brought fresh impetus to training and operations across the ADF. In the months immediately after the 9/11 terrorist attacks against the World Trade Centre and the Pentagon, much of our Navy's attention turned towards the amphibious landing ship HMAS *Kanimbla* and the frigate HMAS *Adelaide* as they prepared to sail to the Middle East on Operation Slipper, our contribution to the war in Afghanistan, and enforce sanctions against Iraq.

I spent some time with Lieutenant Steph Moles, RAN, younger sister and only sibling of my mate Sean, killed all those years earlier while out on a training run. As the Supply Officer onboard, she was steeling herself to sail in *Adelaide*. 'I'm not afraid of dying, Scotty,' she said. 'I'm afraid of not coming home. Can you imagine what that would do to Mum and Dad?'

Having been selected for a second command, my shore time was coming to an end. I watched the world with eyes open anew and wondered where it might all lead.

Journal note, May 2002. *Encourage, coach, lead.*

Joining *Dechaineux* alongside in early May 2002, the boat was in good shape, having recently completed a Mid-Cycle Docking, and the Ship's Company was in fine fettle. With a packed operational program ahead, she was the priority boat for people and had a full complement of eager submariners. As I took on the weight of command once more, the troops were wound up and eager to exercise their sea legs.

Proceeding to sea ten days later and at Deep Diving Depth within the fortnight, we were off to a tremendous start. More relaxed and confident in my approach with the officers and sailors settling into this second command, I nonetheless offered the same challenge as during my first drive, adapted from my high school motto – 'Dare to be the best submariner you can be!' I took a lot from my Jesuit education, including a passion for learning founded on curiosity about the world and caring for others. With the operational limits of the class yet to be discovered, it seemed an apt approach here.

When my Mechanical and Weapons Engineers, the heads of their respective departments, fronted up to my cabin together early one morning, my heart sank immediately. This must be one helluva defect if they were both working the problem. What they reported was not a defect, but an affair. Fraternisation, deliberate and undeniable, and onboard our submarine.

'I can't even guess at who the culprits might be, but this must be dealt with at once. You'll have to tell me who is involved,' I said.

In fact, they didn't have to tell me. When I opened my eyes, I saw it in theirs. My officers were in love with each other. Some difficult conversations followed, and I had cause to read some dull policy in fine detail, but we eventually arrived at the only feasible solution. Driven by the relative posting plots across the Squadron, I arranged a swap draft between my Weapons Engineer and another in HMAS *Waller*. Having invested a lot in her training when she was a Part Three in *Collins*, and thoroughly convinced of her talent, I was sorry to see her go. The fact that I had to rob another seagoing boat of their engineer rather than post one in from ashore was another dramatic example of the dearth of qualified officers and increasing fragility of the Arm.

Nonetheless, our three-month long preparations for the upcoming deployment, both alongside and at sea, continued at a pace. Back ashore in the Command Team Trainer, I was on the preferred side of the glass, and it was my crew being worked up again. This training was at another level, as the Fleet Submarine Operations Officer took us through our pre-deployment paces. Immensely experienced and with a knack for teaching, he guided us masterfully towards the operating standards we needed to meet before the Fleet Commander would sanction our upcoming missions.

Part of those preparations included incorporating a new specialist role into the submarine crew. As we headed out to sea for one of our earlier dives, a young Able Seaman Medic sat on a small, swing-out stool between myself and the Ship Control watchkeepers. When I deployed to Alaska in *Collins*, we took a Petty Officer Medic away with us on a trial basis. Qualifying as a submariner, and contributing as a watchkeeper both dived and surfaced, he was worth his weight in gold. Most importantly, he provided a quantum shift in my ability to look after our people at sea. We had never carried a doctor or medic on the submarines, despite the extended deployments and isolated nature of the operations we routinely conducted. I did my utmost to ensure the subsequent change to the scheme of complement – the standard crewing plan – for the submarines. The young medic in front of me now was an early product of that decision. Watching him absorb everything happening around him, I was reminded of my own first dive, and of how much I had seen since then.

There was no fanfare on the day we deployed. Shaunaugh and Laura were on the wharf, brave enough to stand and wave farewell as we sounded a blast on the ship's horn. It was long enough, and loud enough, but carried a hollow ring.

Mike Deeks, now the Squadron Commodore, was aboard for the first twenty-four hours. With his staff watchkeeping at the central positions onboard, I mustered the entire Ship's Company in the fore-ends for a 'hatches shut' conversation. Exuding profound gravity and complete confidence, his central message was this: 'Security is safety. What you are going to do is vitally important. You must be prepared for whatever that task is … and you are.'

With detailed orders locked in my safe, there was no more information to share just yet. The troops knew that we were heading away for four months and little else. They could see the few short weeks of exercises scheduled with regional navies, but apart from this, the program was largely white space. The 'where to' and 'why for' of the deployment was a mystery to the vast majority of the crew. Yet, with remarkable poise, they sailed away from their loved ones trusting and accepting that they would know what they needed to know, when they needed to know it.

It doesn't mean they weren't intensely curious. One of my senior sailors insisted on bringing his 'random port generator' to the command briefings each evening, a cardboard disc labelled with fanciful destinations: Kure, Hong Kong, Cam Ranh, Bangkok, Kuching, Kota Kinabalu, Colombo, Guam, Disneyland. We kept heading north.

Journal note, August 2002. *Who the hell was that?*

One known objective is MASTEX, the inaugural Malaysian and Australian bilateral maritime warfare exercise, off Peninsular Malaysia. Arriving alongside a commercial berth at Kuantan on a typically glary morning, I squint through the forest fire haze that blankets much of the coastline towards KD *Jebat*. She is a Lekiu-class frigate and our host for the pre-exercise briefings. The Royal Malaysian Navy have recently placed an order with the French for two Scorpène-class submarines, their first. The assembled surface warfare officers understand that there is a great deal involved in safely exercising with submarines. Grateful for the opportunity to work with us, they are super attentive.

It is just as well. As we get underway with *Jebat* and the Laksamana-class corvettes, KD *Tan Pusmah* and *Tun Abdul Jamil*, we are in challenging waters characterised by shallow operating depths and high traffic density. We reduce our safe depth from 60 metres to 30 metres. This leaves around 30 metres between us and the bottom – with sufficient headroom to avoid the shallow draft of the warships, but insufficient to avoid the very deep-drafted merchant ships moving along the trade routes.

Exercise Stardex, conducted immediately after MASTEX, is a second known objective with a broader collection of participating navies. Lining up for a 'shop window' early one morning, I grow increasingly uncomfortable. As an exercise where warships sail by the submarine at close range to train their lookouts on detection and identification of submarine periscopes, a shop window carries an inherent risk of collision. As the warships steam in, we are at periscope depth with both periscopes and every other mast fully raised. When RSS *Valour*, a Singaporean Victory-class corvette, asks us to come to periscope depth, I know things aren't going according to plan. She is less than a mile away and steaming directly towards us, but does not hold us visually or on her radar. I order us deep; they will have to get their periscope detection training another day.

The exercise is put on hold when a Royal Malaysian Air Force Hawk multi-role fighter jet drops from the sky, the pilot surviving after a successful ejection. However, it is not the exercise participants that provide us most excitement, rather the uninvited guests we discover. Patrolling through the exercise areas, we unexpectedly detect – then deliberately close on – an Indian offshore patrol vessel, the INS *Sukanya*. Stopped and silent, but no doubt listening intently to the exercise activity going on around her, she is a long way from home. As we know full well, a combined exercise such as this offers a treasure trove of intelligence on the tactics and capabilities of the participating navies, particularly if the players do not know they are under surveillance.

We watch *Sukanya* get underway as one of the Malaysian warships, KD *Lekiu*, approaches from over the horizon. She steams off *Lekiu*'s track, matching her own speed to the many fishing vessels in the area to avoid attracting attention, and disappears into the surrounding haze. Tracking her on sonar throughout, we later observe her creeping back to resume her station after *Lekiu* has moved through. Sly dog.

A few nights later, we discover there is more than one sly dog in area. As the new kid on the block, we know that the Collins boats are an exceptionally high priority intelligence collection target for all the regional navies.

'Captain to the control room, all compartments assume the ultra-quiet state.'

My heart rate spikes as I leap from my bunk. *We're on. I don't know what it is, but we're on.* As I step through the blackout curtains into the darkened control room, I realise I am barefoot.

Our senior sonar rate, Pony, stands behind our towed array operator, hands gently cupping the long lead headphones on his ears, his face a study of calm concentration.

'Possible submarine contact, Sir. Mel picked it up,' he says in a hushed voice. Not quite a whisper, he knows he has my attention.

This is dangerous. We are dived and deep. We are not scheduled to be working with another boat, so if this is a submarine, she is an intruder and therefore a threat. Given the relatively shallow water we are in, it is also highly likely that we are operating at the same depth. We certainly don't have the luxury of depth separation that keeps us safe in an exercise scenario. Worse still, given the inherent stealth of many regional submarines, she is likely at close range … really close.

'Watchleader, Captain. Conduct close quarters drill.'

Manoeuvring to avoid, we search for further clues to classify the detected contact. I hold my breath and draw ever closer to the sonar consoles. *Step back. Give them room and time.*

The sonar operators are barely here, their minds swimming beyond the pressure hull, combing the sea for a handhold on the intruder. Backs go taut.

'Compressed cavitation, bearing 283,' calls Pony.

Cavitation, the noise created as gas bubbles forming at the tips of a rotating propellor collapse, is one of the simplest and most common ways for us to track a ship. The highly distinctive squeak of 'compressed cavitation' is typically heard off a propellor turning at high speed, and at depth. He is on the move. Either the captain thinks there is no-one out here to hear him or doesn't care. If he's a submariner worth his salt, he cares.

We track him heading south-west for over twenty minutes before he finds deeper water and fades from our sensors. Returning to periscope depth, we report the contact to Commander Dave Johnston, RAN, our Task Group Commander onboard HMAS *Adelaide*. There is little they can do and, for the surface ships, the exercise rolls on.

Days later we are rafted up with RFA *Diligence*, a British forward repair ship, in company with HMS *Conqueror*. With the forays of British warships into Southeast Asia increasingly rare since the transfer of Hong Kong to China in 1997, they are a welcome sight. I leap at the chance to step aboard *Diligence* for a shower under someone else's fresh water, and our chefs delight in a meal they don't cook for themselves.

Journal note, September 2002. *What was different about today? Laura sent me a familygram!*

'Dear Dad, I made it through first netball cut. Party was a success. Love you, miss you heaps, Laura.'

We had been living in our submarine world for weeks on end while life elsewhere rolled on. The lines of connection to home were stretched across both time and space. Though thin and fragile, they were laid deep within me and closely guarded.

Journal note, October 2002. *Now I'm angry!!! You bastards.*

I was in the communications office when the printer began to whirl. We had a heads up from our Submarine Operations (SUBOPS) Room that there was a 'CO's Eyes Only' signal on this broadcast. I waited patiently, but silently. The radio operator busied himself, but was equally apprehensive. Ordinarily, by dint of their job onboard, the radio operators were privileged to see every signal that came into the submarine, regardless of the classification or sensitivity, before it went to the Captain. A 'CO's Eyes Only' signal was different. They carried the potential prospect of grim news from home, either for myself or for one of the communicators. He tore it off the scroll, eyes averted, and handed it over. It wasn't for me, but for him.

Forty-eight hours earlier, we had begun to intercept radio reports of a bombing in Bali. Over time the picture built, and we eventually learned of the 202 innocents killed, including eighty-eight fellow Australians, and the more than two hundred others wounded. My crew and I were safe, but not immune from the effects of the bombings. My communicator was one of several sailors onboard who had family or friends on the island.

In one sense, I imagine, the reactions onboard for us were like those of others elsewhere: confusion, fear, anger and sadness. However, the uncertainty created by the bombings accentuated the ever-present difficulties of life at sea in a submarine. Our signal traffic was heavily vetted by the Headquarters to ensure we got the most essential messages, the intelligence signals related to our task. But there was nothing going out from us. Given our tactical situation, we had to remain silent. So, we could not inquire directly about the welfare of family and friends, nor assure them of our own safety and wellbeing.

At sea for around a month now and not due in port for another month, we focused on the task at hand. But thousands of miles from home, crammed together in our tin can, the stress and tension onboard were palpable, with the sense of isolation and purpose both substantially amplified. This was what war was like – impersonal in the extreme, personal in the extreme. I focused on leadership and service.

In the end, we don't see another overseas port visit during this deployment. The previously long list of foreign destinations where we could guarantee the security of the submarine and crew shrank a lot after the 9/11 attacks and collapsed even more dramatically in the aftermath of the Bali bombings. When our job was done, we shaped course for Australia. Given the long road home, I was immensely grateful the remaining endurance the crew had ensured was still available, having carefully eked out the finite stores of fuel, oils, spare parts and food onboard since the day we sailed. That endurance was in large part a product of the healthy but intense interdepartmental rivalry between the electrical and mechanical sections, led in their own styles by the Deputy Weapons Engineer, Mango, and his offsider the Deputy Marine Engineer, or Chief Tiff, Johnny Ryan.

For months on end, Mango insisted on producing detailed graphs on electrical system defects, failure rates, time between failures and rectification percentages. Johnny was more sparing with his salvoes. At the ultimate evening command briefing for the deployment, Johnny presented 'a detailed analysis and comprehensive depiction of all the defects the stokers had been unable to rectify while at sea'. With Mango straining to see the results, I opened the folder to reveal … a single, completely blank sheet of paper.

Standing on the bridge sailing back into Cockburn Sound in November, we saw flashing light coming from *Adelaide*, resting at anchor. Dave Johnston bade us 'Welcome Home' and waved from the bridge. Keeping it simple, I asked our lookout to pass 'VMT. DBF.'[4] Given that our signal lamp was the least used piece of kit onboard, I wasn't too sure what *Adelaide* read. We either confused them or gave them a good chuckle, perhaps both. Maybe they wondered where we had been in the months since we saw them last, or what we had been doing. Maybe not. Regardless, secure in the knowledge that our mission was a success and we had done what we were sent out to do, we were happy to be back.

---

4   'Very Many Thanks. Diesel Boats Forever.'

CHAPTER 18
FLOOD, FLOOD, FLOOD

Heading out to sea once more early in the new year of 2003, we passed the Nimitz-class aircraft carrier USS *Abraham Lincoln* at anchor in Gage Roads off Fremantle. Her Ship's Company were enjoying a brief liberty ashore while her F-14s conducted bombing runs on the Lancelin range. There was no doubt she was on a war footing, conducting back-to-back deployments into the Middle East. With our own warships scarce, we were set against USS *Honolulu* and our recently commissioned little sister HMAS *Rankin*, honing our anti-submarine warfare skills in preparation for another deployment.

A series of VIP sea days posed a different challenge, with the Governor of Western Australia, Lieutenant General John Sanderson, at the top of a guest list of twenty Perth notables. With the lessons of the USS *Greeneville* tragedy uppermost in my mind, I asked Commodore Deeks to host the guests and my splendid XO, Geoff Wadley, to execute the program as I focused on oversight. I deliberately commanded with a light touch, staying to the side of the action and goings-on throughout the day. When Mike asked if there were any final questions, one keen observer responded, 'Yes. What the bloody hell does the Captain do?'

No harm came our way that day, but disaster would strike deep two weeks later.

Journal note, February 2003. *On the surface, happy.*

The upper accommodation space hatch – the main entry point into the submarine – has been plaguing us with a persistent leak over several running periods. To prove the success of the Chief Tiff's latest repair efforts, we take the boat to Deep Diving Depth. The hatch is bone dry. For the first time since joining the boat, the interdepartmental Priority One defect tally stands at nil all.

'Johnny, super job! Great to see your team back on level pegging with Mango's mob.'

'Flood, flood, flood! Flood in the lower motor room.'

I meet Mango's eyes, just inches from mine. I meet Johnny's eyes; he is as close. A flood means Johnny has at least one new problem and Mango has the lead once again. We share a grin. But there is no time for him to boast. They are gone and so am I.

Within seconds, I am in the control room. Geoff has the weight as Duty Commanding Officer and today it's his boat. The submarine is under immense pressure and flooding uncontrollably.

'Emergency Stations, Emergency Stations. Flood, flood, flood. Flood in the lower motor room.'

'Full ahead. 20 up. Midships. Blow main ballast. Blow emergency main ballast. Shut all hull valves.'

The emergency orders ring out and are immediately acknowledged by the operators. The panel watchkeeper cracks the valves to hear the rattle, blast and hiss of high-pressure air pushing into the ballast tanks. The Chief of the Boat lifts and artfully holds the nose of the submarine. The revolutions come on and we start to surge forward. They know the drill and are already onto it.

In an instant, everything has changed. We have gone from knowing the state of our submarine in intimate detail to endless unknowns.

Breathe.

My heart is beating through my neck. I know – we all know – that if we go down in this depth of water, we will be crushed by the pressure before we hit the bottom. Once the pressure hull splits, the ocean's onslaught will be absolute in its violence. Though it be the world to us, the ocean would fill our submarine as effortlessly as it would fill my lungs, without a moment's hesitation or a skerrick of remorse. There is no coming back.

Breathe.

We've been here before. We've trained for this. Some of us have trained for this our whole adult lives.

'I have the submarine,' I say, resuming full command.

It's much quieter now. Though not very quiet, not in submarine terms. HQ1 reports they are closed up; sonar is calling sweeps for clearance; '20 up' from the Chief on the planes.

But the reaction is over. All of the Emergency Operating Procedures are done and we're pumping on anything that can draw a suction.

Standing between the periscopes in the centre of the packed control room, I feel the eyes of one of my sailors fixed on me. I meet his gaze. He is searching for the answer to a singular question: 'Can we survive?' He sees that I don't know, but I am still in the fight. My eyes return to the depth gauge.

We're sinking. We're beneath Deep Diving Depth, and we're sinking.

There is a moment in time where I know all of me, and I am here. The Captain is here, holding onto his fear to remain calm and offer courage to his crew. Commander Scott is here, observing every single order and every single action, mind racing to understand the present and shape the future. Scotty the husband is here, and so is Laura's dad. Pete, the hopeful boy, still searching for his place in the world, is here. Not wanting to die, not like this. Not taking this crew with him. Yet I can already see myself floating, face down and lifeless, through a cold, dark submarine.

After hanging in suspense for what seems an eternity, the descent below Deep Diving Depth is mercifully arrested. The depth gauge needle twitches … then twitches again … and we finally begin to rise, wrestling from the grip of the depths. Our steadily building speed, driven by the immense power of the propellor, brings life and lift to the hydroplanes. The emergency blow on the main ballast tanks begins to overcome the external pressure, disgorging 400 tonnes of seawater back out into the ocean.

Three eternal minutes after the initial flood, I order the attack periscope raised. On one knee before it, my eyes meet the black rubber cups as they come proud of the deck. As I snap the handles down, willing the submarine to continue its upward trajectory, I search for the glimmer of light on the sea surface.

Breaking the surface at speed, the submarine breaches like a whale, then slumps back into the ocean. Though crippled, I don't know the extent of our wounds. As importantly, I don't know the impact on my people.

Discipline, knowledge, skill, experience, teamwork. Right things in the right order – achieve a safe and known state. This is how you will survive, Scotty.

The motor room is one of the most confined spaces in the submarine. Occupying the narrow cone of the pressure hull at the stern, it is almost entirely filled by the main motor and associated high power electrical cabling and coolers. The lower motor room is much smaller and even more confined. Stationed there to report the watertight integrity of several systems once we were at Deep Diving Depth, one of our Leading

Seaman, Rocker, narrowly escaped a swift death as a flexible hose gave way, flinging pipework through the air and opening the submarine to the sea from two directions. Immediately, the ocean invaded what little space he had in an absolute torrent.

Young Sully, stationed in the engine room, raced aft towards the crack and roar of the flood, colliding with his shipmate, Morrie. Morrie had seen the air in the motor room suddenly fill with froth and spray and bolted forward, away from the deafening racket, to make the initial pipe alerting the crew to the catastrophe.

'Is it bad?' called Sully, as they tear back towards the scene of the flood.

'Yeah, it's bad!'

While he couldn't hear him, Morrie knew Rocker's location. They had played 'Rock, Paper, Scissors' earlier that day to decide who would be stationed down there for the watertight integrity checks. Battered, dazed and pinned underneath the exit ladder by the force of the flood, Rocker was close to drowning. Adrenaline-fuelled arms reached down, took hold of his overalls at the shoulder, and hauled his 90-kilo frame up and out through a 2-foot by 2-foot hatch in the deckplates.

The water filling the lower motor room was cold and chest deep as Morrie headed 'down the hole' to ascertain the cause of the flood and isolate the damage. When the Chief Tiff arrived to take control at the scene, he joined him in the whirlpool. As Sully brought them the tools they needed, they all risked electrocution from the still live high power pumps that occupy the space. The bow up came on, and they watched helplessly as tonnes of seawater ran aft – underneath and around the electric main motor.

Staying on the roof and getting alongside takes every level of redundancy the submarine can offer, and every ounce of energy, shred of intellect and strand of teamwork we can muster. For the next six hours, we engage in a damage control battle to expunge the seawater, identify defective equipment and restore systems and capability, all without causing further damage or killing someone. As we arrive alongside at *Stirling*, Mike Deeks comes down to meet me at the gangway, ahead of the gathering throng of Squadron staff.

'It's good to see you, Scotty!' he says.

'It's good to be here, Sir!'

Finding some free air at the end of the wharf, I call Shaunaugh. 'Ullo. Don't tell me; you're broken again,' she quips.

On hearing her voice, a surge of relief rips through my chest and I struggle to stay calm. *Hold it together, give her the basics, you'll be home soon enough.*

Rocker, somewhat recovered from his ordeal, has a different approach. He also calls his wife, telling her we are back in with a defect. 'Could you come and pick me up? Oh, and could you pick up some smokes along the way?'

'Are you out of cigarettes already?' she asks incredulously.

'Nup. They just got a little wet!'

Surviving the flood was one matter. Recovering from the flood was another entirely and would take a lot more than I had at my disposal. Once we understood the underlying problem, what followed was a docking, material modifications, new operating limits and changes to procedure. It took the combined efforts of the Ship's Company, the Squadron staff, the *Stirling* chaplains, medical and psychology teams, Fleet staff, Navy's senior leadership, accident investigators, design engineers and tradesmen to repair and strengthen the submarine.

Critically, the capacity and effectiveness of the ASC workforce in Western Australia had come on in leaps and bounds. In the months before our next deployment, they brought our total major defects down from forty-five to four. Sailing with major defects of any description typically meant placing heavy reliance on the redundancy designed into the systems and equipment. It added substantially to the cognitive load of those onboard to manage the submarine's performance at sea safely and effectively. But relying on redundant systems from the outset meant greater risk to the mission in the event of further failures or defects. On this occasion, with all our safety systems and highest priority operational capabilities available, we could definitely work with what we had.

My enduring memory of the Ship's Company on the day of the flood was not one of fear, but of cool, calm determination and discipline. It was a memory of courage and strength in the face of a fearful disaster. For weeks afterwards I laid awake all night every night, unwillingly reliving the terror while holding myself as quiet and still as possible lest I wake Shaunaugh. I offered only the merest hint of this to the base psychologist. Some of my ongoing fears were exposing Shaunaugh to the extent of the trauma, and that I would fail in the courage to lead my people back to sea. Put simply, though, what I was most afraid of was death. That fear didn't go away, but once I could see it and put a name to it, I could walk myself past it.

Knowing the detail of the upcoming missions, and the opportunity on offer to really prove the operational capability of the submarine, I understood the importance of keeping it all together. While the majority of the crew had less information than I did, our shared purpose inspired the determination of the entire Ship's Company. But what most enabled our return to sea was our direct and intimate connection with each other – mutual compassion borne of shared experience, and common fear. We had been through and survived the flood together; we would go back to sea together.

When we set sail two weeks after the flood, every man and woman who had been onboard that day was with us. Despite the trauma, they had a renewed sense of belief in their boat, their training and themselves, and in those that support them from ashore. We needed all the help we could get because our mission still stood before us. With warshot weapons embarked once more, the submarine was whole again. Ready to go!

Journal note, 2003. *You will be a long way from home and a long way from help.*
     – Fleet Submarine Operations Officer

Over the weeks immediately before we deployed in April the news was filled with talk of war, the invasion of Iraq and the fall of Baghdad. Precious last hours with my girls were loaded with tension, and I sensed in Shaunaugh a deep dread that I might not come home from this deployment. I was determined that I would.

We were not long departed when we received eerie news of a Chinese Ming-class diesel submarine, No. 361, failing to surface. In an uncommon public announcement, the Chinese reported that she was operating in the Yellow Sea, discovered floating at periscope depth by fishermen, and towed to port. All seventy onboard perished after suffering an engine run-on. Under orders of radio silence prior to the accident, she had not been missed and may have been drifting for up to ten days. As we observed a minute's silence onboard *Dechaineux*, our thoughts were with our own families dealing with their own fears.

In the weeks before the departure, I grew tired of the increasingly scruffy appearance of our sailors. I made a strong 'suggestion' to the Chief of the Boat that a few haircuts and beard trims were in order. Nothing happened. I was disgruntled, and a little nonplussed, but had bigger fish to fry.

Now, after seventeen days at sea and dived, the penny finally dropped when one of the electronic warfare sailors rocked into the control room. He sported a reverse mohawk with shaved sides, the lacquered waves of hair sprouting from his scalp dyed bright orange and gold. Clearly, he needed a head start for this stylistic masterpiece, dodging the barber's chair for months before our sail date. Fringes were spiked, heads were shaved and beards were carved. Within days, most of my crew looked like a walking, talking ice sculptors' exhibition. The officers were not so adventurous – and didn't get the memo ahead of time. The girls were more judicious than the lads, but happy to provide styling tips and product. The levity was a much-needed break from the emotional load we'd all been carrying for weeks and months on end.

'They'd go spare in the skimmers, Sir,' was the reaction from one Petty Officer, who led the team of linguists and cryptologists onboard.

'That's why we're not in a skimmer, mate.'

The days and weeks rolled on. The days were marked by the regular changes in control room lighting, which extended to the upper deck messes and my cabin. White for day, red for dusk and dawn, black at night when we peered to read gauges and dials dimmed to the barest illumination. And the shifts were marked by mealtimes. Breakfast, lunch, dinner and 'midnighters', all timed to feed the watches cycling on and off every six hours.

Our Leading Steward, who doubled as my periscope assistant at Action Stations and as my barber when we were out for a month or more, was at my cabin door. 'For dinner tonight, Sir, we have roast beef, spaghetti Bolognese and *Rankin* Pie. *Rankin* Pie, Sir, is like *Sheean* Pie, except it hasn't been anywhere or done anything.'[5]

I personally spent a lot of some days doing remarkably little. The crew was fully employed executing our operational tasking. But with no fleet exercise program to drive the routines, life at sea happened as it happened, rather than as we scheduled it, so I adapted my approach and style to match. I reviewed the previous watches' records, received a briefing on our remaining fuel and stores, thought ahead to the coming weeks on patrol, walked through the boat and chatted with the watchkeepers, and took an occasional all-round look through the periscope. I grabbed a short kip in the forenoon and another in the afternoon to ensure I was fresh whenever something significant occurred, whether that be in the middle of the day or the middle of the night.

For record keeping purposes, we lived in 24-hour 'Zulu' time, with our clocks set to Greenwich Mean Time. Last night was pizza and tombola, with a rare win for the wardroom, so I knew it was Sunday. The weeks were no longer marked by the traditional non-denominational gathering of earlier years, but Sunday usually offered a less rigid routine. On this patrol, with my own cabin and the luxury of space this afforded, Sunday was 'presents day'. I reached into my seat locker, groped for the bag and selected a gift for the week: rock candies with love hearts and 'Dad' inscribed on them, a jarrah ink blotter, a jar of relish to share, brand new socks, brand new undies. The gifts were small and inexpensive, but they were wrapped and came from home.

And Sunday was tubs day. Proper tubs, not a bird bath. And by proper, I mean a thirty-second spray under the shower, a couple of minutes to suds up and scrub down, and another thirty-second spray to rinse off. I added a minute over the steel basin to trim my non-regulation goatee. I felt clean, shiny and smelled momentarily of soap, rather than diesel and dead skin.

Journal note, May 2003. *I feel very comfortable out here.*

The strain and fatigue of an operational deployment typically built, then plateaued. We continually strove to match the rest and relaxation

---

5   Quiche.

required to endure with the vigilance and vitality needed to achieve our mission objectives, and to survive. Like any submarine patrol, we experienced a great deal of the ordinary, and an unpredictable amount of the extraordinary. The ordinary blurred and faded, the extraordinary electrified and made its mark.

'First watch, stand to. BINT on foreign warship,' crackled over the action broadcast.

'Captain, Sir, Watchleader. Master 34, previously tracked on active transmissions, now gained visual, range 21,000 yards. She is stationed 9,000 yards ahead of the task group. Have stood the watch to for an intelligence take.'

'Captain, roger. Call me at 16,000 yards.'

Dressing in a fresh pair of shorts and black T-shirt, I glimpsed the 'safe to fire' key that had been clipped to the dog tags worn around my neck since we arrived on station weeks earlier. One of the safeguards for our loaded Mark 48 torpedoes, it was ordinarily locked away on the security keyboard. Many years prior I reconciled myself with the fact that I might one day need to order warshot weapons fired, to defend my submarine or to sink an enemy or both, and take life. I'll be happy to sign the key back in once we're done and headed back to Australia. There were some days when I just hoped it all ended with a cup of tea in my comfy chair at home.

As I moved through the boat, the watchkeeping was tight everywhere and the mood relaxed, though less so in the control room. When I offered one of the less experienced officers a two-hour stint as Watchleader during a relatively quiet period, the XO handed the watch over to him with a warning. 'I don't want to end up in a bamboo cage as a result of this, chum!'

The comment was made in jest – the younger officer knew the XO would be close by and ready to back him up – but was borne of a certain sincerity. For a submarine on patrol, there were no friendlies and no back-up. The troops knew we were wholly and solely reliant on ourselves to look after each other, look after the boat, bring the pieces of the puzzle together and get the job done, whatever that may be. All that said, I was completely at ease. With time and experience came acceptance, comfort within discomfort and the commitment to both perform and endure. I was a submariner and a master of my duty as Commanding Officer, relishing the gift of a fully operational boat and blessed with a crew who excelled in their trade, matching challenge with skill and determination hour by hour.

Journal note, July 2003. *What was different about today?*

I saw and felt Grandad. His hand was on my shoulder, though at first I just saw his face. He was smiling.

'How did you find me down here?' I asked.

I've only seen Grandad's ghost a few times, but always at sea. He was with me when I needed him most. He came to give me encouragement and faith in what I was doing. His presence was vivid and strong, and most welcome. Courage faded; courage gleamed. *I think I'm doing OK.*

'… anyway, it was good to be with you, Grandad.'

As we sailed from Darwin on the return leg home, we operated under Peacetime Rules of Engagement once more and it was time for some sport. A powerful Carrier Battle Group, led by USS *Carl Vinson* with her air wings embarked and including the Ticonderoga-class cruiser USS *Antietam*, the Oliver Hazard Perry-class frigate USS *Ingraham* and the fast combat support ship USS *Sacramento*, was known to be transiting north along our west coast. I took a back seat, handing Duty Command to Geoff, the XO, with everyone else onboard also stepping up one position, and told the Americans we were coming for them.

Four days later, after they first detected the warships off Port Hedland, it took a further twenty-four hours to track, close and penetrate the screen. Evading the searching aircraft and ships, Geoff warily brought *Dechaineux* back to periscope depth and took an all-round look. It was the middle of the night and pitch black, but the horizon was not empty.

'Standby set-up, the carrier,' he called, with a clear periscope view of the beast through our thermal imaging.

Our USN Acoustic Intelligence Specialist, who had been with us as my tactical advisor throughout the deployment, let out a holler of delight. With green grenades lighting up the night sky, Geoff called them up on the pre-ordered tactical circuit.

'*Carl Vinson*, this is Australian Submarine. I bear 190, range 3,500 yards from you. Do you hold me?'

'No, but I hold your flares!'

Confidence and pride, borne of mastery, pervaded. *Beautiful. Well done, team. My work here is done.*

PART III

CAPTAIN AND STRATEGIST

CHAPTER 19
TO WAR

Stepping out of submarine command, I wanted to find a new mark in the wider Navy and ADF. After a decade and a half of intense seatime, I needed a change and some respite. And while I considered myself a submariner first and foremost, I was also a naval officer, senior Commander and professional warfighter in the broadest sense. Driven along in part by the prevailing view that submariners lacked breadth of experience, over the next few years I found myself posted into a series of joint – or tri-service – organisations that required officers with naval command expertise. While none of these roles could compete with the thrill and satisfaction of submarine command, they each offered distinct advantages and learning opportunities.

In June 2006, I was on my first deployment into a land operation, heading into Timor Leste. An operation had been launched a month prior to quell unrest and restore stability following the attempted military coup led by Major Alfredo Reinado. I knew Reinado personally, having met and observed him while he was attending the Australian Command and Staff Course during the back half of the previous year. Charismatic and personable when engaged, he kept a low profile, avoiding any unnecessary attention.

With the collapse of security and resulting violence, an Australian battalion group of about 1,800 personnel had been deployed ashore with support from the RAN and RAAF. I was asked to lead a team of specialists from the ADF Warfare Centre to conduct an evaluation of the operation. It began with a series of interviews with the most senior leaders in Canberra that focused on strategy and policy outcomes. Those findings would then be tested against the views and position of the Commander and forces on the ground in Timor Leste.

The welcome from the Australian Headquarters in Dili was borderline cordial and left me with the distinct impression they didn't appreciate us peering over their collective shoulders. Regardless, we set about our task. In the space of three intensive weeks, we completed the interview program and extensive pre-deployment preparations, were on the ground moving through unfamiliar and dangerous territory on the violence-scarred streets of the East Timorese capital, and then back home again. Accustomed to the range of thoughts and emotions that are part of naval deployments, the rapidity with which we moved through the cycle was unlike anything I had experienced in my career.

The return to normalcy was both abrupt and discrete. Departing Dili one morning and landing at RAAF Base *Richmond* after dark the same day, there were no week-long passages back to Australia, nor the arrival statement of a warship or submarine sailing back in through Sydney Heads. Over the following days, I walked through the boutique shops and shaded suburban pockets of Lane Cove, with civil life here entirely uninterrupted – self-absorbed with today's business and oblivious to the deathly tension that hung over Dili. Finding myself in between realities – here now but still there – was a strange emotional space.

My second deployment into a land operation was not long following, with news of a posting into our national headquarters in Baghdad, Iraq. While the pre-deployment preparations were intensive, the day before flying out was the first day of the war for me. I wrote a letter to Laura. Her Headmistress, who already held similar letters for all her classmates, had asked for it – to be read by Laura on graduation from high school three years hence. Emotion poured from me as I strained to capture my hopes as a father, and the enormity of my love and admiration. My head pounded as I scrambled to distil wisdom worth taking forward in her life, and beyond mine.

Weeks prior, I had been increasingly worried. With my departure looming, there was no emotional reaction or kickback coming from a decidedly level Laura. Taking her aside, I asked if she understood where I was going and if she had any concerns.

'I know that you're going off to Iraq, Dad. I know where it is, what your job will be and how dangerous it is,' was her forthright response.

'I understand that people are dying and having their lives torn apart, but at least I know where you will be. I have spent my life not knowing where my father was, knowing that he loves me and I love him, but not knowing where he is. It has been the most difficult thing to have one of my friends say, "Where's your dad?" and have no answer. Not "he's in the city", or "he's in Moss Vale". I had no idea where you were. You were at sea, but that meant nothing to them and not enough to me. At least in Iraq, I know where you are.'

While immensely relieved that she wasn't wrestling with difficult emotions on her own or that they might boil over when I was gone and unable to console her, I was impossibly sad and wholly ashamed for all the times she felt that desolation in the years gone by.

On the morning of departure, I could not sit still in the house. Everything was done, nothing can be done and it was not yet time to leave. Shaunaugh and I were together, but already apart in our own torment. There was no truth or assurance that could allay the overwhelming fear that we might never see each other again. We took the dog for a walk around the block, sniffing at every gate, and past my old primary school, kids tumbling into the yard, laughing. Sick with worry and grief, Shaunaugh was on the point of collapse.

'Don't be nice to me!' she commanded. She was hapless while I was helpless.

In a quiet moment a few days earlier, my Uncle David had said to us, 'It came to pass ... but it didn't come to stay. You'll be back'. Unbeknownst to me, my already waning faith in organised religion was about to be dealt a death blow in Iraq. Regardless, these simple words from a holy man I had trusted my entire life gave me inordinate comfort and just enough courage to keep moving forward.

Journal entry, September 2006. *Measures of success on departure: to survive. To survive with honour. To understand. To lead. To inspire. To serve. To succeed?*

Orange lights glowing in the haze over Darwin on take-off were my last sighting of Terra Australis as we set course for Diego Garcia, the Middle East and war. The Chief of Staff for Headquarters Joint Task Force (JTF) 633 had travelled from Baghdad to meet me on arrival in Kuwait. As his relief, he was keen to see me get off the plane. I noted his assessment that 'the Americans are putting a tremendous effort in, but it's sliding backwards, and they can't stop it'. After four days of final briefings in Kuwait, I felt prepared, equipped, armed and generally at ease.

I got a lesson in angles and dangles 'Ronny RAAF style' as our C-130 Hercules, Callsign Mambo 33, piled into Baghdad airport. The approach was nothing like the steady line and easy descent of a commercial airliner, as the young Flight Lieutenants dramatically twisted and contorted our flight path to magnify the targeting challenge for any missile-armed assailants on the ground. My boss, a Brigadier, was there to greet me on landing. He was the National Commander for all ADF personnel operating in the Middle East Area of Operations, which included Iraq, the Persian Gulf and Afghanistan.

My job was to run the JTF Headquarters so he could command the Force. It was no short order, given that we were operating across three totally different war zones. Within the Joint Task Force there were about two thousand Australian sailors, soldiers and airmen within ten or more different task groups. They constituted a truly diverse range of capabilities, performing tremendously varied roles in unique environments. On the ground, Army Security Detachments protected the Australian Ambassador in Baghdad, and Army engineers re-built communities destroyed by the Taliban. In the air, long-range RAAF aircraft conducted overland surveillance patrols to locate roadside bombs in Iraq, while Chinook helicopters flew combat support missions over the mountains of Afghanistan. And at sea, Navy frigates defended the Iraqi oil terminals.

Journal entry, October 2006. *One hundred and seventy attacks in Iraq yesterday. The figures on killed and wounded are staggering.*

The violence of Iraq was not often in my face, but it was everywhere. The airfield was rocketed on the day I arrived. The margins were finer as we lined up for take-off in a Hercules on a subsequent departure. As a senior guy, I had a ticket to a seat in the cabin with the pilots and saw the rockets hit the tarmac a few hundred yards ahead, smoke and debris spewing into thin pillars above. Every now and then, the deep-seated blast and rumble of detonated truck and car bombs climbed up through my boots and into my bones, even when they were a couple of kilometres distant. The thick pall of black smoke mushrooming into the sky was the next indication of which crowded market, square or mosque had been targeted for that day's mass murder event.

We were headquartered within Camp Victory, the sprawling complex of palaces erected by Saddam Hussein during his dictatorship and occupied during the invasion of 2003. Rockets launched from the suburbs of Baghdad impacted within the camp every other day, landing where they will, on a routine but irregular basis. Firefights raged in the streets outside the wire daily, and stray rounds commonly flew in over the high surrounding walls.

My digs, shared with about a dozen of the more senior Australian officers, were in one of the smaller lakeside buildings known as Kirribilli House, although it was less luxurious than its namesake. Tucked away in the House early one November evening, we were shaken by the hefty explosions of multiple 122 mm rockets impacting close by. Misjudging the strength of the attack, I decided to get back to the Headquarters. Out in the open, as more rockets fell around me, my otherwise oversized helmet and hefty battle-rattle felt decidedly puny and flimsy. Momentarily sat on my arse by one explosion, I crossed the 70 yards to shelter at break-neck speed.

As luck would have it, I arrived in Iraq at the start of Ramadan, in a critical phase of the Baghdad Security Plan and during a particularly violent period. Monthly US combat deaths exceeded those suffered during the initial invasion in 2003. The war took a toll of about five hundred deaths a week across the country. Two-thirds of those killed were Iraqis, rather than foreign forces, and over two-thirds of those deaths were Iraqi civilians. I was reminded of the Bali bombings but realised that ten times that carnage was occurring around me every month. In December 2006, the month Saddam Hussein was executed, there were more than two thousand sectarian murders; Shia killing Sunni and Sunni killing Shia, all in the name of Allah. And most of those atrocities occurred in the dishevelled streets of Baghdad. Before I left Iraq in March 2007, it wasn't five hundred deaths a week, it was over a thousand.

Laying my head down at the end of any given day, I was deeply impressed by the professionalism of our troops and the niche capabilities they represented. I was also clear on how our Headquarters role supported them in theatre and linked us all with higher command in Australia.

Complex, dynamic, unrelenting and exhausting as it was, doing my job as Chief of Staff was the easy part. Try as I might, crafting a coherent and resonant story that authentically connected us with the fractured, chaotic and disordered identity of Iraq remained beyond me. The really difficult piece was coming to grips with the violence and misery, which left me bereft.

The Force had been built up over the years since the invasion in 2003, with various elements joining and their respective missions set at different times. As a result, our written orders to the Task Group Commanders lacked coherence. In early November 2006, we took on the task of rewriting the operational orders across the Task Force. Our aim was to give the deployed troops the best possible chance of success, without overstepping the mark and ensure the Headquarters wasn't adding to the inherent chaos of Middle Eastern wars.

The potential of the Australians in theatre to make a real difference was significant. They were all working at difficult, highly specialised tasks, a long way from home, often under personal threat in hostile situations and nearly always under strain. Crucially, those in Headquarters roles had to understand and respond to the reality of the challenges faced by the Task Group Commanders, and it was equally important that they understood the strategic realities and how their task group could best contribute to our national objectives.

This meant some of us in the Headquarters needed to get out into the theatre and into the heads of the Task Group Commanders, so we could subsequently get out of their way. We could do nothing to reduce the general snarl, disarray and violence, but worked hard to give the troops greater clarity on our objectives and on their levels of authority. Most importantly, our combined efforts gave us a shared and much improved contextual understanding of the various battlespaces. It was a minor victory in a battlespace that had few wins at the time.

Getting around the theatre was never smooth. On one trip, after hopping from Baghdad to Tallil, Kuwait, then Qatar, I was positioned to fly into Afghanistan. Moving in with an Infantry Company of the 1st Reconstruction Task Force, I led them across the tarmac in the predawn stillness, Red Hot Chili Peppers blaring from the dark, and strode into the bowels of our 37 Squadron Herc. After a long haul, our approach into the capital of Uruzgan Province, Tarin Kowt – known to all as TK – was altered to avoid flying over a Taliban roadblock set up just three miles out of town.

Landing at Kandahar later that day, the centrality of this airfield and the highly kinetic and reactive nature of the war were immediately apparent, with abundant Harriers, Falcons, Apaches, Black Hawks, Chinooks and Cougars engaged in continuous flying operations. Early one morning, I witnessed the Canadians' Leopard tanks and Bison armoured personnel carriers departing base en masse – track and engine noise deafening, diesel smoke and dust everywhere. They lost their Regimental Sergeant Major in a suicide vehicle-borne attack just outside the city the previous day, taking their killed in action to forty-five, and were intent on redressing the score.

The violence in Afghanistan was escalating, with casualty figures exceeding those suffered at any time since operations began in 2001. Over several days in Kabul – a filthy and hectic city completely overgrown by Hesco barriers, checkpoints and barbed wire – I moved with greater confidence, knowing that my escort was sticking close by. An Army major, his unofficial mandate was to keep the naval captain upright and breathing, and get him back to the Headquarters in one piece. It seemed this was my year of body armour, loaded weapons and other people's miserable streets.

Our Deputy Commander in Afghanistan accompanied me back to Kandahar as we tried to return to TK to visit the 1st Reconstruction Task Force. This element was the most recent addition to JTF 633, having arrived in September to work in partnership with Dutch forces supporting the people of Deh Rawood, Chora District and TK. Thwarted over several days by the vagaries of a war zone, the nearest we got to TK was in a US Army Chinook, bundled aboard among a stuffing of stores. But closing visibility and dropping temperatures forced us to turn around short of our destination. On landing back at Kandahar, the aircraft captain informed us that we were close, having turned back just 23 miles south of our objective. He was adamant that he pushed every possible limit to navigate us through the worsening weather and over the mountain range. Disappointed but appreciative, we thanked him for his efforts.

Our flight took on greater significance when we heard reports of a missing Hind MI-26 heavy-lift helicopter with eight people onboard. Flying only fifteen minutes ahead of us on the same route, it failed to arrive at TK. When the weather finally lifted, the wreckage of the Hind was discovered; the incinerated airframe, scattered across the mountainside, was 22.5 miles south of TK. Not for the first or last time, we owed our lives to the skill and the professionalism of our pilots. With news of the fatal Black Hawk crash off HMAS *Kanimbla* during Operation Quickstep near Fiji just two days earlier still fresh in our minds, it reminded me once again how closely death skirted us.

Over the tour, I experienced an endless stream of juxtaposition and contradiction. Iraq, the Gulf, Afghanistan. Normality, abnormality. Clarity, confusion. Beauty, atrocity. With the ever-present prospect of violence, I moved through each day in a state of near hypervigilance. Yet, without wishing for or desiring death in any way, I accepted the fact that I might die over here. I was more accepting then of a potential death in service than when I was at sea in submarines, knowing there was less within my control. We were there to serve, and I could find honour in a death suffered among Australian servicemen and women.

Yet being killed was not what I feared most – it was the threat of being overwhelmed physically, emotionally or intellectually. In particular, the risk that I might succumb to the chaos, and thereby fail to lead the Headquarters staff and fail to fully support the task groups deployed across the theatre. Challenged on an hourly basis across streams of exceedingly long days, leaning into the complexity and adversity helped me find the courage to wear and absorb the chaos and the tumult. I became comfortable within it, knowing that I needed to and could manage the associated fear.

Most days I got out for a run along part of Camp Victory's massive perimeter. Ostensibly, I ran to maintain my physical fitness to sustainably survive the grind. More truthfully, I ran to feel alive and free. Most outings were uneventful, but more than one was interrupted by a headlong dive into a roadside ditch to avoid incoming small arms fire. Nonetheless, I leaped at the opportunity to take an early morning run with

Air Chief Marshal Angus Houston, touring Iraq as our Chief of Defence Force. Enjoying a relaxed conversation, we took a boyish delight in steadily outpacing the menacingly fit soldiers of his personal security detachment and the Major General in command of all Australian Special Forces. We were out in front as General George Casey, Commander of the Multi-National Force – Iraq, appeared, running towards us with his own party. For whatever reason, the Chief had been unable to secure a meeting with Casey during his visit, so he made the most of this fortuitous interaction. It also gave the troops a chance to catch up to the pilot and the submariner!

One of the most difficult experiences was the sense of being at war and at home simultaneously. Over the years at sea, I became entirely capable of putting aspects of my life – family, friends, connection with wider society – away for a time. Not disconnecting from them, more like taking them off the chart table and placing them on a nearby shelf. I often chose a moment to bring my family to mind in detail, remembering a soft touch, loving smile or reassuring voice. Strangely in Iraq and Afghanistan, unlike during any of my submarine service, there was opportunity to connect with family by phone. Earnestly trying to keep a promise to Shaunaugh to call every day, and to be present with and for her when I did, I quickly learned the impact it had at home when I missed a call, much like putting a spark to the tinderbox already stacked with fret and worry. It helped no-one when the crump of an inbound rocket found its way down the line. Brief and difficult as they sometimes were, the thin but consistent connection we held through these calls did a lot to help us move through the days.

The prospect of a fortnight's leave mid-tour also brought the total duration of absence from home down to manageable chunks. Rather than me returning to Australia, we chose to meet up for a family holiday in Thailand. Having ably dealt with the endless complexities and intricacies of running the JTF Headquarters for months on end, I stumbled. Filled with anticipation, I arrived at Dubai International Airport with several hours in hand before my connecting flight, but failed to take into account the one-hour time zone difference in the Gulf. On presenting at the unattended departure gate, I was at first confused, then aghast, then distraught with the realisation that my aircraft was gone.

Unarmed, out of uniform, on leave and on my own, my underlying fatigue and fragility became all too apparent. Intensely embarrassed and hugely ashamed by the disappointment looming for the girls, I struggled to regain composure, but managed to reunite with them the following day. Remarkably, no single day throughout my tour brought me such intense personal distress. It became known within the family as the 'worst day of the war'.

February 10 2007 was a big day in Iraq. After two and a half years in command, it was the day General Casey handed over to the incoming US General David H. Petraeus who was set to implement 'the surge', a strategic injection of an additional 30,000 US Army and Marine Corps troops to strengthen the existing force of 140,000, break the momentum of the insurgencies and regain control. It was an irrefutable demonstration of the US commitment to prevail despite their mounting casualties.

By any measure, the Australian effort paled in comparison. The absence of Australian combat-related fatalities during the Iraq war was in one sense a commendable outcome and, in no small part, a testament to the professionalism of the sailors, soldiers and airmen and women operating in that highly dangerous theatre. However, it stood in clear contrast to the thousands of US combat deaths suffered over the course of the war and the more than 600 Coalition Forces killed in action during my time in theatre alone. We were in Iraq, but not in strength, and those capable and battleworthy forces we did have in country were restrained from fully engaging in the fight.

One night when I was sixteen years old, a deranged local lad with a reputation and a knack for violence decided that my best mate Roger and I were to be his evening's entertainment. We had seen the thug at the far end of the bar earlier that night and steered clear. But he was waiting in ambush beyond the pub as we left hours later. There was no time to run and nowhere to go. With the build and the heart of a prop forward, and a full-tilt attitude to life, Roger was a bloody good brawler. He repeatedly went on the offensive, but was struck down again and again.

I didn't join the fray, but I wasn't frozen. I stepped out of reach, abandoning my mate to a savage beating. It wasn't discretion in action, it was cowardice and betrayal. *What would my grandfather think of me now?* Desolate with shame, I was left with an intact nose and a fierce determination to never again fail in the courage to stand by a mate.

At times in Iraq, we drew the direct and vocal criticism that rather than standing by our allies we stood behind them. Given my longstanding personal conviction to step forward and be present when it counted, it was a penetrating accusation. Certainly, the mismatch between our political rhetoric and our actual strategic commitment, in relation to the scale and gravity of the challenge on the ground in Iraq, was inescapable. I consoled myself with the knowledge that, magnitude aside, the quality of the Australian contribution was second to none.

Much of my last week in theatre was consumed with the organisation and execution of the Prime Minister's tour of both Afghanistan and Iraq. Over several days, John Howard met with the deployed troops, who he later described in Parliament as 'our finest patriots and our finest internationalists'. Speaking with the Iraqi Prime Minister Karzai and later with the Afghan Prime Minister Maliki, he signalled continued Australian commitment to supporting each nation.

As a monstrous golden dust storm rolled over Baghdad, I watched the Prime Minister's aircraft ascend and climb away, protective F-16 Falcon fighter jets high overhead. Turning for the Headquarters, I was ready to hand over the weight as Chief of Staff to my relief, a resolute Group Captain who was keen to take over.

Journal note, 18 March 2007. *Phoned Shaunaugh. Told her I was out of a job and coming home.*

CHAPTER 20
CAPABILITY IN DECAY

The welcome home party Shaunaugh and Laura threw when I arrived back from the Middle East was a terrific way to start feeling at home again. For the girls, it was a chance to draw a line under yet another deployment. For me, it was a moment to reconnect with wider family and friends, and acknowledge those who were there for the girls while I was away. It was also a moment to be aware that there were limits to what people might comprehend about my experiences, and what they were willing to hear and absorb.

Cold beer in hand, I looked out from the kitchen at the familiar faces filling the living room of our little Federation rental. Crowded and noisy, Cold Chisel pushed up the volume and filled the spaces between. The distinctive laugh (more a man-sized giggle) of a mate and navy veteran of 'the Stans' bounced round the room. He could and did relate to much of my life experience. Another friend stood tall in the crowd, holding court. Like most others in the room, he had shared certain days and experiences in my girls' lives that I had missed. A shard of envy came and went. My diminutive mum was harder to spot, even close by. She and Dad were immensely proud of me, which was confounding, given my intimate knowledge of my failings and their limited visibility of my successes. While I still endeavoured to do them proud every day, I sometimes felt our lives could not be more different.

Most importantly, after the disruption of the previous years, I resolved to re-establish family life with my girls and hopefully avoid the familiar sense of playing catch up. In the week before I flew out of Baghdad, a padre had queried my ambition to 'regain what we had before'.

'You will be different. They will be different. Life will be different. Meet your family where they are and go from there,' was his wise counsel.

I had some settling down to do in the first instance. Although I had been able to live and function quite well over in the Middle East, I'd been on my guard for most of the past nine months. The stomach ulcer and burned oesophagus I brought home as souvenirs were testament to the stress and strain. Time in Iraq and Afghanistan drastically shifted my sense of what was dangerous or not, and it was seriously out of whack with living responsibly in suburban Sydney. Within three months of getting back, I ran through all of the points on my driver's licence, copping speeding fine after speeding fine.

By then I had stepped through my post-operational psychology screening, commonly known as POPS, careful not to create any fuss or draw attention to myself. In the naïvety of my youth, and perhaps influenced by my experience with Grandad, I firmly believed that I could and would one day go to war and return unchanged. I had long since disavowed myself of that myth. Grateful to have survived, and with a two-year shore posting ahead of me, it was time to move forward once more – even if I was living with some emotional homework undone.

Soon enough, as Laura lined up for her HSC year, we bought a small brick home in Gladesville. We painted it throughout to match the few stained-glass windows brightening the bedrooms and accentuated the warmth of the simple fireplace in the living room. The galley kitchen at the back of the house had just enough room for a little square dining table. With a hedge to trim, a lawn to mow and a tidy garden to tend, the backyard was my new happy place. It was old and a squeeze, but it was ours, and we were together.

Journal note, May 2007. *Living with my girls is living.*

On Day One as Commander of the Submarine Task Group, I breezed through the familiar maze of cypher-locked doors and tempest defences that protected the goings on of our Submarine Operations Room at Fleet Headquarters. Assuming responsibility for the planning, preparation and conduct of all submarine exercises and operations at sea, I had reporting lines to both the Fleet Commander and the Chief of Joint Operations. Thrilled at the prospect of taking up a job I had aspired to for many years, I was even more excited to take it on as a four-ring Captain – the role recently elevated from a Commander's position in response to the growing understanding of the strategic importance of the submarines.

Settling into the new office, I was encircled by restricted, secret and top-secret computer screens and keyboards. Several weeks earlier, a near tragedy had unfolded onboard one of our submarines at sea and it was the first matter my staff briefed me on. It was apparent from the CO's signalled reports that the crew performed marvellously in some extraordinarily difficult circumstances, collectively achieving a phenomenal outcome. However, the situation demanded an independent review of the circumstances, the decision-making and the lessons to be learned. As we discussed it, the Deputy Fleet Commander was ushered into the small entry hallway outside my office.

'Welcome aboard, Scotty. I have a job for you,' said the Commodore, wasting little time. '*Farncomb* will be alongside in Thailand in four days' time. I need you to conduct the Inquiry. Your flights are booked.'

Deployed into Southeast Asian waters, *Farncomb* had surfaced under the cover of night to disentangle fishing nets and lines that had fouled her propellor and were affecting her operations. Five of the crew were swept from the casing of the submarine by rough seas, including the ship's diving team, some of the regular man overboard recovery team and the XO.

Eyes fixed to the periscope, the CO switched on the image intensifier to try and keep those bobbing in the dark turmoil in sight. To enable a recovery, he manoeuvred the submarine away from the men in the water, necessarily steaming into the gloom of the night before turning to make a fresh approach. Calling for volunteers, he sent another team onto the casing.

Putting people on the casing at sea in anything but the calmest conditions is inherently dangerous. The low freeboard, smooth deck and lack of guard rails meant that the prospect of ending up in the drink was an ever-present hazard. In open ocean, in the middle of the night, with a rising sea and rapidly deteriorating weather, *Farncomb* was operating independently and unsupported by any Allied forces. There was no prospect of outside assistance.

Once the CO brought the submarine back within striking range of those in the water, one of the boat's cooks leaped into the roiling seas, armed only with the heaving line tied around his waist. A senior sonarman clung to the side of the boat and helped him haul one of the recovered divers aboard. One of the Chief Petty Officers, a stalwart of the Secret Harbour Surf Life Saving Club back home, also swam out to his shipmates without hesitation.

Battling worsening conditions, the intensive recovery effort ran for more than an hour and a half, as those on the casing worked feverishly to hold their footing against continual assaults from the sea. Once those washed overboard were brought back alongside, it took herculean efforts to haul them up off the ballast tanks and onto the casing, then lower them to safety below. Through the persistent efforts of the entire Ship's Company, they finally located, reached and recovered all five of their shipmates.

I met *Farncomb* on arrival in Sattahip and briefed the CO on the parameters of the inquiry. My senior intelligence officer, who had an eye for detail and was a veteran of multiple inquiries, set up shop for us in the tiny, cramped ship's office and we started interviewing the key players to ascertain the facts and reconstruct the night. Speaking with them, the officers and sailors were variously nonchalant, matter-of-fact or downright shaken up in recounting their tales. Notwithstanding the passage of time – the submarine stayed at sea and on task for several weeks after the event – the experience made a deep impression on them all.

I would wager that most sailors have, at some stage, contemplated the lonely terror of finding themselves overboard and separated from their ship. Recalling the mounting seas and worsening weather as the only discernible features of the surrounding ocean, those washed overboard were under no illusions as to how perilous their situation was. Their confidence in their own abilities and innate trust in their Captain and shipmates was severely tested, particularly as the black unlit form of the submarine initially moved away from them, and the time adrift in the ocean stretched out. Ultimately, their faith and trust was vindicated.

Occurring at the front end of my posting as the Task Group Commander, the whole saga was a forceful reminder of the inherent risks our submarine crews face at sea and the gravity of my responsibilities when I ordered the boats out on exercises and operations.

Later that year, the Minister for Defence, Dr Brendan Nelson, took the time to write personally and individually to the Officers and Ship's Company. He acknowledged that, in the custom of their chosen 'Trade', the details of their work would be purposely obscured from public view. He expressed his appreciation and admiration for all they achieved during their five-month deployment, thanking them and their families for their efforts, sacrifices and contribution to the defence of the nation.

Unprecedented in my experience, it was a simple but meaningful gesture. Through my time in the Navy, I have observed that some politicians operate as the Minister *of* Defence, while others find a way to act as a Minister *for* Defence. Dr Nelson, who understood what submarines offered, was one of the latter.

The work at SUBOPS was great. Given responsibility as the Submarine Operating Authority (SUBOPAUTH), I approved the orders and allocation of waterspace for underwater operations in the Australian theatre, and for our boats deployed beyond. Much like air traffic control, water is precisely allocated in time and space to enable navigational safety, avoid collisions between submarines and, in the event of hostilities, prevent 'Blue on Blue' engagements. Running the broadcast was equally key, vetting the signal traffic to the submarines to make sure they have what they need but are not overloaded with communications. It was deliberate and dynamic work, requiring meticulous attention to detail. Our role in directing and supporting the submarines at sea was as close as you could get to the operating boats while working ashore. Supported by some great staff, I was entirely at home leading my team.

In August 2007, as part of my SUBOPS duties, I headed back to Pearl Harbor and represented the RAN at the Asia Pacific Submarine Conference (APSC). An unclassified annual forum promoting regional cooperation in submarine escape and rescue, the APSC was established by the USN in the wake of the *Kursk* disaster.

'We are our own guardians!' began the Commander of the US Pacific Fleet, Admiral Bob 'Rat' Willard, USN, launching into a heartfelt spiel on our collective responsibility as mariners to guard against and contend with misadventure on and below the high seas. Taken by his passion, I later asked him whether there was anything in particular behind his obvious conviction. Bob told me he was embarked in the carrier USS *Kitty Hawk* in March 1984, at the height of the Cold War, when she collided with the K-314 (an early Victor-class Russian submarine) in the Sea of Japan. Tasked with shadowing the US task group, the K-314 surfaced close ahead of the *Kitty Hawk* in the middle of the night. Unable to avoid collision, the carrier steamed over the submarine, driving her forward and rolling her onto her back. *Kitty Hawk* suffered only minor damage, but the submarine was desperately crippled and unable to dive or get underway. They almost certainly suffered severe casualties and probably fatalities. It was unimaginable that they were not at ongoing risk, including from the nuclear reactor and weapons onboard.

Bob also spoke to his experience flying over the ailing submarine the next morning, and the Russian Captain's staunch refusal to accept any offers of assistance from the USN. She was eventually recovered by a Soviet seagoing tug days later and dragged back to Vladivostok. His experiences as a Cold War warrior aside, Bob was adamant in his belief that we could do better with the fundamentally humanitarian task of submarine escape and rescue. I wholeheartedly agreed.

The conference was a great lead-in to Exercise Pacific Reach 2007, which the RAN hosted in Perth later that year. As the Australian Submarine Search and Rescue Authority, it was mine to lead. The exercise involved a wide array of ships, submarines and aircraft, as well as saturation diving teams and underwater medical specialists.

The Republic of Korea submarine ROKS *Lee Eok-Gi* made a 4,000 nautical miles passage to take part – a phenomenal journey for the little 1,200-tonne Chang Bogo-class boat. The other stand-out unit was the Japanese rescue ship, the JDS *Chihaya*. Replete with its own Deep Submergence Rescue Vessel (DSRV), launched through a moon pool in the centre of the ship, this modern 6,000 tonne masterpiece was the envy of every submarine operating nation in attendance and certainly outshone our Australian capabilities.

In all, nineteen navies participated or were represented, plus the NATO-sponsored 'International Submarine Escape and Rescue Liaison Office'. Over several weeks, we put the various units, systems and specialists through their paces in submarine abandonment, escape and rescue.[6] Notwithstanding the complexity of the at-sea operations,

---

6   Abandonment relates to a distressed submarine on the surface. Submarine escape relates to a distressed submarine on the bottom in water depths that permit escape through a hatch to the surface. This contrasts with rescue via a submersible that mates with the distressed submarine and carries survivors to the surface.

the real intricacy as Exercise Director came in the dynamics of trust among the various nations.

In a domain where stealth and secrecy are the stock in trade, submariners are renowned for the zealous protection of their capabilities. From an international relations perspective, the participants included historical and contemporary adversaries, such as the United States and Russia, China and Japan, India and Pakistan. These dynamics made the core objective – building trust and confidence across the navies – difficult, but not impossible. With a submarine in distress, in what would inevitably be a race against time, no one nation could be assured of having all the capability required in a given scenario. It was in everyone's interest that these navies shared the trust required to 'make the call' and the confidence that the call would be answered.

The counterintelligence threat that needed to be dealt with was real, especially with actual submarines in action. The Russian delegation had little to lose in this regard but were clearly cautious. They had reason to be wary. This was the first occasion their attendance had been sanctioned; the loss of the *Kursk* continued to evoke national shame and they had narrowly averted a disaster with their Priz-class rescue submarine, the *AS-28*, two years earlier. At a depth of 190 metres, she became entangled in undersea cables off the Kamchatka Peninsula. After three days stranded in the dark and freezing submarine, she was cut free by a British Remotely Operated Vehicle (ROV) and the seven crewed saved. The Russian approach at our exercise was to be present, but entirely mute. And it was messing with the vibe, so something had to be done.

'Good afternoon, Comrades!' I said, stepping onto their minibus at the end of Day Three. 'Today I am coming to Fremantle with you.'

With no Russian language skills to support my forward-leaning approach, it was an awkward trip. They had booked their accommodation in Fremantle when they landed in the country, presumably out of suspicion of being bugged. Inviting myself into their serviced apartment was even more ambitious, but I was resolute and pressed on. A hesitant offer of tea eventually turned to an offer of vodka, a bottle of Stolichnaya into several more.

Apparently language was less important than common experience as we yarned about submarines and submariners long into the night.

Emerging into the night somewhat worse for wear, I was down a pair of dolphins but up a Russian submarine CO's badge. The following morning, the Russians found their voice. It was one of the few occasions when my willingness to drink stupendous amounts of alcohol paid actual dividends.

The Chinese delegation from the People's Liberation Army (Navy) took a different approach. Their contribution of a navy scuba team, ever ready to dive on and survey our submarines, was a pointed choice. They were on the front foot from the get-go; so much so that one of my more creative staff cheekily assigned them all code names before morning tea on Day One. One Chinese lieutenant, a linguist supporting the Senior Captain, got extra attention.

'Shut the fuck up alert! Red Sparrow in the room and closing fast,' my guy would whisper into my ear with a mischievous grin on his head.

Of itself, the exercise was a great success, but for me and others it brought the parlous state of Australian submarine escape and rescue into stark relief. A year earlier, one of the cables securing our submarine rescue vehicle ASRV *Remora* to her mother ship had parted in heavy seas during a certification exercise off Rottnest Island in Western Australia. Two men were stranded at a depth of 140 metres for more than twelve hours before being rescued. *Remora* was not recovered for a further five months and never recommissioned, leaving the RAN without a local rescue service. While we had an agreement with the Royal Navy to call on their globally deployable rescue capability if required, this was thin comfort for a submarine service that had long been at the forefront of regional escape and rescue expertise and capability.

To make matters worse, while we had a purpose-built Submarine Escape Training Facility (SETF) at *Stirling*, the DMO contracts with industry to maintain it and support pressurised escape training were close to collapse. When I first did the training as a young submariner, we completed multiple ascents through the 22-metre vertical freshwater tank, including many wearing the distinctive, orange-hooded escape suits. Locking yourself into the exceedingly cramped single-man escape tower before it was deliberately and rapidly flooded to equalise the pressure and spring open the upper hatch called for a great deal of faith in the theory, systems and training. Racing up through the column of water as the pressurised air in your suit and your lungs vented beneath you in a whale-worthy display of expanding gas was a spine-tingling experience, culminating as you burst through the surface at the top of the tank.

Even at the relatively shallow depths of 'the Tank', failure to follow the training, such as by momentarily holding your breath during an ascent, could result in pulmonary barotrauma – commonly known as blowing your lungs. The instructors had our undivided attention. Providing the skill and confidence to enable exit from a stricken submarine down to a depth of 180 metres, this training was a quintessential element of qualification for all new submariners and currency for those already at sea.

But as our own $25 million facility lay idle, we spent the next three years flying trainees overseas to qualify with our allies in the Canadian Navy while the disputes were settled. Working with the vast array of other navies capabilities assembled on our shores for Pacific Reach, it was obvious that our own was seriously eroded and we had lost any regional pre-eminence in this domain.

Journal note, June 2007. *A boat at sea is worth two in dock.*

Coming off the back of Pacific Reach, HMAS *Rankin* was announced as the winner of the prized Gloucester Cup, awarded annually to the premier fleet unit across the whole RAN. From the mid-1980s until the early-2000s – a drought spanning nearly two decades – no submarine wore the highly coveted 'Gold Star'. Phenomenally, we now had a flurry of success, with a submarine winning the Cup three times in the past four years.

But the recent triumphs veiled a darker reality. These tactical victories by individual submarines were an aberration, rather than a barometer of the health of the Arm and the class. The Arm was being hollowed out, and the class laid up. When he lifted the Gloucester Cup, the CO of *Rankin* had more accumulated submarine seatime than all of his seaman officers combined – and he had spent eight years out of the Navy working in private enterprise! The recent successes were achieved with the newest submarines just out of build, but that honeymoon was over. Limping home from their final deployment to New Zealand with a rapidly failing battery, taking a short stop in Eden to de-ammunition, *Rankin* was delivered into the maws of the dockyard in Adelaide once more.

Down to just two working submarines in the Fleet again – *Collins*, which had been used as an alongside training boat for most of the year due to the lack of qualified submariners, and *Waller* – the remaining four hulls were in the yard at Adelaide. In February 2008, when the Fleet Commander turned to me looking for options to respond to the next constitutional crisis brewing in Fiji, his not unreasonable claim was, 'This is something we need to be able to do!' The dearth of available submarines was a grim reality.

While sea rides were rare and most of my days involved a commute to work in the concrete confines of the Headquarters, there was plenty of international travel with the SUBOPS gig. Visits to Yokosuka, home of the US Seventh Fleet in Japan, and out to Guam, Hawaii, and Washington, D.C., to engage with senior USN leadership were regular occurrences.

There was a peculiar dichotomy in the way we worked with our counterparts in the USN, an Allied but foreign navy, and with our own wider Australian Navy. The foreseeable differences, principally borne of either the different types of submarine we operated or the scale of our operations, were readily accommodated. The stranger fact was that a conversation with senior American submariners almost invariably kicked off a notch or two above the starting point when working within our own Navy and senior leadership. And it didn't matter whether there were strategic, operational or tactical matters on the table.

Critically, as submariners, they knew and understood the challenges presented and opportunities on offer without the need for explanation, or the call for justification that so often preceded any conversation at home. Equally, given the nature of submarine operations, they knew what to challenge us on and what really mattered when it came to putting forces to sea in the underwater domain. It was a no bullshit environment.

Having been on the receiving end of more than a few tactical lessons on the prowess of our submarines, the USN were keen to see their Allies prosper and help wherever they could. One of my early challenges was acting as the Theatre Anti-Submarine Warfare (ASW) Commander for Exercise Talisman Sabre off the east coast of Australia; and I was the first Australian officer assuming this command. With operational control of the assigned anti-submarine warfare forces, including US space-based assets, ships, aircraft and submarines, we were on a steep learning curve. To ensure our success, the US flew in a score of trained and experienced watchkeepers to support my staff. It was more evidence of the ever-expanding trust and collaboration across the two submarine forces and stood in stark contrast to our 'beyond arm's length' relationship with the submarine forces of most other navies.

Regrettably, our ability to contribute to our own defence and the strategic stability of the wider Asia-Pacific region was crashing. When the Commander of US Submarine Forces, Admiral Jay Donnelly, USN visited Australia at the back end of 2007, international alliances and China were at the top of his agenda. While the one or two submarines we could get to sea were doing good things, we were failing his benchmark of 'credible combat power continuously postured'. And a couple of things he said in conversation with our Admirals resonated with me. 'We recruit sailors, but retain families,' was one truism in particular. Speaking of his own Navy, but allowing the comparison to be drawn, Jay also noted that, 'Sailors love the work at sea, it's what they have to put up with ashore that sees them leave the navy.'

Spoken out loud, this seemed simple and common sense. With our fragile Arm still scattered across the country – our people jerked from one high priority billet to the next, and a widening gap of expectation and actual at-sea experience at all levels – it was uncommon wisdom for us. Masking the true state of the workforce, our submarines were increasingly crewed by 'operational reliefs' – officers and sailors posted ashore after their sea rotation but sent back to sea at short notice to fill a vacancy.

With no respite, little quality seatime and diminishing prospects of operational deployments, the total strength of the Arm declined to around 420 qualified submariners in 2008 – a 35 percent shortfall in requirements by the most generous estimate. At 433 athletes, we sent more people to the Olympic Games in Beijing that year! Worse still, while occasionally able to qualify a few new submariners out of the heavily throttled recruiting pipeline, we were losing experienced people at a greater rate. The overall proficiency in the Arm was dissolving through the deck plates.

Arguments about whether the submarines were alongside because of their poor material state or a lack of crews were by now inconsequential.

Trust across the DMO, ASC and Navy was practically non-existent. 'Own goals' – defects occurring on the boats while in refit – were so frequent that they led to suspicions of sabotage to deliberately keep submarines under ASC material control and attracting revenue. Chronic overruns in the duration of maintenance periods and shortcomings in their effectiveness were grinding the Submarine Arm into the dust.

Without the ability to proceed reliably and consistently to sea and operate its submarines, no defence force can generate and sustain a professional, high-quality submarine force. We weren't dealing with the occasional twenty-four hour delay in the life of a single submarine, but with rampant industrial disease. There was a common, not entirely paranoid, view that the sea was not the greatest threat, rather there were enemies much closer to home. The cumulative impacts of more than a decade of repeat offences were borne at inordinate cost to Navy's people and capability, measured in lost years of seagoing submarine service and operational effect. When my pleas to the Fleet Commander that he join the battle to get our submarines to sail were met with a lackadaisical 'Will the sun not shine?', I realised I was banging my head against the wrong brick wall.

Journal note, 2008. *Friday a very tough day.*

Throughout my time as Commander Submarine Task Group, I matched our exercise and operational commitments to the prevailing and forecast reality, which meant continually scaling back the submarine programs over time. The few submarines at sea did continue to do good work: *Collins* proved our new Dived Entry and Re-entry capability for Special Forces operations, and *Waller* gave us a thrill when she sank the Ex-USS *Fletcher*, a decommissioned Spruance-class destroyer. Proving her new combat system and the latest Mark 48 torpedo variant jointly developed with the USN, they broke the destroyer in half, sending her to the bottom within minutes.

Unfortunately, occasional highlights couldn't mask the lack of available and reliable support for all but the most rudimentary levels of training and unit readiness. By the middle of 2008, not only were we unable to respond to emergent tasking, but we were also unable to fulfil the few classified operations still on the schedule.

A tremendous effort and a lot of resources had been expended preparing one of our submarines for some particularly demanding and highly classified tasking within what was already a lengthy and complex deployment. Given certain strategic circumstances, there was a great deal to be gained. For those few senior ADF officers and others who knew of and understood it, this top-secret operation had an exceptionally strong profile. Expectations were commensurately high. However, in the weeks preceding the operation, I decided that it had to be cancelled. There was no single factor that undoubtedly or absolutely precluded the operation going ahead, but next to nothing was robust. With a fulsome appreciation of the strategic consequences of either a failed or successful mission, it was a simple but painful decision to take. *We are at the stops. Deal with that reality and do not carry the Squadron into the abyss.*

To judge myself compassionately, I made a courageous decision grounded in specialist knowledge and experience, and took the necessary action. To judge myself more harshly, I was paralysed by uncertainty, lacked aggression and determination, and denied the Navy and the Arm an opportunity to achieve a particular success. In the end, I trusted my instincts. Even in hindsight, the wisdom or otherwise of my decision is difficult to discern. Certainly, the capability slide was by now unstoppable. A year later, despite heroic efforts within the Squadron, there would be no dependably operational Australian submarines.

CHAPTER 21
IN THE STRATOSPHERE

Journal note, December 2008. *What's surprising? The politics. So nice, so nasty.*

Though I still thought of myself as a submariner first and foremost, there were only so many trade-specific roles for senior dolphin wearers; particularly those keen to remain focused on command and warfare rather than become embroiled in acquisition projects and the like. So, I considered it an immense privilege to be selected for a one-year posting as Chief of Staff to the Vice Chief of Defence Force (VCDF), running Lieutenant General David Hurley's office in the cauldron of high command in Canberra.

Day One of the handover from my predecessor, a particularly sharp Colonel who was not yet at the end of his tether but definitely holding on tight, was long and frenetic. Our uninterrupted view from the Vice Chief's office over the lake and across to the majestic Brindabellas lost some of its shine as the gravity of the terrorist attacks and bombings unfolding across Mumbai began to sink in. Still in Asia but closer to home, the intensity rose even further when we received news of a combat fatality in Afghanistan. A young officer with 4 RAR (Commando) was killed by an Improvised Explosive Device (IED) in Uruzgan Province.

It was a grim start to an astonishing and eye-opening year. Fourteen-hour days labouring to make the most of every precious minute for the General bought me a front row seat to the strategic theatre in a year dominated by the aftermath of the Global Financial Crisis and punctuated by immense challenges for the ADF. The Defence White Paper of May 2009 held much promise, but contending with the associated Strategic Reform Program while protecting operational performance at home and abroad seriously tested the senior leadership of Defence. The tremendous devastation of the Victorian bushfires, the worst the nation had ever seen; the challenge of illegal immigration ramping up, highlighted by the tragic explosion and fire aboard SIEV 36 off Ashmore Reef; plus the war in Iraq and Afghanistan all compounded the tension felt across the Force. Nothing stood still.

I saw something of this environment five years earlier. In 2004, I took up a role as the Maritime Operations lead within Strategic Operations Division (SOD). With domain expertise drawn from across the ADF, we served as the Chief of Defence Forces' strategic operations staff in Canberra. Working as the conduit between CDF and the Joint Operations Command (JOC), our role was to convert political direction and command intent into action – assigning forces and drafting the Warning Orders, Execution Orders and Rules of Engagement for every ADF operation large and small. The job had an interesting ring to it, but it was a long way from submarine command at sea. Immensely proud of my extensive sea service, I had diligently avoided postings to the 'head shed' in Canberra for the first twenty years of my career. Fresh from the thrill of seagoing command, the struggle to find meaning and connection in the role, let alone traverse the essentially foreign landscape of Russell Offices and the National Capital, became a daily reality.

Physically located several floors beneath the main Defence Signals Directorate building, the inner workings of SOD were heavily protected. Navigating myself to the desk was my first challenge each day. Running or riding the fifteen kilometres from our pretty home in the Canberra suburb of Curtin was the simple part. I then had to pass through a total of thirteen barriers, beginning with the armed guards at the front pass office and including fingerprint detectors and eye scanners, to arrive at my desk deep beneath ground level. It was like going to work with Maxwell Smart.

A year into the SOD job, Shaunaugh, Laura and I headed out of Canberra on a sunny Boxing Day in 2004 to join the in-laws for Christmas in the Southern Highlands. We had just dropped down onto the Federal Highway by Lake George when news of an earthquake and tsunami in the Indian Ocean came over the car radio.

'I knew I should have put a CD on,' said Shaunaugh, as I turned us around and headed for Russell.

The following weeks were packed with briefings and meetings, day and night, bringing together an Interdepartmental Task Force to shape and support the ADF relief effort. The earthquake, with its epicentre off the west coast of northern Sumatra, was one of the most powerful ever recorded. Inundating coastal areas of Indonesia, Thailand and India, the ensuing tsunami wreaked havoc on hundreds of thousands, but none suffered more than the inhabitants of Banda Aceh, who were still reeling from the aggressive Indonesian military campaign of 2003 to suppress the separatists of the Free Aceh Movement (GAM). That campaign resulted in acceptance of special autonomy under Indonesian rule for the indigenous people, but the turmoil and lingering instability added a difficult force protection dimension to the deployment of Australian troops onto foreign soil to support the relief effort.

Sailing from Sydney on New Year's Eve, the amphibious transport ship HMAS *Kanimbla* deployed as the linchpin of the operation, embarking two Sea King helicopters from 817 Squadron, the bulk of the medical and engineering assets and many of the 900 ADF personnel involved. Having played a central role in the strategic planning and execution of the operations, I shared in the widely felt sense of achievement when *Kanimbla* berthed in Singapore in late March, marking the end of a highly effective three-month long operation.

Kanimbla had been alongside for just two days when a second earthquake struck Sumatra. In proposing the ship for immediate redeployment for Operation Sumatra Assist II, I wondered if we were pushing them, and our luck, just a little too hard. While I raised this as a concern, I didn't press it home with anyone. It was more instinct than calculation, and we were collectively flush with the success of the earlier operation.

Regrettably, Sumatra Assist II resulted in a tragedy for the ADF when one of the helicopters crashed on landing at Nias, killing nine. Not for the first or last time, I pondered just how far back, and how far up the line, culpability should run. The Board of Inquiry found the accident was caused by a failure of the flight control system, the result of non-compliant onboard maintenance two months earlier. But it also pointed to a Squadron culture forged over the preceding years within the high operational tempo that had 'resulted from strategic and government tasking.'[7] Since that time, I have carried a share of the weight for those lives.

Journal note, February 2009. *The US Alliance is not a purpose.*

In 2009, with our commitment in Iraq winding down towards the cessation of Operation Catalyst mid-year, our commitment in Afghanistan was escalating once again. By the time Prime Minister Kevin Rudd announced in April that Australia would increase its troop commitment in Afghanistan from around 1,100 to over 1,500 personnel, I'd had ample opportunity to absorb the strategic deliberations that led to that decision. There was an obvious near-term focus on support to the upcoming Afghan presidential elections in a deteriorating security environment, although the wider stated objective was to lift our training of the Afghan National Army, enabling them to take responsibility for security in Uruzgan Province and pointing to an eventual drawdown of our presence.

Though I spent limited time on the ground, as an Afghanistan veteran I had some personal experience of the conflict, which had seen another three Australian combat fatalities in recent months. I was readily convinced that freedom from oppression for the Afghan people and freedom from the threat of fundamentalist terrorism for Australians were worth fighting for, and that Afghanistan might be the place to do that. I was heartily in favour of an Alliance strengthened through pursuit of coincidental ideals and security from common threats, and was even willing to accept that the world was complex and there was no singular answer for the question of 'why be in Afghanistan?'

What I personally tussled with throughout the year was the obfuscation of purpose. Over time, I heard more than enough of the hollow political reasoning from the hardline strategists that allowed 'the Alliance' to assume primacy as the justification for our commitment. There was no doubt that paying homage to the US Alliance brought forward a satisfying sense of realpolitik, but it was perverse reasoning. Critical to our national security framework, our deep and longstanding alliance with the US was far more than an insurance policy. However, it did not constitute an inherent purpose in and of itself. If an endeavour is

---

7   Royal Australian Navy. *Nias Island Seaking Accident Board of Inquiry Report, Executive Summary*, 2007, Australia. Accessed 31 Aug. 2021

worth the lives of Australian servicemen and women, then they should be committed to the full extent of their capability, with the weight of the nation behind them. If it is not, then perhaps they should not be committed at all.

Working close by Angus Houston and David Hurley as they navigated their responsibilities and grappled with these issues, I was in awe of their humble approach to service. I saw Houston strive day by day, and long into most nights, to 'help the politicians make the right decisions' while he avidly championed his ADF. I saw Hurley deliberately placing his values alongside the big decisions, while converting his emotion and passion to resolution and action. It was heartening to observe first-hand the sagacious influence they exercised across Defence and into government, ever watchful of honouring the trust and respect of senior ministers and junior troops alike. Together, they opened my eyes to new dimensions of capacity to accept and discharge responsibility and new standards of loyalty and devotion to duty. It was inspirational and highly personable leadership at its best, and I was willingly led.

Journal note, 2009. *What is most important? My family.*

Given that the posting into the VCDF office in Canberra was for only one year, and I had no idea of what might follow, we decided to keep the family in Sydney. We knew it would mean lots of separation through yet another year, but mostly in shorter, week-size bites. The decision also kept Shaunaugh in her job at North Shore Private Hospital and allowed Laura to pursue her degree at Sydney University. Navy helped the decision along by providing me with an apartment in Barton. It meant working long days through the week, and a four-hour commute up and down the highway every Friday and Sunday night.

The Friday night drive was a bastard. Straining against the headlights of oncoming trucks and cars, drained and fighting fatigue, at least I was heading home. Weekends were usually full but included an obligatory Saturday afternoon nap to keep me level and a long Sunday run to spend time outdoors. The Sunday night drive was another bastard. Drive, work, drive, relax, repeat.

The commute afforded plenty of time to count the cost of separation and dislocation from the girls and the wider family. When my Uncle John passed away that year, I was unable to get back to Sydney for his funeral. On the road home that Friday night, I drafted a letter in my mind to Aunty Elv, explaining what kept me away. Service to a General fighting a war for peace in Afghanistan and a war for resources in Australia was my excuse, which I felt John would have understood.

I also tried to articulate what he meant to me. John was a fellow serviceman, also following in my grandad's footsteps, and growing up I borrowed heavily from his mischievous spirit and sense of humour. With metaphoric pen in hand, I found I was drawing mostly on the impressions of my youth. In fact, I had seen little of John for decades. We were close when I was young, but with my absences at sea and at war over the years, he was lost to me long before his death.

The threads tethering me to my close-knit family also slackened over the years. My parents, siblings and their families remained tightly bound, and they joked that the 'Scott Family radar' alerted them to each other's presence and movements as they jostled about the suburbs of Sydney. Though always welcomed, I was rarely on the screen. The lack of dependable interaction and recent shared experience loosened bindings, as did the growing catalogue of my own adventures and misadventures that couldn't be shared or I felt wouldn't be understood. Year on year, I continued to serve in the name of my family and my country; year on year, the fabric of my wider family life continued to wear thin. Some of it was worn through.

Shaunaugh, Laura and I were travelling okay as a family, regaining some connection during my time in Sydney over the previous two years. In part, this was because the extent of my responsibilities at SUBOPS, and now with the Vice Chief, meant there was simply no time in a day or a week for me to drink, and therefore no prospect of getting wrecked. While I welcomed the general sobriety, the current pattern of life was relentless and unsustainable, and the future uncertain. All three of us carried some emotional scars and the underlying fragility became apparent at odd times.

Travelling to the office in Canberra one morning, I took a different route from my apartment and drove past St Clare's College, a Catholic girls' school in Griffith. When we moved to Canberra together back in 2004, I went to some lengths to select what I thought would be the best school for Laura, knowing what a wrench it was moving away from her friends in Perth. I was adamant this was the place for her. It wasn't, and she was miserable there for two years.

Coming home one day just before at Christmas, with news of a promotion and crash posting, I had asked, 'Anyone want to move out of Canberra next week?'

'Yes, please!' was Laura's immediate response.

'Wanna know where we're headed?'

'Nup, don't care!' came just as quick.

The memories washed over me as I passed the school on this morning's commute. My heart sank as I confronted the possibly irrational but unshakeable belief that I had let Laura down and caused her needless pain. I pulled over to the side of the road in time to open the car door and vomit. I vowed to limit the impacts of my service on my family into the future.

'Sir, the Chief would like to see you,' reported our Major, as he hung up the phone.

'CDF?'

'No, Sir. Your Chief. The Chief of Navy.'

In a year of working up the hall, I had seen plenty of Vice Admiral Russ Crane, RAN and was singularly impressed by his leadership at the helm of our Service, but he hadn't had any cause to call me to his office. Perhaps I had unwittingly transgressed some lore and put my career in jeopardy. Perhaps, having been promoted in rank beyond submarine command, my requests for command of a senior warship were about to be answered.

'Scotty, when the signal is released this afternoon, your name will be on it. I want you to command the Surface Task Group. And I need you to bring anti-submarine warfare out of the dark ages for these guys,' he stated.

So, not a single ship command, but command of the task group and the Fleet Battle Staff. When I shared the news with Air Chief Marshal Houston and General Hurley, Angus drew breath and said, 'Now that's a statement!'

As a helicopter pilot who made it to the top of the pile in the fast-jet jungle of Air Force, he understood the tribal implications of a clearance diver appointing a submariner in command of entire task groups of surface ships – the sacred domain of surface warfare officers. I was a little surprised myself. Though ancient history now, I was conscious I had never achieved a bridge watchkeeping certificate on a warship, let alone commanded one at sea. I was also ecstatic … though not everyone in Navy would be.

Sharing the news with family, my father-in-law, Kevin, reasonably asked, 'What do you know about surface ships anyway?'

'Well, I know how to sink them. That's gotta help when you're trying to keep them afloat!'

CHAPTER 22
AMONG THE FLEET

In 2010, I spent the year in my pyjamas. Striking a deal with the Deputy Chief of Navy, I forewent attendance on the senior staff course in Canberra in lieu of a year at home in Sydney reading for a Master's degree in Strategy through correspondence. He listened when I told him I needed a circuit breaker if I was going to keep both my family and my career, and that another year 'married-separated' wouldn't cut it. It became a running joke in the family that I was at my desk in PJs when the girls left in the morning for work and uni, and still there when they returned home each evening.

By year's end, I was well and truly primed to get underway again and, in November 2010, marched into Fleet Headquarters in Sydney with my packed seabag. I was there to command the Surface Task Group and lead the Fleet Battle Staff – our afloat Headquarters for maritime operations, joint operations with the other services, and combined operations with other nations.

'Jeez, mate, timing is everything,' said my envious predecessor as he handed over.

We had just taken a briefing on the North Korean artillery bombardment of the South Korean island of Yeonpyeong, near the disputed Northern Limit Line in the Yellow Sea, and subsequent retaliatory fire from the Republic of Korea forces. Causing widespread damage and numerous fatalities on Yeonpyeong, the bombardment triggered a serious escalation of tensions on the peninsula, with the carrier USS *George Washington* sailing in support of the South Koreans the following day.

There was immediate speculation about the deployment of an Australian naval task group. Tensions continued to rise over the next several months, peaking with the sinking of the ROKS *Cheonan*, a 1,200-tonne Pohang-class coastal defence corvette, by a North Korean submarine in the same disputed region. The *Cheonan* was literally ripped in two by the torpedo attack, killing forty-six sailors, which was nearly half the crew. Incredibly, the South Koreans kept their cool in the midst of this grievous aggression, resisting the temptation to take retaliatory strikes against the recently nuclear armed North.

It's a function of life in uniform that you need to be continually prepared to deploy, particularly in a role such as this one. Unavoidably there are some false starts, but just thinking you are off to war is both invigorating and emotionally taxing.

Although nothing eventuated for us out of the Korean conflict, it was not long after joining the Headquarters that I deployed – but not overseas and not even to sea. A Joint Task Force was established on New Year's Day 2011 to respond to the deadly floods ravaging South East Queensland. As the weight of ADF assets rapidly escalated over the coming week, I flew to Brisbane with a small staff to lead the planning for the maritime recovery effort.

With the release from the Wivenhoe Dam a day earlier, the Brisbane River was swollen and angry, flowing relentlessly downstream and out into Moreton Bay. Flying low over the river in an SK-50 Sea King, much of the destruction was evident, with yachts cast adrift, ferry wharves monstered into masses of twisted steel and flotsam piled high against the footings of the numerous bridges spanning the river. A great deal more damage was concealed beneath the dirt brown mask spreading out from the banks into the valley towns and city suburbs.

By mid-January, the Navy commitment and presence grew substantially. Flying in, at times, atrocious weather conditions, our helicopters conducted search and rescue, and aerial survey, as well as taking Prime Minister Julia Gillard over and into the flooded areas. Bull sharks were sighted miles upstream, so the Navy Clearance Diving Team took the opportunity to test their new shark repellent devices as they assessed underwater hazards and the structural integrity of the bridges. In time, three Navy hydrographic ships arrived to survey the river and cleared it for commercial traffic while the minehunter HMAS *Huon* scanned Moreton Bay to clear the shipping channels and anchorages of submerged debris.

The number of ADF personnel deployed to the area eventually rose to around 1,600, making it the largest disaster relief deployment since Cyclone Tracy in 1974. I watched on as sailors pitched in with the locals of the Lockyer Valley, clearing away the ruined belongings and once loved possessions that were now so much dross and debris. It was service, up close and personal, and it was a privilege to be a part of it.

For the first time in a couple of years, I was scheduled be at sea for several weeks rather than one or two days. Stepping off the baking tarmac at RAAF Base *Darwin*, I climbed in through the rear loading door of the C-2A Greyhound, also known as the 'COD'. In company with eight of my Fleet Battle Staff officers and sailors, I donned a helmet and ear protectors and strapped in for the ride out to the USS *George Washington*. GW, as she is known, was deployed out of Japan for Exercise Talisman Sabre 2011 and operating with her Carrier Battle Group in the Arafura Sea. After a noisy ninety-minute flight amid the roar and rumble of the twin engines, we were all pretty damned excited with the prospect of our first carrier deck landing.

With a massive jolt and breath-busting wrench, the wheels hit the deck, the arrestor wires took hold, the throttles were thrown down and the COD abruptly stopped in her tracks. As the rear door opened to deposit her human cargo, grand expectations were met as we emerged onto a movie set of fighter jets, helicopters and flight deck crew in their primary-coloured jackets and helmets. Steam rose from the catapult rails as the wind pushed across the deck, snapping at our legs. Heads low, we scurried for the closest bulkhead door on the island-like superstructure.

Warmly met by the Commodore of Destroyer Squadron 15 (COMDESRON 15) – a permanently deployed squadron of Arleigh Burke-class destroyers stationed in Japan and part of the US Seventh Fleet – Captain John Schultz, USN was embarked in GW as the Sea Combat Commander. My staff and I were embarked to work mostly with his team, commanding the tasking and movements of the Squadron destroyers and other assets involved in the exercise and across the region beyond.

John, an anti-submarine warfare specialist throughout his career, was exceedingly generous with his time. He had a few years on me but displayed a boyish delight in what he did and the way he saw things. We first met months earlier in 'the Cave', the DESRON 15 Headquarters ashore in Yokosuka. Originally part of the labyrinthine network of tunnels dug into the hillside during the Second World War to fortify the Imperial Japanese Navy arsenal, their bunker was one of the few sections still in use.

John was acutely aware of the growing threat posed to freedom of navigation and to US naval dominance in the Pacific by the increasingly capable submarines of several regional navies, but none more so than the PLA(N). By 2011, the Chinese militarisation of the South China Sea was well underway as they put enormous energy into conjuring legitimacy around their 'nine-dash line', an artefact falsely implying Chinese sovereignty over large swathes of the region.[8] As such, anti-submarine warfare in the Western Pacific, and the Allied ability to 'hold at risk' every foreign submarine at sea, was foremost in his mind.

It took a few days to find our way into the organisation onboard, particularly as our presence was shining a light on some dysfunction between the embarked Commander Task Force (CTF) 70 staff and the DESRON 15 staff. CTF 70 deliberately focused on honouring their Talisman Sabre exercise commitments, while DESRON 15 were flat out working the ships here with the carrier, as well as the destroyers deployed on actual operations elsewhere in the Western Pacific. I spent a little time with the Chief of Staff to CTF 70 to iron things out on my side. As a fellow dolphin wearer, we had more in common than I realised.

'The submariners think I'm a traitor, the surface guys and aviators think I'm an imposter,' he confided. I knew exactly what he meant.

A day off the GW gave me a look at things from a different perspective. Embarking in one of the Seahawks, I transferred across to USS *Cowpens*, the Ticonderoga-class cruiser providing the Carrier Battle Group with a great deal of their reach and firepower, and then to HMAS *Darwin*. The CO and the Ship's Warrant Officer, another submariner, welcomed me aboard. *Darwin* was in a comfortable slot, embedded with the carrier for several months now, although some of the crew felt the 'sameness' of life aboard a frigate where they weren't the centre of the naval universe. Operating seamlessly with the US ships and aircraft, and adding strength to force, it was 'the Alliance' at work.

Strapped back into the COD at the end of our Talisman Sabre tour, the catapult fired shoving us into our seats like astronauts on take-off.

---

8   China's claim to the 'nine-dash line' was invalidated by the Permanent Court of Arbitration in the Hague on July 12, 2016.

My seabag had some extra weight, courtesy of a departure gift from John. An ashtray made from the cut-down casing of a 5-inch shell fired by one of his destroyers, the USS *Fitzgerald*, it was a perfect memento of the immense power of a Carrier Battle Group patrolling the Indo-Pacific. Although unintended, it was also a reminder of their potential vulnerability and vincibility.

Journal note, 2013. *More accepting, more effective, less anxious.*

It was over these years that I started to go well and truly 'off-piste' with my running. With the encouragement of my old kindergarten mate, Tom Silk, I ran my first trail ultra-marathon, the renowned 'Six Foot Track', in 2005. Set over 45 kilometres between the Explorers Tree in Katoomba and the Jenolan Caves, the whole course is only three kilometres longer than a classic road marathon, but the terrain makes all the difference. Hikers typically traipse the track over three days. The race, including river crossings, tortuous climbs and hair-raising descents, was tackled over a matter of hours.

Lulled into a false sense of security by the knowledge that Tom would occasionally run the 'Twelve Foot Track' – there and back – for fun, I had no idea what I was getting myself into. Trail novice that I was, I ran the whole thing in a flimsy pair of road racing flats. By the end of the race, my feet and legs were so battered by the loose and jagged rocks and steep descents that it took me years to summon up the courage to attempt another, but a spark had been lit and smouldered away.

I was never a superior athlete. Winning the school cross-country championship in the final year of high school was a personal triumph, crossing the line ahead of some truly talented runners. They were far better than me on any given day, and my only advantage was they didn't see me as genuine competition. In the months beforehand, I ran the race course scores of times, rehearsing my cunning plan. Overtly working hard to take the front early on race day, I deliberately used bends on the bush track sections to push beyond myself and lengthen a short lead. It was a challenge run entirely in my own head, and it was a massive punish. But when we came into the open with under a kilometre to run, I was too far ahead for them to reel me back.

The day stuck in my mind as a time when I took on a challenge that stretched beyond my own belief in what I could do, then worked my butt off to see it through. It was an approach that held me in good stead throughout my submarine career, especially when I doubted my ability for the roles ahead.

In the years after my return from Iraq, I was increasingly attracted to spending time in the bush. It brought both challenge and serenity, particularly up in the Blue Mountains outside Sydney. It carried something of the majesty of being at sea yet was more readily accessible. Through 2010 and 2011, I built up my experience running and racing on the trails, targeting my first 100-kilometre ultra-marathon in 2012. Though daunting, I found encouragement and inspiration during a couple of days spent as support crew for Tom when he ran the 240-kilometre Coast to Kosciusko ultra. Kicking off in Eden on the New South Wales far south coast and threading inland to summit Australia's highest peak, he was on his feet from sunrise to sunset, then sunrise and sunset again. It was a dramatic lesson in what a human can do with a little belief and a lot of determination.

Beyond the simple joy of movement, the strict and demanding training regime of the 'ultras' carried a couple of benefits. The daily workouts and occasional social engagement with like-minded folk on long Sunday runs were great for my general mental health. Importantly, running also gave me a socially acceptable rationale to avoid drinking completely. 'A beer? No thanks, mate, I'm in training for an ultra-marathon.'

Despite being off the grog, across 2011 and 2012 it was increasingly apparent – to me and those closest to me – that my life was more difficult than it had to be. While I was highly functional and capable of some exceptional professional performance, I suffered continually from excessive and unnecessary anxiety. My effectiveness at work was enabled and buttressed by a massive internal overload.

I prized my identity as a naval officer, particularly as a submariner and seagoing Captain, immensely. Over many years, my professional life demanded detailed preparation and precise execution, where the consequences of error or failure could be the loss of billion-dollar platforms and loss of life. As my responsibilities grew, I was increasingly consumed by my accountability for the safety and welfare of others. Worst-case scenario planning was part of my daily life, and I knew what a really bad day in uniform looked like. The associated stress devolved into a damaging pattern of habitual worry and rumination. Running helped short-circuit this to a degree, but an accepted state of worrying over everything had become my comfort zone – a coping mechanism gone wrong.

Linking my continual anxiety to the stressful demands of the job and the impacts of multiple service-related traumas at sea and in theatre ashore, I was more willing than in previous years to use the support offered within the Navy system. With selection for command appointments and promotion increasingly competitive, being treated for anxiety wouldn't add any shine to my resume. But I knew I needed help to continue moving forward without imploding. With a great deal of professional success behind me already, I decided 'protecting' my career was less important than preserving my mental health to avoid spiralling back into depression.

However, I was not drawing any attention to myself as I made my way to the office of the resident psychologist at Garden Island in Sydney. He promptly identified my perfectionist tendencies, helping me see and understand that while such a trait might appear praiseworthy, it was not necessarily health inducing. Several months of cognitive behavioural therapy taught me to identify and name my thoughts, emotions and related behaviours. It did nothing to reduce the work-related stress, but dramatically reduced my overall anxiety levels and gave me the confidence to keep leaning into my career.

Selected for promotion to Commodore in mid-2013, I decided to return to therapy to consolidate our previous work and prepare for the shift to 'One Star' performance. We continued our campaign against perfectionism, aiming to achieve the 'right' standard. It became clear that most often the first conversation I had with myself, on just about any subject, came from a position of doubt and negativity. Although this was a totally unfounded premise, I didn't always get to the less judgemental, more accepting and creative one-on-one chat that allowed a positive vision to emerge. My psychologist helped me see that it was in this second conversation where the true value and opportunity resided.

Journal note, February 2012. *You can make a real difference here.*
Do what you do – hour by hour, day by day.

Selected in advance as the inaugural Commander, my 'other' job over the previous six months involved designing and creating the Australian Maritime Warfare Centre (AMWC). The ambition was to create a single, coherent organisation responsible for maritime warfare development and optimise the warfighting effectiveness of the Fleet. It was a powerful mandate.

Thankfully, the main component parts already existed. The functions of writing warfare policy, proving tactical doctrine, deploying an expanding array of targets, analysing weapon system performance and managing signature ranges were all happening somewhere in Fleet, but the effort was disparate and disjointed. I needed to concentrate and co-locate those who could contribute. There was no shortage of expertise available, with discrete teams of warriors, scientists, technicians and analysts – and their respective histories – offering the makings of a magnificent opportunity. They were also the principal source of my main challenge – achieving cultural alignment.

"We're ready to go, Sir."

"Thanks, Scotty, lead on," said the Fleet Commander, who had just arrived to officiate at our little ceremony to open the AMWC.

Setting up shop in one of the larger heritage-listed buildings on Garden Island, for once in my life I had an office above ground, replete with windows and a view down the length of Sydney Harbour. Having seen active service as a Lieutenant and the Air Intercept Control officer in HMAS *Sydney* during the first Gulf War, my immediate boss had a straightforward vision and was committed to instilling the highest professional standards and a true warfighting culture within the Fleet. Given that the AMWC was a key pillar in that ambition, I was all for it.

Unfortunately, there was a dichotomy between the warfare standards we wanted to achieve and the material and personnel state of the Fleet. The Fleet was in a deep hole, and the widening gaps in the Defence budget only exacerbated the situation. A high-level review into the material state of the Fleet – instigated after Navy failed to respond to government direction in the wake of Cyclone Yasi, with all three amphibious ships in an unseaworthy state – was released in mid-2011. The situation was symptomatic of the internal collapse of the maritime engineering workforce across Navy and the DMO, and a prevailing culture that discouraged forthright reporting and action in the face of sour realities.

Recruitment and retention were headed in the right direction, but they came from a low base and there was a massive imbalance between the trained and untrained force. A decade of continuous single-ship deployments conducting counter-terrorism and counter-piracy operations had achieved some distinct successes in the distant Middle East. However, they did nothing for our ability to concentrate our forces and operate in strength against an adversary at sea, which was what we were now asking of the Fleet.

Despite the challenges, we had some wins along the way. The prospect of writing doctrine hadn't thrilled me through much of my earlier naval career, which is just as well as I probably wasn't equipped to do it then anyway. But the time had come for that to change. The lack of a coherent approach to deal with the growing submarine threat in the region was the gaping hole in our doctrinal guidance, so we set about creating a bespoke 'Australian ASW Concept for Operations'.

One of the stalwarts of the Fleet Battle Staff, who I brought across to the AMWC, broke the back of this work. Leaning heavily on his former Royal Navy experience and the US Navy approach to undersea warfare, we developed a concept that took a tiered approach, focusing on defeating the adversary submarine mission at every stage, and an integrated structure built on theatre, force and local ASW capabilities. Drawing extensively on my own experiences, it was intellectual work grounded in necessity and resulted in a critical piece of doctrine that stood to shape our Fleet's ability to combat submarines – and survive at sea – far into the future.

Related to this work was the introduction of Complex Group Warfare events. Deliberately driven by real world intelligence and operational analysis, these at-sea exercises drew on a multitude of specialist skills while focusing on a particular warfare domain, such as countering an intruder submarine. The scenario-based events ran over multiple days, rather than a few hours, and helped lift performance beyond the heavily serialised programs of staged procedural exercises that had long characterised the Fleet's activity at sea.

HMAS *Perth*, recently out of a major combat and weapons system upgrade, was one of the ships that got plenty of attention and support from our target and weapon analysis specialists. I joined her off the NSW coast to witness test firings of her evolved Sea Sparrow missiles, designed to defend the ship against incoming missiles. Stationed in the crowded ops room as the missiles streaked from the waist of the ship to track and destroy incoming targets, I had a line-of-sight view of the beaming CO. He was even happier when the ship deployed to the US missile range at Point Mugu in California to prove her new Block II Harpoon missiles. Classically designed as anti-ship weapons, a series of successful firings hit their marks, proving the RAN's newfound ability to attack targets ashore at long range.

After nearly a decade serving in mostly Joint and Fleet jobs, amassing a wealth of professional experience and a profound appreciation for much of what goes on in the wider Defence Force, I yearned to get back to the boats. It was where I belonged, and where I was most needed.

CHAPTER 23
CAPABILITY REINCARNATED

Journal note, 25 March 2013. *It's where your little black heart belongs!*
– Shaunaugh

When I got the call from the Chief to say that I would be promoted to Commodore and posted as Director General Submarines I was both delighted and disconcerted. My little black heart did belong to and with the submariners. To take up responsibility for strategic leadership of the Arm as the senior submariner within Navy Headquarters and assume the mantle as the professional head of the Submarine Arm was more than I had dared to dream for during much of my career. However, over the past decade, most of my service had been in roles not directly associated with the Submarine Arm. While I maintained a listening watch on 'all things boats' throughout, I would be returning to the submarine fray with a relatively fresh set of eyes. Unfortunately, what I could see from the outside had little appeal and I had some deep reservations about what could be achieved.

Since the early 2000s, the Submarine Arm had been dragged to its knees and repeatedly kicked in the guts. Now the bitter taste of my experiences with industry and DMO during the years I was in command was quick to lace my tongue. The successive cancellation of top-secret operations while I was in command of the Submarine Task Group still galled me. For the past five years, four of the six submarines had been locked away in dockyards, more liability than capability.

As I saw it, ASC still persisted with its self-imposed organisational identity crisis. They comprehensively failed to make the transition from submarine builder to submarine maintainer and were quite possibly close to insolvency. Since 2008, sustainment of the Collins-class had been under intense ministerial scrutiny as a 'project of concern' and supporting companies, like Raytheon and Thales, desperately ducked and weaved to avoid getting caught in the crossfire.

The presiding DMO reminded me of the caricature Fat Controller, helplessly watching the wreck of an entire train set. Prime Minister Kevin Rudd's White Paper commitment of 2009 – to double the size of the submarine fleet – had amounted to precisely nothing, and punting the submarines had lost none of its sporting appeal for politicians and journalists alike.

One of the early outcomes of a review into the collapse of the Australian submarine capability – conducted by British engineer John Coles in 2011 – was the establishment of a 'Submarine Enterprise' across Navy, the DMO and industry, principally ASC. Looking to enable the submarine fleet over the next fifteen years of service life, Coles established international benchmarks of effectiveness and efficiency for sustainment of a modern submarine capability – how many submarines does a navy get at sea and for how much? Drawing a line under our collective performance, he showed that we had been achieving less than half the average availability of other nations' submarine programs at much more than twice the benchmark cost. No-one could hide from this.

'Scotty, it's shifting! Trust me, I'm a submariner!' was Captain Matt Buckley's reassuring claim, and paired disclaimer, about Navy's newly invigorated relationships with submarine industry and with the DMO. Matt was already in place in Canberra and would be my Director in the Submarines Branch. I trusted his judgement and insight, and wanted to understand how far forward things had moved, if at all.

With a shared view on our respective roles across each organisation, it appeared there was emerging clarity around the overall purpose of the Submarine Enterprise, and it related to getting submarines safely and reliably to sea. Navy adopted Coles' benchmark 'submarine days and dollars' as their requirement, and collectively the Enterprise had set a series of targets to achieve over the next several years. Matt assured me that we had indeed hit the nadir and were on our way back up together. I would need to see it to believe it.

Despite the promise on the industrial front, I gave long and serious thought to resigning my commission and stepping away from Navy at this time. Even from the sidelines, I could see that the state of the submarine workforce was parlous. Lack of boats and workforce shortfalls had been chronic problems throughout my career, but the situation was extreme. There were just on five hundred qualified submariners across the entire RAN. Within that number, there were discrete, highly specialised streams of warfare, electrical, engineering and intelligence officers, marine and electronic technicians, sonar and electronic warfare analysts, communicators, linguists, cooks, stewards and medics. The Arm was so weak that most of the twelve specialist submarine categories fit our human resources criteria for 'critical' or 'perilous.'

While the total had increased marginally since I was in SUBOPS five years prior, most submariners desperately lacked experience for want of seagoing submarines. Many were exhausted after years of trying to hold together a once proud and capable Squadron and project some semblance of a naval force. With resignations at an all-time high, we were losing more officers and sailors than we could qualify. Our total numbers had shrunk over the previous year, at a time when we desperately needed to grow. Largely because of the lack of seagoing submarines, morale was shot and the Arm accelerated into a downward spiral.

Things were grim and the emerging demands were unlike any we had previously experienced. With a worsening geostrategic situation, the government was shaping up to make some big decisions about the next class and an expanded fleet of submarines. This would go nowhere if we couldn't demonstrate vastly improved performance with the Collins-class boats. Scrutiny on the workforce issues was sporadic, but as the platform availability began to rise, it was obvious that our shredded workforce would find itself in the headlights. Submarines do not win wars without submariners, and Navy would not be able to deflect the criticism for failing to generate the submariners it needed.

What gave me most pause was not the sorry state of affairs, but the fact that I couldn't for the life of me envisage a way forward. How could I possibly take on this responsibility when I had no idea how I would make a difference? Still, as David Petraeus told me in Iraq, 'hard is not hopeless!' I slowly built the courage to accept that I might fail, that I might well be the man who leads the Submarine Arm during the years it rusts away and dissolves into the sea. Accepting that possibility, and fully suspecting that no-one else had the answers either, I decided to head for Canberra once more. I would find a way.

Journal note, 19 September 2013. *ASC are talking to Navy's targets!*

During my first hectic months in the job, I spent most of my time on the road and in the air. I needed to engage with the Squadron Headquarters in Perth, and the yards in both South and Western Australia. In quick succession I sighted, if not climbed aboard, our LR5 Deep Submergence Rescue Vehicle (DSRV) and each of our six submarines, which were variously in maintenance in Adelaide or Perth or deployed at sea. A dynamic start to building my appreciation of the strategic context, it was illustrative of what it took to touch the key elements of our submarine capability.

Early connection with the USN, our closest ally, was a must. Touching down in the States, I discovered there had been a mass shooting at the Washington Navy Yards that morning with twelve fatalities. The Yards, home to their Naval Sea Systems Command, was one of my priority destinations. Notwithstanding that all the Australian exchange officers working there were safe, I had enough friends and colleagues working in the Yards that the assault felt personal.

While the travel never really let up, life folded into interminable rounds of committee meetings, cabinet submissions and briefings to ministers and prime ministers. At one of the earlier Submarine Board meetings, I realised the ASC executives were genuinely speaking to and working toward the jointly set submarine availability targets, and it struck me forcefully that they did indeed understand the requirement. They acknowledged that we were falling short and that something had to be done about it. It was a level of responsiveness I had not previously encountered.

Working in our favour was the unanimous commitment to achieving benchmark performance and beyond, with a raft of metrics measuring our progress. For its part, Navy adopted a set of requirements stated so plainly that they could not be misunderstood or misconstrued: at all times, two submarines must be deployable from four submarines available to the Fleet Commander, with two remaining submarines in long-term maintenance and upgrade.

The introduction of a '10+2' Usage and Upkeep Cycle was a fundamental change. It involved a ten-year schedule of operations and maintenance for each submarine, followed by a complete refit during a two-year Full-Cycle Docking. The principle of 'single-stream' Full-Cycle Dockings, with one submarine delivered to the yard at the end of its ten-year schedule just as its predecessor emerged from refit, was key. While it would take several years to grow into the new cycle, in time it would generate a stable, enduring and consistent program for both Navy and the industrial base, allowing us to shape policy and direct resource to progressively achieve greater availability, reliability, capability and deployability. Sticking to the plan would be the tough bit.

Beyond these constructive developments, there had been more profound changes over the past decade that impacted my role as Director General Submarines. Our Defence Force had changed, principally through action in Iraq, the Persian Gulf and Afghanistan. Our nation had changed, with the contrasting impacts of a global financial crisis and a resources boom. Most significantly, our place in the world had changed, with substantial shifts in the national power base of our allies, our neighbours and potential adversaries. These shifts made the capabilities of our submarines even more relevant and their raison d'être all the more apparent, to me at least, but not to everyone.

Early in my tenure, the CEO of Thales Australia put it bluntly when he said to me, 'People don't understand why we have submarines.' By people, he meant most people, across every layer and every part of Australian society. Even across the Enterprise, we told ourselves that our purpose was to 'generate a potent and enduring submarine capability', but this statement was missing a core element. It spoke to what we needed to do yet assumed an understanding of why we might invest in submarines in the first place. With a quarter of a century of experience as a submariner, that understanding was ingrained within me. Speaking with the officers and sailors in the Arm, it was clear that most understood what they could do and how they could do it. They implicitly knew it was special, but they couldn't consistently and convincingly articulate *why* it was important to the nation.

I decided the Submarine Enterprise purpose statement needed to be amplified to carry real meaning. With my own motto as Director General Submarines of 'deter and defeat' in mind, I changed it to read: 'to generate a potent and enduring submarine capability *to serve as the Nation's principle strategic deterrent*'. This higher purpose was immediately and enthusiastically picked up by the whole Submarine Arm and beyond; it made sense to them and answered the question of 'why submarines?' for ourselves and for others.

With clarity on our strategic relevance and value, I settled into a state of comfortable discomfort and calm urgency. We had all the time in the world, and there was no time to lose! My staff and I used the guiding principles of preserving stealth, generating expansion, assuring potency and achieving deterrence to drive our day-to-day decisions and actions on the way towards a reconstituted and revitalised submarine capability. The whole lot came close to crashing down around our ears in late February 2014.

Beavering away in my office one afternoon, I took a call from the watchkeeper at SUBOPS.

'There's been an engine room fire onboard *Waller*, Sir. She's on the surface, fire has been extinguished with halon. Four casualties. Extent of systems damage not yet known,' she said.

'Thanks, Louisa, keep me informed,' I replied.

Waller, just out of a major refit, was lined up for a long running period at sea. Her CO had her moving smoothly through work-ups over in the West and she was on track to be our next RIMPAC deployer. With three submarines still locked away in extended dockings, *Waller* was designated as one-third of our seagoing capacity through 2014. The damage onboard was extensive, with machinery and electrical cabling destroyed beyond repair.

The desperately needed bounty of seatime, training and experience derived from work-ups and a long deployment was gone. The loss of overall redundancy and flexibility in dropping from three running boats to two was massive, particularly when we were under such intense scrutiny from elsewhere in Navy and from government. The immediate impact on Navy was apparent, although just how long we would bear the pain was not.

The fire was a strategic shock that sat ASC on their corporate arse, stunned and frozen. Instinct told me to demand that ASC get her repaired and back to Navy as soon as possible, but there was a wider question about our collective response. With the repairs likely to run into the tens of millions of dollars, the sustainment budget didn't have room for a contingency like this, and the industrial workforce was already fully committed on other submarines.

Paul Gay had just taken up the role as General Manager for Collins' sustainment, after spending time with ASC's troubled shipbuilding program. He was still lobster red and steaming as he was pulled from one cauldron and dropped into another. Together with John Chandler, my partner in the DMO, we hatched a plan to keep the Enterprise on the rails. It meant progressing the *Waller* repairs as expeditiously as practicable, aiming to maximise her seatime in the following year, but without throwing our existing plans for other submarines out the window.

When additional resources were brought in by way of cabling expertise from our American strategic industrial partner, Electric Boat, and surface Navy technical sailors to augment the ASC staff, we began to make ground. There were months when it seemed the repairs would go on interminably. When *Waller* did finally re-emerge nearly two years later, we had folded in additional capability and preserved the programs for the other submarines in dock and at sea, all without breaking the grand bargain with industry. A painful episode, but a massive success story for the wider Submarine Enterprise.

When I had arrived in Canberra, the staff were toiling away trying to implement the recommendations of the latest workforce review. Conducted a few years earlier, it suffered from the same faulty premise that derailed a string of reviews before it. With myopic focus on the crews, they sought to 'fix the problem' while accepting and perpetuating the paradigm of a Submarine Arm valiantly struggling beneath critical mass. While they identified tactical-level causal factors and near-term remedies, these reviews were consistently silent on the root strategic cause of endemic weakness in the Submarine Arm: Navy's decades-long failure to consistently provide the right number of quality people to generate sufficient strength and assure the total capability. We were in a stern chase. Worse still, we were chasing the wrong target.

'Where will you find the crews?' was a common enough refrain in the halls of Navy Headquarters. The difficulty in responding was that submariners are not to be 'found' anywhere. They are not a naturally occurring species, just as a Submarine Arm is not a naturally occurring organism, even within a first-rate navy. They need to be created, fostered, nurtured and championed, particularly when they comprise the most specialised workforce in the ADF, but represent less than one-twentieth of the Navy.

Within six months, we devised a workforce growth strategy to ensure provision of qualified and experienced submariners at sea, ashore and across the wider Navy and ADF. Linked directly to our projected submarine availability, it laid down a path to double the number of submariners within a decade and set the foundations for further growth beyond. Originally scoped out to the year 2040 to include the final demands of an expanded, multi-class fleet, the Chief cut it down to a 2025 time frame prior to signing off on it. Even in a strategic headquarters the appetite for far-reaching designs and decisions can be spoiled.

We would be walking a tightrope – balancing the training of record numbers of submariners with the safe and effective conduct of intense operations and extended deployments. To rig a safety net, I brought a select handful of experienced submarine COs in from retirement or allied navies to command the boats at sea. We would act as our own guardians. The whole endeavour was mammoth and daunting, but the mere creation of the right strategy had an immediate and positive impact on morale and retention.

However, the criticism levelled at our work, sometimes directly but more often indirectly, tested the limits of my commitment and self-compassion. I battled against deeply ingrained, and at times, insidious resistance from some quarters. Rather than welcoming it as a strengthening of the Navy overall, there were those in senior ranks who simplistically equated growth of the Submarine Arm with deficiencies in the surface fleet.

I found my allies elsewhere and used the political pressure to advantage, but the friction within Navy intensified as we embarked on the next step: nice fat pay packets. The 'submarine pay' that attracted many of my contemporaries into boats decades earlier had been steadily and comprehensively defrayed over the years. It was time to restore the differential.

The Defence Force Advocate, an esteemed silk, became my new best mate as we built the argument to take to the ADF Remuneration Tribunal. The military is not unionised, so sailors don't get to argue their lot. Pay scales and allowances are decided by the Tribunal, much as a court determines guilt or innocence. I had long held the view that if we paid our submariners so much that they couldn't afford to leave, we would probably be paying them what they were worth.

We built a package of conditions to help lift the Arm from the abyss and carry it forward. While it was multifaceted, the cornerstone was an annual Capability Assurance Payment. Crucially, it was tiered to match and reward seagoing submarine experience, and was paid both at sea and ashore. As the name implied, this was less about recognition of skill or hardship and more about signalling the value that Defence and government placed on the capability. Navy's uniformed workforce had been the perennial risk to the strategic deterrent for too long.

A landmark decision from the Tribunal came our way in late 2015, and by the end of 2016, the downward spiral was reversed. While we were still under strength and fragile, we had brought the number of 'critical' categories down to the low single digits. Retention was at an all-time high and the Arm had grown by a staggering 40 percent over the previous three and a half years. The confidence and momentum we generated through successive years of growth, despite the ongoing challenges, finally had the buttressing it needed to carry it forward long into the future.

CHAPTER 24

CENTENARY OF SUBMARINES

In many respects, it was a brilliant time to lead the Arm. By luck and happenstance, my tenure as Director General Submarines coincided with a landmark year. In February 2014, I donned my dress uniform and medals to attend Navy's launch of our 'Centenary of Australian Submarines' commemorations, presided over by the Minister for Defence and self-confessed submarine tragic, Senator David Johnston. My old ship, HMAS *Vampire*, now a literal museum piece, and the submarine HMAS *Onslow*, also long since decommissioned, set the stage at the National Maritime Museum in Darling Harbour.

It was a most appropriate location, given that our first submarines, HMAS *AE1* and *AE2*, had sailed into the port of Sydney to join the newly formed Fleet of the Royal Australian Navy in 1914. Just over a decade after Federation, and just under a decade since the global naval powers made their first serious ventures into the submarine domain, the submarines were ordered by Prime Minister Alfred Deakin. Built at the Barrow-in-Furness naval shipyards in the United Kingdom, they endured an arduous passage under escort and tow. The formation of the Fleet – now replete with its submarine element – was significant on many accounts, particularly as a statement of the nation's intent to uphold its sovereignty and protect its interests, and an irrefutable demonstration of the capacity to do so. At the outbreak of the First World War, *AE1* and *AE2* were immediately deployed into action with the Fleet, securing Australian and regional waters, escorting our troops overseas and, for *AE2*, conducting combat operations during the Gallipoli campaign. War being war, things didn't end well for either submarine.

Later in our centenary year, I had the privilege of leading an RAN contingent to Rabaul, Papua New Guinea to commemorate the loss of *AE1* a hundred years earlier. Both *AE1* and *AE2* had sailed with the Australian Naval and Military Expeditionary Force, tasked with seizing or neutralising the German territories in the Pacific and contending with Vice Admiral von Spee's East Asiatic Squadron. Regrettably, *AE1* failed to return to Rabaul harbour after a patrol searching for the enemy. Under the command of Lieutenant Commander Thomas Besant, RN, she was lost without a trace and with all thirty-five souls onboard.

In the commemorative address, I spoke about the proud tradition of service, sacrifice and warfighting spirit established by *AE1* and *AE2*. Marching through the township of Rabaul, the Ship's Company of the minehunter HMAS *Yarra* and the Navy Band brought a great sense of dignity and ceremony to the day. *Yarra* had recently conducted an intensive but unsuccessful search for the wreck of *AE1*; one of many fruitless searches conducted by the RAN since 1976.

The occasion was all the more poignant for the presence of a score of descendants of the crew of *AE1* who had travelled from all parts of Australia and beyond. In the fortnight before I arrived in Rabaul, the volcano Tavurvur had erupted violently, partially burying the town under layers of ash and scoria. It was a forceful reminder of the dynamic geography of the region. Speaking with the descendants, I was filled with admiration for their determination to honour these sailors, but struggled to offer them hope that we would ever know precisely where their ancestors and their diminutive submarine lay in an everchanging seascape.[9]

The Centenary also took me to a somewhat peculiar destination to commemorate Anzac Day – Holbrook in rural New South Wales. This quintessentially Australian country town, situated in the Riverina and nearly 400 kilometres inland from the nearest coastline, had long been an unlikely place of retreat for submariners. With an appropriately quirky connection to the Squadron, it is one of the few places in Australia where most people know of and celebrate our submarine heritage.

In 1915, amid waves of imperial sentiment, the locals erased 'Germanton' from the map and renamed their town in honour of Lieutenant

---

9   Contrary to my expectations, the wreck of AE1 was discovered in December 2017 by the *Fugro Equator* during a search led by retired Admiral Peter Briggs. Lying in 300 metres of water off the Duke of York islands, her precise location is not publicly disclosed.

Norman Holbrook, RN. Holbrook was the first submariner to win the Victoria Cross, awarded for actions in command of the submarine HMS *B-11* when he entered the Dardanelles, known to the Turks as the Canakkale Strait, to sink the battleship *Mesûdiye* at her station. The old ironclad, a bulwark staged at the entrance to the Sea of Marmora and the approaches to the Ottoman capital of Istanbul, was sent to the bottom by a single torpedo.

Eighty years later in the mid-1990s, the casing and fin of the decommissioned HMAS *Otway* was acquired as a centrepiece for the town's submarine museum. For decades, the people of Holbrook and the surrounding sheep and wheat stations generously welcomed raiding parties of submariners arriving in convoy from Sydney, their pub verandas and streets wide enough and quiet enough to tolerate some of our excesses. Although the connection diminished with the relocation of the Squadron to Perth, it seemed an appropriate place to absorb the breadth of experience and emotion that Anzac Day evokes for many service men and women – from the solemnity of acts of remembrance, to the wholehearted celebration of camaraderie and esprit de corps.

Lieutenant Holbrook was not the first submariner to penetrate the Strait during the fateful Gallipoli campaign. That distinction went to Lieutenant Commander Henry Stoker, RN in command of HMAS *AE2*. In April of 1915, the Canakkale Strait (which separates and connects the continents of Europe and Asia) was the most dangerous waterway in the world. With the fate of their mates onboard *AE1* still fresh, the crew of *AE2* willingly faced the combined threat of torpedo boats, shore batteries, field artillery, searchlights and minefields operated by prepared and determined Turkish forces defending their homeland.

The Turks had already expelled the combined Fleets of the Royal Navy and the French Navy from the Strait. They also imposed severe losses on the Allied forces, including sinking three battleships and two submarines. When *AE2* emerged into the Sea of Marmora, somewhat battered for the experience, she was ideally positioned to threaten the supply lines reinforcing the Turkish divisions on the Gallipoli peninsula, until her ultimate loss in combat to the Turkish gunboat *Sultanhisar*.

A century later, I travelled to Turkey with the Chief of Navy to represent the Submarine Arm as we commemorated the 100th anniversary of *AE2*'s actions. The formalities took place aboard HMAS *ANZAC* as she held station over the site of *AE2*, with a Turkish frigate in close escort. Now considered an archaeological relic, her resting place was discovered at a depth of 72 metres during a 1998 expedition.

Standing alongside the Turkish Fleet Commander, we recalled the courage of the crew, acknowledged the compassion of the Turkish forces who accepted their surrender after *AE2* was scuttled, and honoured the memory of the four sailors who did not survive the ensuing years interned in prisoner of war camps. Our earliest submarines, operating forward in the littorals of our then German and Turkish enemies on deterrent and offensive operations, foretold the purpose of the force throughout the ensuing century.

We were connected to the sailors onboard *AE1* and *AE2* in other ways. The immense courage and selfless patriotic devotion to duty of those crews matched the character of the submariners I knew at home, and stood as an enduring exemplar of what could and should be expected of the modern Arm. The submariners I knew existed within a tribe where membership and respect were achieved through acquired knowledge, shared experience, common practice, a unique language, distinct markings and long heritage. The arduous conditions, confined quarters and profound isolation they faced called for tolerance and sacrifice. The threats they were prepared to meet demanded exacting professional standards and a healthy respect for the sea and the enemy alike.

Perhaps, as we celebrated the passing of one century of Australian Submarine operations and embarked on the next, the thread that connected us more than any other was the willingness of our submariners to serve in perhaps the most persistently hostile environment imaginable to deter and defeat the nation's enemies. This is at the heart of what it means to be part of the submarine tribe. This is what it means to be an Australian Submariner.

CHAPTER 25
STRATEGIC PARTNERS

A few months before the trip to Turkey, I joined the CEO of the DMO and his party of advisors for a whirlwind fact-finding tour of selected European capital cities and their submarine dockyards. The mission was to verify those nations we might partner with to develop our own sovereign submarine capability – an enduring Australian submarine capability untrammelled by foreign design, build or sustainment dependencies. Our observations would shape the ensuing evaluation conducted by DMO, later the Capability Acquisition and Sustainment Group (CASG), throughout 2015.

The details of that evaluation still remain highly classified. It encompassed our requirements, but also elicited sensitive and closely protected data on the naval, technical and industrial capabilities of the prospective nations; secrets they did not offer without receiving the strongest of assurances.

Our visit to Stockholm and Malmö was illuminating but disappointing. While our Swedish hosts pointed to a century of submarine production and our close association through Collins, there was no escaping the facts that their Navy operated two small coastal submarines with scant ambition of expansion or evolution, and their yard at Malmö was long devoid of life. This was not the naval or industrial powerhouse on which to rely for our next class of submarines.

The atmosphere in Berlin and Kiel was different. Like the Swedes, the Deutsche Marine operated a single class of small diesel electric submarines. With only four boats, their squadron was also smaller than our own and rarely put to sea, but it was their contemporary industrial record and capacity that stood out. As submarine exporters, ThyssenKrupp Marine Systems (TKMS) presented as the archetypal proponents of German engineering and efficiency, with more than

160 boats built across the previous five decades. German submarines already operated with half a dozen regional navies across the Indo-Pacific.

With key criteria set by us, and a certain way of working for them, the Germans would design and produce a crop of submarines in the colour of our choosing, much as you might order a fleet of Mercedes-Benz buses, only a tad more complex. A tour of the latest Dolphin-class boat under construction in Kiel for the Israelis, finished in a lovely shade of Mediterranean green, made the point persuasively.

What struck me with the French in both Paris and Cherbourg was their complete understanding and sovereign capability across the full spectrum of submarine design, production and operations. Bolstering their nuclear submarine industrial resilience and capacity, they also designed and exported diesel electric submarines, including the Scorpène-class operated regionally by Malaysia and India. Strikingly, they had an established production sequence across the two types of ocean-going submarines they operated: nuclear-powered attack submarines and nuclear armed ballistic missile submarines, which lay at the heart of their national security. The French, having delivered an at-sea deterrent continuously since 1971, know boats. Their collective determination to achieve assured and credible presence at sea was writ large in their whole approach. As the highly charismatic head of French Military Strategy, Vice Admiral Charles-Henri du Che, remarked to me when he visited Australia in 2015, 'If you have twelve submarines, it is to have them at sea!'

In April 2016, I travelled to Adelaide for the announcement by Prime Minister Malcolm Turnbull that Direction des Constructions Navales Services (DCNS) of France was selected as the preferred strategic partner to develop our sovereign submarine capability. While much anticipated, it wasn't widely predicted. The senior executives of the newly minted CASG now had a massive project on which to cut their organisational teeth.

For Navy, in the near term, this meant a rapid escalation of our engagement with France's Marine nationale. There was a great deal to gain from close cooperation, including at sea, but these were uncharted waters. Our interaction between the two navies in recent decades had been sparse and the interaction between the submarine forces almost non-existent, so we were running at it from a near-standing start.

Dispatched to Paris with a selection of my submarine experts in late 2016 for navy-to-navy talks, I carried no French language proficiency with me, but did have a mariner's portfolio of diplomatic skills. By remarkable coincidence, I had worked with each of the officers in the French delegation, generally through our escape and rescue networks. While each delegation explored the art of the possible, we also protected the operational and alliance matters closest to the heart of our respective deterrent forces. The success of the talks stood to set the trajectory of our Navy's relationship for years to come.

I opened in an unexpected way, telling them of my grandfather's war and of my connection with their country and their values, as well as the legacy of service and sacrifice of thousands of Australians who still lay in French soil. My remarks were brief but heartfelt, and helped connect us as servicemen, acknowledging the heritage we shared beyond our submarine brotherhood. We were off to a good start at least.

Thanks, Grandad. Still serving, still remembered.

For submariners, submarines are our core business – everyone's submarines, everywhere. The submarine forces of allies or potential adversaries are highly relevant to our profession, to our existence and to our survival. While the threats we might face and the missions we might execute can vary widely, it's in working with or in combat against other submarine forces that we face the greatest test, and the truth of our capabilities comes into sharpest relief. We do not exist in isolation, but within the context of other submarine forces and of the strategic environment surrounding us. In this regard, the submarine forces of regional navies are especially relevant and important.

While working with the French had come on late in the piece, working with the Japanese was a highlight throughout my time as Director General Submarines. In mid-2013, just prior to assuming the role, I travelled to Yokosuka, Japan for the triennial Exercise Pacific Reach. We were in the happy position of having HMAS *Waller* deployed for the exercise, our farthest deployment in recent years. It was here that I first met Vice Admiral Masakazu Kaji, the recently appointed Commander Fleet Submarine Force, as he cracked open a sake barrel at the welcome ceremony.

Drinking with the Japanese could result in some truly regrettable whiskey hangovers, but I judged it was worth leaning in unguarded and accepting some personal risk to bond with leaders such as Vice Admiral Kaji. A magnetic officer and absolute statesman, we became firm friends in quick order.

While Japan became the third potential partner nation for our next submarines, much of my work with them was not premised on any potential build, but rather deliberately focused on the mutual benefit of strengthening our operational connections at sea in the Western Pacific. In early 2014, I met with the Japanese Director General of Operations and Plans for the inaugural navy-to-navy Submarine Operational Talks at the Japanese strategic headquarters at Ichigaya in Tokyo.

Together we mapped out a plan for strategic-level engagement and created opportunities for our submarines to work together in coming years, including through Japanese deployments to Australia. Operating principally around their home waters, the Japanese submarine fleet was contending with a persistent and rising sense of menace across the Northeast Asia region and running at an intense operational tempo, so potential deployments to Australia were highly ambitious.

It was during one of many official visits to Japan that I had the privilege of going to sea in the Blue Dragon, JS *Soryu*. Taking one of my experienced Commanders with me as an extra pair of eyes and ears, we were the first foreign naval officers ever to searide this class of submarine. Domestically designed and built, these boats were the result of decades of investment and evolution. Operating both surfaced and dived over several days, we transited from the shipyards in Kobe down to Kure naval base on the Inland Sea. We were treated like royalty, given almost entirely free rein of the boat and as much chicken katsu as our bellies could hold. Though my Japanese was barely better than my French, the capabilities of the submarine and the proficiency of the crew were on open display. She was a most impressive boat, precisely matched to the requirements of the Japanese and their operating environment. And while the ghosts of the Imperial Japanese Navy were hidden from sight, it was clear that the warfighting spirit born of samurai traditions was deeply inculcated into their sailors.

This golden opportunity to searide a Japanese submarine had arisen after we extended a similar privilege to Vice Admiral Kaji during a visit to Australia months earlier. Acting as his escort, I accompanied him as we sailed in HMAS *Sheean* to exercise with the Virginia-class boat USS *Hawaii* off the West Australian coast over several days. To understand the capabilities of a submarine, there is no better place to stand than between the periscopes, at depth and at Action Stations, while tracking another navy's submarine. And in the closely guarded world of submarine operations, it was an irrefutable demonstration of trust and partnership across all three nations.

There was a lot we might learn from the Japanese, including from their national response to their changing strategic environment. The Japanese had set up two of their industrial powerhouses, Mitsubishi Heavy Industries (MHI) and Kawasaki Heavy Industries (KHI) to build their submarines, each churning out one boat every two years. Over time, they progressed from one class to the next and built up a force of eighteen modern submarines, including a dedicated training squadron. The deliberate evolution of their submarine capabilities was ample proof of what a medium-power navy could achieve over time and with persistence, and a prime example of what Australia might create with equal determination.

As tensions rose through the middle of the decade, the Japanese deliberately and overtly kept some of their older boats in their order of battle and retained more of their submariners, rapidly expanding the size of the force-in-being by a submarine a year. Faced with an expanding Chinese military and an emerging North Korean nuclear weapons program, this was a conscious and, in strategic terms, near immediate response to the increasingly coercive environment.

The Japanese were not the only ones looking to submarine capability to shore up their sovereignty. Within a decade, the Vietnam People's Navy rapidly acquired a small fleet of six new-build Kilo-class submarines from Russia, sailing them out of their major naval base in Cam Ranh Bay. Although I had been to Vietnam on an official ADF visit previously, in mid-2016 I had the chance to spend several days with Rear Admiral Do Minh Tha. Towards the end of that visit, the diminutive Vietnamese submarine commander based in Haiphong offered me a brief but compelling history lesson.

'I was born in 1958 and spent much of my childhood traipsing the countryside of North Vietnam dodging the US aerial bombardments. Has Vietnam ever invaded China, Korea, Japan, the Philippines? No! Yet we have a history of near continuous conflict on our borders. And we have been repeatedly subjected to invasion and occupation, defending our sovereignty against foreign powers, such as the American War. You are familiar with this.' Minh spoke slowly, in precise English, to ensure he was not misunderstood. 'Over the centuries, China has invaded Vietnam fourteen times.'

Minh's final assertion carried extra weight. Their need for an effective deterrent was, in his mind, absolute.

The South Koreans too had built up an impressive submarine capability over the years in the face of incessant provocation from North Korea. I first met Rear Admiral Youn Jeong Sang as a Squadron Commander in Busan, South Korea in 2012. Later, as the Commander of their Submarine Force, he was rightfully proud of the ROKN's success in generating a modern, comprehensive and professional submarine force. Standing as a model of steadfast expansion, the establishment in 2015 of his Two Star Force Command, headquartered at Jinhae Naval Base, was no accidental occurrence. Since 1990 they had evolved from a small squadron of mini-subs to a modern force operating sixteen boats across three classes.

Touring their latest Son Won-il-class boat in construction at the massive Daewoo Shipbuilding and Marine Engineering (DSME) yards in Geoje, where they were also refitting and building submarines for Indonesia, it was evident that the South Koreans had grafted technical skill with industrial heft to forge ahead with in-country design and build of sophisticated diesel electric attack submarines. They also supported their boats with a full suite of training and support facilities ashore, including a comprehensive rescue capability.

It was in their LR5 rescue submersible that I nearly came to grief during my last official visit to Korea in 2016. I was one of several senior foreign officers embarked in their purpose-built submarine rescue ship, the ROKS *Cheonghaejin*, to observe a series of exercises in the Tsushima Strait. Offered an opportunity to dive in the LR5, ranged on *Cheonghaejin*'s aft deck, I stepped forward immediately; as much to demonstrate my genuine confidence in our hosts as out of any desire for more dived time.

Clambering through the top hatch of the small white submarine, which looked like a science project gone wrong, I cringed involuntarily as escort officers pointed cameras and called for a pose. Superstitious as they are, submariners prefer to have photos taken on their return from a dive or deployment, rather than on departure.

With the hatch sealed, we were plopped into the sea and disconnected. Taking up a cramped position directly behind the two Korean pilots, I scanned my close surrounds. Beyond the array of instruments and gauges I had an unobstructed view through the large bubble window to the crystal blue sea outside. *Finally, I get to dive in a proper submarine with a window!*

A calm procedural demeanour prevailed through the short series of pre-diving checks. Then, moments after we began to dive, the craft took an unexpectedly sharp bow down angle. My eyes darted back to the depth gauge; we were not diving so much as plummeting. The chatter in the cockpit picked up noticeably.

Looking aft into the belly of the submersible, my fellow seariders were unperturbed. Not being submariners, they were oblivious to the drama whereas I was all too aware that the option set diminished substantially once the rescue submarine crashed into the seabed! The crew had miscalculated the trim and we had dived demonstrably heavy. The skipper hit the emergency blows, ejecting ballast to arrest our descent and bringing us back to bob about at the surface.

Fifteen minutes later, we gave it another go. Now deep underwater and in control, they handed me the joystick. Cruising 6 feet off the sandy bottom, tormenting ugly bottom-dwelling fish with the powerful searchlights, it occurred to me that my personal tolerance for at-sea emergencies had grown pretty bloody thin. Whether you the think it's your first day at sea or your last, the sea neither knows nor cares. I wondered how long it would take for my submariner mates to find the humour in the irony if it had all ended badly. Likely not long at all!

CHAPTER 26
IT'S TIME

Journal note, January 2015. There will be a call on your courage either way.

Challenges notwithstanding, across my final years in the Navy I carried a sense of immense gratitude for my life, and a growing appreciation of all that I had experienced and the people surrounding me on the journey.

For decades I endeavoured, day after day and night after night, to muster the courage to step through my trepidation, anxiety and fears. The courage to set sail in our submarines, deploy to our war zones, or direct our operations and capabilities from headquarters ashore. Not to appear courageous, but to serve. In that time, few days went by when I did not ask myself the question, *'Why am I here?'* Quite often, it was more like, *'What the bloody hell am I doing here?'*

I didn't always find an adequate answer. Most days, it didn't matter since I was already deeply committed. In choosing to join the Navy and volunteering for submarines, I accepted a seeming loss of autonomy in daily life. Throwing in the towel wasn't really an option when on watch with a crew, at depth, in a faraway sea. Almost inevitably, whenever the next real decision came around, I pondered it for a while, discussed it with Shaunaugh, then took up the posting. The big wheel turned another revolution, carried forward by the value and enjoyment I found in service, and the excitement of challenges not yet met.

But the courage to persist came in different forms at different times, whether it was the courage to risk my relationships, my reputation or my life. It often seemed that the direction that appeared most difficult also required the most courage, and was therefore the right path for me to take. Challenge and reward came year on year. As Director General Submarines, I was still striving for the courage to see through the task at hand, with all its consequent separation and solitude, and to make the difference I was meant to make.

257

Journal note, April 2015. *What happened today?*

The drive to Canberra is still a bastard. By mid-2015, after consecutive years of pushing up and down the highway each week, the pattern is set. I creep out of the house in the dark hours of Monday morning and get behind the wheel. But this day feels different. Rolling past Goulburn after a couple of quiet and solitary hours on the road, it is time to call Shaunaugh. She would be up by now, getting ready for her day at work. She would also be alone since Laura, living in Dubai and travelling the world as an Emirates flight attendant, is not due home again for another six months. Living and working in three different cities, we couldn't be more separated.

'Call Shaunaugh,' I say to the hands-free operator who resides within the dash. There is never much to talk about, but a quick chat at the start of the day connects us and always lifts my spirits.

'Have a good day, Shaun. I love you!'

As the orange sun jabs its way into the car, I begin to scream. A long, nightmarish, howling scream. The anguish of forever driving away from my family for the sake of others suddenly shreds me. *Where the fuck am I going?*

My body and my soul feel as if they are being torn asunder. Ripping at the steering wheel in an absolute rage, my foot is on the accelerator and the big engine is roaring. My eyes shut, open and shut again. I am out of control, still screaming, and the car is out of control, still roaring. So much fucking noise! *Am I making that noise? Where is it coming from? It's fucking terrifying. When will it stop?*

I'm in the gravel. *I don't care. Yes, I do! Hit the brakes. Jesus Christ!*

The car slews to a stop. A dust storm rolls over the car and down the road in front of me, and I panic momentarily. *Oh, my God. Did I hang up? Did Shaunaugh hear that?*

I flick on the hazards and just sit there, totally wired. The relief valves on my frail equanimity are well and truly lifted. Sometime later, I check the side mirror, ease out and drive on.

The day passes, though the discordant and unsettled feelings stay with me. Walking out into the evening twilight, something has shifted. I have had enough and done enough. With a powerful sense of completeness, satisfaction and acceptance, I am ready to step ashore and explore new horizons, keeping my family at the centre of my life – not for their sake, but for mine. I will finish this job, then find the courage to move on.

By the end of 2016, we have moved through one program – aimed at creating efficiency across our supply chains and maintenance regimes – and onto another that will modernise the onboard systems and sensors. Quite separately, I discovered the unexpected delight and indescribable relief of moving stalled acquisition projects through the seemingly interminable committee processes to achieve full government approval. Upgrades for sonar, communications and electronic warfare suites, all to be sequentially installed in the submarines within the time frame of the scheduled dockings over the next several years, could now go ahead.

At the same time, the engineering studies were well underway to support a now inescapable Life of Type Extension for the class, which involved replacing major equipment sets, including the diesel generators and the main motor. The path was set to substantially add to the stealth, lethality and durability of the boats for a decade or more, while our next class of submarines was being built and commissioned into service.

Importantly, our escape and rescue capability was reinstated when we brought two new support vessels into operational service. *MV Besant,* a purpose-built Escape Gear Ship, and *MV Stoker,* the larger Rescue Gear Ship, had been named to honour the Commanding Officers and Ships' Companies of the submarines we lost in the First World War. In combination with our locally operated LR5 submersible, our ability to support a distressed submarine was now among the most comprehensive in the region. Hosting the Asia Pacific Submarine Conference in Fremantle, we were once again able to look our submarine operating neighbours, and our own sailors, in the eye.

We were making ground in other dimensions as well. In 2013, as part of my preparations to speak as the senior RAN representative at an annual meeting with the most senior submariners in the USN and RN, I went into the vaults to review our performance at sea in recent years. Anchored in my own fond recollections of operational success in command of *Dechaineux* in 2002 and 2003, I was embarrassed and dismayed at what I saw, or rather what I did not see. Our participation and performance against national training and exercise commitments over the intervening decade was sporadic and exceedingly thin. Our performance meeting international exercise commitments to work alongside regional defence partners, such as Japan, Malaysia and Singapore, was demonstrably worse. More critically, by any relative measure, but particularly in comparison with the USN Pacific Submarine Fleet, our contribution to the strategic stability and security of our region was virtually non-existent. We had barely held ourselves together, let alone made any persistent operational contribution by way of effective operations or credible presence beyond our own shores.

The contrast on my last official trip to the US in late 2016 could not have been more striking. Over the past three years, we had conducted fourteen major deployments, including seven overseas deployments covering the Indian and Pacific Oceans, Southeast Asia and Northeast Asia. The boats had visited twenty-four disparate ports across eight different nations, including India (regrettably, we had not sailed to the sub-continent for twenty years, despite operating out of Western Australia). One of the boats conducted a nine-month deployment from home port, now the longest on record for the Squadron. And with the sole exception of HMAS *Collins* in a full refit, every submarine had deployed at least once in the past year.

The seatime laid coats of experience on our submariners, just as every successful docking, with three out of every four now occurring in the West, added new steel to the armour of our industrial workforce. Yet despite all the good news, I remained painfully aware of our shortfalls, including the gaps in our uniformed workforce and some serious fragility around obsolescence and supportability as the boats aged. Nonetheless, with industry doing their part to consistently deliver the boats out of major maintenance periods, on time and in a robust material state, we were meeting Navy's availability requirements, enabling more and more deployments and expanding the horizons of the Submarine Arm once again.

Fundamentally, with seaworthy and battleworthy submarines, we were achieving greater at-sea presence, meeting operational commitments and delivering an increasingly credible strategic deterrent effect. We went from having a plan and a sense of optimism to gaining results, a sense of trajectory and real momentum. It was a much better story to tell.

In December, I flew to *Stirling* for my last annual Squadron Forum. With the boats alongside for Christmas, it was a chance to gather en masse, reflect on the year and just be together. Submarine operations being what they are, not all the best tales could be told, but we openly celebrated *Rankin* snatching the Gloucester Cup once more – a full decade since the last time a submarine was judged 'Best in Fleet'. Winning a trophy at home doesn't mean you'll survive the war, but it was public acknowledgement that we were back in the game.

On the Sunday morning, we gathered wharfside with swords and medals. Submariners aren't big on ceremonial, and there were no dignitaries gracing our presence or inspecting the ranks, but this was an occasion worth a dress up.

After years of struggle, five of the six submarines were finally being maintained and operated out of their home port of Perth, with just a single hull in refit elsewhere. For one day only, all five were alongside together at HMAS *Stirling*.

By any reasonable notion, it should not have been a remarkable occasion. Yet it was the first time we achieved this level of availability and force concentration in a quarter of a century. In too many respects and for too long, we had been in a deep, dark hole, but today it felt like we were emerging from that abyss.

I chose this occasion to hand over the reins to my successor, figuring there was still enough work around for him to earn his pay over the next couple of years. Acknowledging the challenges that still lay before them and the threat of enemies not yet known, I offered the men and women of the Submarine Arm some final words of encouragement and my humble opinion: 'It is within you – and it is worth it!' Taking Shaunaugh's hand, we headed for home.

Journal note, December 2016. *Very proud. Away you go.*

EPILOGUE

Journal note, April 2001. *The enemy is there. He is learning about you. One day, he will come to kill you.*

Early one morning in September 2021, while penning the final chapter of this memoir, I receive a text from a friend and mentor. An Air Force type most animated when talking about fast jets, he knows the ABC News headline will grab my attention.

'Australia to get nuclear powered submarines,' it read.

Our submarine seascape has shifted again as Prime Minister Scott Morrison, British Prime Minister Boris Johnston and US President Joe Biden announce that Australia will acquire at least eight nuclear powered submarines through an enhanced trilateral security partnership named AUKUS. It is the death knell for our collaboration on the Attack-class with the French, and the most significant reversal in government direction on submarine capability in the history of the Arm. For the first time since 1960 – when the USS *Triton* demonstrated the range, speed and endurance of nuclear submarines by completing a dived circum-navigation of the globe – our directed submarine capability matches the real demands of our geographic and geostrategic circumstances.

A like decision might have been usefully made by a courageous government sometime in the previous two decades as the service life of the Collins-class wore inexorably on. While there has been no short-age of government announcements regarding submarines in that time, action to match the rhetoric is less evident. Logically, prime ministers weigh contemporary political risk against future national security, making decisions and investments accordingly. Thus, democratic nations build the navies and the submarine forces that they deserve.

Our collective failure to assure the future potency of our submarine force in past decades has sent a strategic message to the region, whether we intended it or not, and emboldened potential adversaries like China.

Perhaps AUKUS presents the opportunity to advance our timelines on a multi-class submarine force-in-being and restore the balance. Either way, the time is probably coming when Australians will know if the navy and submarine force that we deserve is also the navy and submarine force that we need.

Twenty years ago, alongside in Darwin after recently returning from a Southeast Asian deployment, the sun rose with a bite as I walked the casing, clutching one brew tight and seriously regretting the many brews of the night before. I spied a lone, but familiar, figure high above on the wharf. Standing off at a distance, he was obviously contemplating the submarine. I invited him onboard for a tour and gathered a few officers and sailors into the wardroom to talk submarines, navies and nations.

I'm not sure what brought Kim Beazley to Darwin that day, or to the wharf that morning. I do know that submarines appear before those who know them and disappear before those who do not. In a war fought at sea, fortune will favour those who genuinely fathom submarines and submariners.

Working my way through discharge medicals in my last few months of naval service, I asked for a referral to see a psychologist. To get over the threshold and step into what might end up being a long, dark cave, I initially approached therapy much like a final dental check. *I think I might just need a filling!* One session turned into two, two turned into four, and finally into months of intense emotional work.

For years I had tolerated and lived with the recurring images of past traumas intruding on my thoughts. No day or night, sometimes no hour, would go by without recalling a flood, a fire, a rocket attack. Externally at least, and for now, I was doing okay. I was happy enough, focused, functioning. But there was a layer of underlying tension and heat in my life that continually threatened to spill out or erupt.

Previously diagnosed with Generalised Anxiety Disorder and now exhibiting symptoms of PTSD, I began a program of Eye Movement Desensitization and Reprocessing (EMDR) therapy that involved deliberately recalling and cognitively processing past traumatic and threatening events. This was not a quick flick through the photo album of my mind. It was remembering and repeatedly reliving the moments and hours that had scared the life out of me, in full and vivid emotional and sensational detail. It was gut-wrenching, mortifying and extraordinarily difficult.

I approached the sessions with a willing dread. Mounting the softly lit timber stairs within the Federation-era terrace, I often trembled with anticipation of what might be laid bare and fought back the urge to turn and run. I knew I had to persist, for the sake of my life beyond. Each week, I came away exhausted and spent, but emerged back into the day feeling lighter and more open to life beyond the rusty iron gate.

Turns out, it wasn't a cave to be lit but rather a mangrove creek at high tide with a lot of crocodiles. They are still there, some of them monstrous. The difference is the tide is out and they are now in plain sight. No longer lurking beneath murky waters, ready to show their snout and bite on a whim, they are much easier to deal with. Crocodiles still, but demons no more.

In late 2019, my beloved mum passed away, succumbing to pancreatic cancer after a stoic three-year battle. In the short years since, Dad has uncovered and passed on some of her keepsakes, including an archaeological record of her son's naval career; a life she shared from a distance but kept close to her heart. There were boxes of postcards from faraway ports, press clippings of interviews long since forgotten, a business card for every posting since my first command. She collected them over the years as she sent reams of long letters to me, all to stay connected to her son.

Year after year in living their lives, my parents, my grandparents and countless others taught me that courage and compassion need know no bounds. Over time, I understood that allowing what I value to steer my direction in life – and accepting myself, others and the world around us – helped me chart a determined and ambitious life.

Like my grandfather Jack, I know something of survival, resilience, leadership and honour. I also know what it is, what it takes and what it means to be an Australian Submariner. I can find the courage to endure and overcome adversity, having survived everything life has thrown my way so far. With commitment, I can advance on any worthwhile challenge and find resilience beyond success or failure. And I know it is compassion – for myself and for others – that unlocks genuine belonging and offers endless opportunities to be led and to lead.

On leadership, I most admire those who humbly choose to inspire. Those who lift people to achieve what they might believe is beyond them. Those who enliven and embolden a crew, even in the most extreme and demanding environments, and deliver what is impossible through individual endeavour alone. I found those leaders everywhere – in moments of opportunity and adversity, at sea and ashore, as men and women, as Admirals and Able Seamen – and I am grateful to them all.

Now, I have one calling ahead – to be my honourable self.

ACRONYMS

ADF	Australian Defence Force
ADCAP	Advanced Capability
ADFWC	Australian Defence Force Warfare Centre
ADI	Australian Defence Industries
ASW	Anti-Submarine Warfare
AMWC	Australian Maritime Warfare Centre
APSC	Asia Pacific Submarine Conference
ASC	Australian Submarine Corporation
ASRV	Australian Submarine Rescue Vehicle
AUKUS	Australia, United Kingdom, United States of America
BINT	Basic Intelligence Take
CASG	Capability Acquisition & Sustainment Group (formerly DMO)
CFMETR	Canadian Forces Maritime Experimental and Test Ranges
CDF	Chief of Defence Force
CSC	Conspicuous Service Cross
CDS	Commendation for Distinguished Service
CEO	Chief Executive Officer
CO	Commanding Officer
COD	Carrier Onboard Delivery
DCNS	Direction des Constructions Navales Services (later Naval Group)
DoD	Department of Defence

DMO	Defence Materiel Organisation (later CASG)
DSME	Daewoo Shipbuilding and Marine Engineering
EBS	Emergency Breathing System
EMDR	Eye Movement Desensitization and Reprocessing
GAM	Geurakan Aceh Meurdeka (Free Aceh Movement)
GPV	General Purpose Vessel
GW	USS *George Washington*
HMAS	Her Majesty's Australian Ship / Submarine
HMAT	His Majesty's Australian Transport
HMCS	Her Majesty's Canadian Ship / Submarine
HMS	Her Majesty's Ship / Submarine
HNLMS	Her Dutch Majesty's Ship / Submarine
HNoMS	His Norwegian Majesty's Ship / Submarine
IED	Improvised Explosive Device
INTERFET	International Forces East Timor
IRA	Irish Republican Army
ISMERLO	International Submarine Escape and Rescue Liaison Office
JMSDF	Japanese Maritime Self Defence Force
JOC	Joint Operations Command
JTF	Joint Task Force
KD	Kapal Di-Raja (His Majesty's Ship)
KHI	Kawasaki Heavy Industries
LOTE	Life of Type Extension
MASTEX	Malaysia Australia Tactical Exercise
MGR	Main Generator Room
MHI	Mitsubishi Heavy Industries

NATO	North Atlantic Treaty Organisation
NUWC	Naval Undersea Warfare Centre
PD	Periscope Depth
PIPRS	Pulse Intercept Passive Ranging Sonar
PLA(N)	People's Liberation Army (Navy)
POPS	Post Operational Psychology Screening
RADAR	Radio Navigation and Ranging
RAF	Royal Air Force
RAAF	Royal Australian Air Force
RAN	Royal Australian Navy
RAR	Royal Australian Regiment
RIMPAC	Rim of the Pacific
RN	Royal Navy
RNLN	Royal Netherlands Navy
RNZAF	Royal New Zealand Air Force
ROKS	Republic of Korea Ship/Submarine
ROV	Remotely Operated Vehicle
SASR	Special Air Service Regiment
SCTT	Submarine Command Team Trainer
SEAL	Sea Air Land Teams
SEAFAC	Southeast Alaska Acoustic Measurement Facility
SETF	Submarine Escape Training Facility
SOD	Strategic Operations Division
SONAR	Sound Navigation and Ranging
SSE	Submerged Signal Ejector
SUBOPAUTH	Submarine Operating Authority
SUBOPS	Submarine Operations
TK	Tarin Kowt
USN	United States Navy

UUC	Usage and Upkeep Cycle
VCDF	Vice Chief of Defence Force
WRANS	Women's Royal Australian Naval Service
XO	Executive Officer

GLOSSARY

Slang terms are shown in *italics*

Action Stations	Whole submarine manning for major offensive or defensive action
alongside	Next to or together with a wharf, another ship or submarine
athwartships	Across the submarine from side to side
attack	Watchkeeper on the attack periscope
Attack Teams	On the watch crew positions for ship attack or similar event
AUKUS	Trilateral security pact between Australia, the United Kingdom and the United States; jointly announced on 15 September 2021 and focused on military capability for the Indo-Pacific region
Australian White Ensign	Flown by His / Her Majesty's Australian Ships and Submarines in commission
ballast	Weight carried in a ship or submarine to make her seaworthy in various conditions
ballast tanks	Tanks that enable a submarine to dive or surface by changing her buoyancy
battle rattle	Body armour and webbing
beam	Literally the widest part of a ship or submarine, but also used to identify objects, such as ships, on the port or starboard side of the submarine
black pig	Submariner's nickname for a submarine
Blue on Blue	Fratricide caused by friendly fire
brass hat	Commander's peaked cap, adorned with gold-coloured oak leaves
brew	Generally refers to coffee or tea, but also to beer

bulkhead	A wall of a compartment onboard a ship or submarine other than the ship's side. Watertight bulkheads form watertight and gastight sections within the submarine
cable	Unit for measuring short distances at sea. Equal to one-tenth of a nautical mile, 200 yards or approx. 182 metres
Captain	Refers to either the rank of Captain (four rings) or a role as the Captain of a ship or submarine. This role is also known as Commanding Officer (CO)
cart	Navy slang for a bunk/bed; also known in submarines as a 'rack', 'farter' or 'fart sack'
casing	A free-flooding streamlined form built around external fittings, such as the capstan gear, towed array handling gear, conning and escape towers and other protrusions to reduce noise and frictional drag
cheer ship	Naval tradition where a Ship's Company line the rails at the ship's side to perform a collective salute, paying respect to a reigning monarch or other high ranking dignitary, or another warship.
Chief Tiff	Contraction of 'Chief Artificer', the senior marine technician onboard
coaming	Lip of the hatch designed to prevent water from flowing below
Collins-class	Swedish-designed, Australian-built diesel-electric fleet submarines; in service with the RAN since 1996
Commander	Refers to either the rank of Commander (three rings) or a role, such as the Commander of a task group or task force
commission	Officers in the RAN receive a commission from the Governor-General as Commander-in-Chief on appointment. Ships and submarines are similarly commissioned on acceptance into service

commissioning crew	Personnel selected to bring a ship or submarine from build into commissioned naval service
con	Nautical term to direct the course and speed of the ship by giving wheel and engine orders
conning tower	Classically a small watertight compartment above the control room from which an attack would be conducted; the conning tower on modern submarines refers to a watertight tower within the fin providing access between the control room and the bridge
continental shelf	The edge of the Australian continent that lies under the ocean extending from the coastline to a drop-off point called the shelf break
Coxswain	The senior Chief Petty Officer and most experienced planesman onboard a submarine; known as the Chief of the Boat onboard the Collins-class
crash sail	Proceed to sea in an emergency or urgent situation
Crush Depth	Design depth at which sea pressure will overcome and collapse the pressure hull of a submarine
Diving Stations	Whole submarine crew positions for diving the submarine or high-risk dived operations
dolphins	Qualification badge of all Australian Submariners; also known as a 'set' or 'pair' of dolphins. Similar badges are worn by qualified submariners of other navies
downtrot	Sentry posted below when alongside
embarked	Brought onboard for a particular purpose or duty
Emergency Stations	Whole submarine crew positions for emergency situations, such as fires or floods
evolution	Generic term for any simulated event or training exercise designed to develop individual or team skills

familygram	Short, coded messages sent from family members to crew, and vetted by the Commanding Officer, while at sea.
fathom	Traditional nautical unit for linear measurement of depth of water and soundings. Equal to 6 feet or approx. 2 metres
feather	Distinctive plume of white water created ahead of and around a periscope as it cuts through the surface of the sea
fin	A streamlined, free-flooding superstructure encompassing the conning tower, masts and periscopes
Five Power Defence Arrangements	A military consultative agreement established in 1971 between the UK, Australia, New Zealand, Malaysia and Singapore
Full-Cycle Docking	Major submarine refit conducted approx. every ten years over approx. two years
graving dock	An excavation connected with a harbour or river and closed by use of a caisson or dock gates to permit flooding and draining
gyro / gyroscope	True North–seeking electrically powered compass to indicate direction and provide input to navigational and combat systems
hardstand	A strip of concrete built across the foreshore to facilitate the hauling up of ships or submarines
hatch	Circular opening piercing the pressure hull or deck to allow access to the submarine or compartments below
hydroplanes / planes	Forward and aft hydroplanes operate much as a rudder does, but to control submarine depth; cruciform planes on Collins-class control both course and depth

in theatre	Within a defined theatre of operations
knot	Unit for measuring speed at sea. Equal to 1 nautical mile per hour, approx. 1.85 kilometres per hour
lid	Watertight hinged hatch cover, such as the conning tower upper and lower lids
Life of Type Extension	Replacement of major onboard systems to extend the in-service life of each submarine
Mid-Cycle Docking	Major submarine refit conducted approx. every five years over approx. one year
midnighters	Meal served as watches change over in the middle of the night
nautical mile	Unit for measuring distance at sea; equal to 10 cables or 1,852 metres
Nav	Navigating Officer
Next of Kin signal	Details every person onboard for the purposes of notifying next of kin in the event of loss of the submarine; released and acknowledged prior to diving
Number 1 dress uniform	Ceremonial uniform. Naval uniforms are traditionally numbered for ease of ordering the required dress for different activities
Oberon-class	British-designed and built diesel–electric fleet submarines in service with the RAN between 1967 and 2000
Officer of the Day	Delegated responsibility for the safety and conduct of a ship or submarine alongside
Officer of the Watch	Delegated responsibility for the safety and conduct of a ship or submarine at sea
on the roof	Submarine slang for being surfaced

onboard	Term used to describe being embarked in ships and submarines as well as being on a base
opened up for diving	All onboard systems aligned in the correct state to dive the submarine
oppo	Opposite number or counterpart on another watch
Ops	Operations Officer
passage routine	Defined state of submarine systems, crewing and routines for extended transit
patrol routine	Defined state of submarine systems, crewing and routines for extended operational duty
periscope depth	A shallow depth which allows use of the periscopes and other masts
posting	Appointment to a position in a ship, submarine or establishment
pressure hull	Built to withstand the pressure of the sea and preserve the structural integrity of the submarine at depth while maintaining normal atmospheric pressure within to enable habitability
Q-tank	Internal ballast tank in Oberon-class used to rapidly change the forward trim and dive the submarine; operated through the use of related valves and vents
quiet state	Ordered states of machinery line-up, personal movement and other restrictions designed to match submarine tasking and threat levels; typically referred to as patrol-quiet, search-quiet or ultra-quiet states
rack	See 'cart'
Range Hut	Facility ashore used to conduct ship or submarine trials and to record measurements taken on an instrumented at-sea range
rank	Officer ranks in the RAN are: Midshipman, Sub-Lieutenant, Lieutenant, Lieutenant-Commander,

Commander, Captain, Commodore, Rear Admiral, Vice Admiral, Admiral.
Sailor ranks in the RAN are:
Junior Rates – Seaman, Able Seaman, Leading Seaman; Senior Rates – Petty Officer, Chief Petty Officer, Warrant Officer, Warrant Officer of the Navy

rate	Sailors are rated within specialist categories, such as cook or electronic warfare analyst
re-scrub	Requirement to re-submit to an examination or event, such as a work-up
Red Ensign	Flown by ships and vessels registered in the United Kingdom or Commonwealth countries, and by naval ships and submarines when undergoing trials prior to acceptance into service
refit	Full or partial program of works to test, service and renew major onboard equipment and systems. Generally, requires substantial time in dock and an extensive program to re-constitute and progressively prove full operational capability
rig	Uniform. Hence, 'out of rig' is out of uniform
salvo / salvoes	The action of firing multiple torpedoes or missiles at the same time
search	Watchkeeper on the search periscope
serials	Separate sequential parts of an exercise, typically addressing specific objectives with identified participants following set procedures and instructions
shake down	abbreviated work-up normally conducted after a short period alongside to verify the state of the submarine, and safety and operational standards
shoulder boards	Epaulettes
signal traffic	Messages to and from higher headquarters or other units, including intelligence updates, weather forecasts, defect reports, exercise instructions and operational orders

single ship steaming	Surface ship conducting independent passage and not in company with other ships
skimmer	Collegial slang for a warship or sailor that 'skims' the surface of the oceans
skirting	A ship sailing close by the Go Deep Circle of a submarine at periscope depth
snorting	Operating diesel electric generators to charge a submarine's main batteries, either on the surface or dived
stoker	Marine technician responsible for onboard power generation and mechanical system
stripe up	Achieve a promotion in rank
Submarine Arm	Comprises all those submarine-qualified officers and sailors serving in the RAN
Submarine Enterprise	The Submarine Enterprise was established in the wake of the Coles Review and comprises Navy, CASG and related industry, principally ASC; also known as 'the Enterprise'
tail-end Charlie	Army slang for the last soldier in line of a foot patrol, often the first to be dispatched by an ambushing enemy
tannoy	Audio-system brand name applied generically to the main broadcast system used for making verbal orders and reports onboard
Task Force	A formidable collection of naval or military assets formed to conduct a specific mission or campaign, generally comprised of several smaller task groups
The Trade	Service in the Submarine Arm has long been known as 'The Trade', a term popularised in the Rudyard Kipling poem of the same name[10]

---

10   Kipling, Rudyard. *Rudyard Kipling's Verse, Inclusive Edition, 1885–1918*. Garden City: Doubleday, Page & Co., 1922.

Torps	Torpedo Officer
towed array	Array of sonar hydrophones towed behind a submarine or surface ship on a cable, as opposed to a hull-mounted array
track manager	Control room position responsible for assigning and managing sonar, visual and other tracks in the combat system
trim	Horizontal inclination of a ship or submarine; hence bows up or down. Also, a generic term for the overall state of balance of the submarine against hydrodynamic forces
trim tanks	Movement of water between trim tanks located forward and aft enables adjustment of inclination while maintaining a state of neutral buoyancy
tubs	Submarine slang for a shower
Turk's head	Spherical, ornamental knot on the end of a rope
up top	Naval slang for the countries and waters of Northeast and Southeast Asia
warner	Generic term for electronic warfare equipment used to detect radars
wheel over	Point at which a ship or submarine commences a turn to maintain a planned navigational track
work-up	series of drills and exercises conducted over weeks or months to prove the state of the submarine and achieve safety and operational standards
zeds	Navy slang for sleep

A note about speed, distance and depth:
Speed at sea is stated in knots, while distance at sea is stated in yards, cables and nautical miles.
Submarine depth and depth of water are stated in feet and fathoms during my Oberon service, and in metres from my Upholder service onward.

INDEX

(Note: Page numbers in **bold** refer to images)

ACKNOWLEDGEMENTS

I would like to acknowledge those who inspired my submarine service and thank those who taught, tolerated or ran with me along the way.

I am immeasurably grateful to the following people in particular for their contribution to the creation and publication of this book:

Mum and Dad, Mark Scott, Annie Watt, Cath Batson, Maree Todd, Kevin and Sonja Worthington, Frances Andrijich, Kim Beazley, Mark Berridge, Matt Buckley, Mike Carlton, Garth Callender, Sir Peter Cosgrove, JJ Cupples, Teresa Curman, Armelle Davies, Mike Deeks, Chris Donald, James Goldrick, Cassandra Goodman, John Gower, Rachel Hanson, John Harvey, Sir Angus Houston, Glyn Hunter, His Excellency General the Honourable David Hurley, Kelly Irving, David Johnston, Peter Jones, Ian Lees, James Lybrand, Denis Mamo, Sarah Martin, Anna McDonald, Bill Merz, Claire Miller, Jess Nakakawa, John Oddie, Paddy O'Dwyer, Tom Phillips, John Quinn, John Raymond, Georgia Richter, John Ryan, Allan Sicard, Jodie Spiteri-James, Mark Todd, Geoff Wadley, Mark Wales, Chloe Walton, Jans Wibrandts, Bron Williams and Scott Wright, not to forget Ruby, Olive and Pigwidgeon.

Shaunaugh and Laura – thank you for being us.

ABOUT THE AUTHOR

Peter Scott joined the Royal Australian Navy as a seventeen-year-old Midshipman, hopeful but uncertain, and over three decades rose to be the professional head of the Navy's elite: the Submarine Arm. During that journey, he served among the dedicated crews of the most highly specialised capability in any Navy in the most complex and demanding environment on earth: the undersea battlespace.

He survived and led others through at-sea fires, floods and explosions, and passed the most demanding military command course in the world, Perisher. Peter commanded the longest deployment ever conducted by an Australian submarine and led the Arm through an unprecedented period of expansion.

In all, he served in ten submarines and twenty different command and leadership appointments over thirty-four years. A veteran of multiple Special Operations with the Submarine Arm, he also saw war service in Iraq, the Persian Gulf and Afghanistan during 2006 and 2007.

He was awarded a Commendation for Distinguished Service in the Australia Day Honours List 2008, having previously been decorated with the Conspicuous Service Cross for achievements in command of HMAS *Collins*.

Peter holds a Master's degree in Coaching Psychology from the University of Sydney and now works as an executive coach to unleash the courage, compassion and wisdom of leaders. When not writing or coaching, Peter can be found on the trails running ultra-marathons or relaxing at home with his family.